# The Poetics of Transition

*New Americanists*

A Series Edited by Donald E. Pease

# The Poetics of Transition

Emerson, Pragmatism, &
American Literary Modernism

Jonathan Levin

Duke University Press
Durham & London 1999

© 1999 Duke University Press
All rights reserved
Printed in the United States of America on acid-free paper ∞
Designed by Rebecca Filene
Typeset in Minion by Tseng Information Systems, Inc.

Library of Congress Cataloging-in-Publication Data
Levin, Jonathan.
The poetics of transition : Emerson, pragmatism, and
American literary modernism / Jonathan Levin.
p. cm. — (New Americanists)
Includes bibliographical references (p.   ) and index.
ISBN 0-8223-2277-3 (alk. paper).
ISBN 0-8223-2296-x (pbk. : alk. paper)
1. American literature—20th century—History and criticism.   2. Modernism (Literature)—
United States.   3. Emerson, Ralph Waldo, 1803–1882—Philosophy.   4. Emerson, Ralph Waldo,
1803–1882—Influence.   5. Influence (Literary, artistic, etc.)   6. Pragmatism in literature.
I. Title.   II. Series.
PS228.M63L48   1999   810.9′112—dc21   98-8840   CIP

*For Milton and Rona,*
*and for Halina*

# Contents

# Preface

I HAVE ATTEMPTED in what follows to reconstruct the history of a metaphor, transition, that has exercised a powerful hold over a great many American imaginations. Emerson provides one key formulation of the metaphor in "Self-Reliance": "Power ceases in the instant of repose; it resides in the moment of transition from a past to a new state, in the shooting of the gulf, in the darting to an aim" (*EL* 271). Repose is a figure here for the deadening grip of habit. Once we settle into a condition of repose, we compromise the vital energies that should constitute our power or, to put it less personally, we compromise the energies that should constitute power in our always elusive relationship to it. Power is *in* transition and serves the interests not of any settled condition (the interests, say, of a determined self) but rather those of the tendencies-in-realization latent in any given condition.

There is, however, a paradox embedded in this formulation, one which indicates the complexity of this dynamic for Emerson and for those who would later adopt his metaphor, however consciously or unconsciously. What, after all, could it possibly mean to reside in a moment of transition? Residence carries the same negative connotation Emerson already associates with repose in this passage, a connotation made explicit in his comment in the later essay "Fate": "Every spirit makes its house; but afterwards the house confines the spirit" (*EL* 946). It is as if Emerson's effort to make the transition from repose to a state of unsettled possibility is compromised, in advance, by the language in which that effort is destined to be realized. According to Emerson's poetics of transition, repose and transition are at once mutually exclusive and irreducibly entangled tropes.

This study proposes to analyze the paradoxical poetics of transition: to trace its background in Emerson's conception of self, his aesthetic and poetic theory, even his prose style; to uncover its central role in William James's psychology and later in his radical empiricism and pragmatism, as well as in the differently inflected pragmatisms of John Dewey and George Santayana; and to follow its continuing evolution among such experimental American literary modernists as Henry James, Gertrude Stein, and Wallace Stevens. As a distinct American intellectual and literary inheritance, the poetics of transition offers not a set of ideas or concepts but rather a general attitude toward ideas and concepts. This attitude is often manifest as a pervasive formal or stylistic restlessness. The poetics of transition is stimulated by a core dissatisfaction with all definite, definitive formulations, be they concepts, metaphors, or larger formal structures. Of course, communication would hardly be possible without concepts, metaphors, and formal structures. Hence the poetics of transition requires the very forms it ceaselessly attempts to overcome. It rejects these forms even as it draws on them to posit new ones that will, in turn, set the same transitional dynamic in motion again.

The poetics of transition is almost universally ignored by neopragmatists, who are less interested in such formal, literary dynamics than in pragmatism's bearing on questions of knowledge and truth. As Stanley Fish suggests in his essay "Consequences," antifoundationalists set out "to demonstrate that the norms and standards and rules that foundationalist theory would oppose to history, convention, and local practice are in every instance a function or extension of history, convention, and local practice." In other words, nothing outside history and local practice grounds the knowledge or values that we habitually invoke within that history and practice. This does not imply, for Fish or for other neopragmatists, a release into rampant subjectivity, but calls instead for a more detailed understanding of the conditions of subjectivity: "Thus the lesson of anti-foundationalism is not only that external and independent guides will never be found but that it is unnecessary to seek them, because you will always be guided by the rules or rules of thumb that are the content of any settled practice, by the assumed definitions, distinctions, criteria of evidence, measures of adequacy, and such, which not only define the practice but structure the understanding of the agent who thinks of himself as a 'competent member.' "[1] Such situated, conditioned knowledge forms the only real basis from which to evaluate and intervene in matters of social and political consequence.

Richard Rorty's discussion in *Contingency, Irony, Solidarity* of the contingencies of language, community, and self reflects the same understanding of conditioned subjectivity. Rortian pragmatism rejects the classic philosophical project of establishing rational foundation for our thoughts and beliefs and attempts instead to describe a "post-Philosophical culture" in which situated human intelligence can be applied to concrete scientific and social problems. Pragmatists were among the first modern philosophers to insist that truth is not found but made. What is true, like what is beautiful and good, is not located outside (or above) our material and cultural experience, but is instead conditioned by that experience. There is no meaningful conception of the true, the beautiful, or the good apart from our culturally and historically specific imagination of them. Neopragmatists extend this insight by underscoring the contingency of all available foundations of knowledge and belief. Hence the term *antifoundationalism.* What we count as true, beautiful, or good is necessarily determined by prevailing practices and the conditions of subjectivity to which they give rise.

Such neopragmatist formulations are, however, subject to a certain irony, an effect of the considerable eloquence and authority with which critics like Rorty and Fish analyze and expose the contingencies of everything we hold on good authority. Their deconstructions of authority are delivered in impressively unified, coherent, and assured critical voices. This study, which at least aims at the same style of critical authority, will focus on another phase of pragmatism, one in which such authority is suspended, even if only temporarily. Of course, all of the authors I will discuss in what follows assume authoritative voices, even Gertrude Stein (who goes further than any other writer I will discuss in staging the limits of that authority). Still, these writers also cultivate forms of unauthorized experience, moments or passages of transition that suggestively put prevailing standards of authority in question. While pragmatism did indeed contribute to the present antifoundationalist consensus, that consensus is to some extent bought at the cost of something more profoundly unassimilated and unassimilable within the pragmatist project.

This is why it is important to pay careful attention to what might be designated the foundational tropes of pragmatist antifoundationalism. Only close analysis of the language of pragmatism will reveal the defining instabilities of pragmatism and their relationship to American literary culture more generally. Most neopragmatists conceive pragmatism as a form of historicized and even politicized intellectual practice, the perfect conclusion to nineteenth-century trends in philosophy epitomized by Hegel's historicism and the natural prelude to the explosion, in the twentieth century, of Rorty's post-Philosophical culture. Accordingly, neopragmatists typically reject any formulation that hints of metaphysical idealism, approving just those writings and passages that concretely historicize intellectual, moral, and scientific culture. In this view, the authentically pragmatic content of pragmatism takes its place alongside other postmodern (or protopostmodern) perspectives, ultimately advancing the liberation of humankind from the last vestiges of Enlightenment illusion. Hence Cornel West's characterization of pragmatism as "a future-oriented instrumentalism that tries to deploy thought as a weapon to enable more effective action," a formulation which leads him to announce that his own "prophetic pragmatism" will take up "the 'postmodern' themes of degraded otherness, subjected alienness, and subaltern marginality, that is, the wretched of the earth (poor peoples of color, women, workers)." [2] Despite West's spirited call to arms, there is little agreement among neopragmatists as to whether this most recent liberation is itself a politically progressive accomplishment or is finally moving us beyond such liberal illusions of steady political progress. This is, of course, a division that runs straight through postmodern theory itself.

One reason I am skeptical of West's narrative is that it ignores the unsettled, unsettling quality of the Emersonian moment of transition. A moment of transition may ultimately have what will eventually come to be defined as politically progressive consequences, but as it unfolds it remains undetermined in ways obscured by such retrospective characterizations. This is precisely what is unsettling about a poetics of transition. Although many pragmatists have followed Dewey by linking pragmatism to specific, often radically democratic political perspectives, pragmatists have also recognized something in pragmatism that is constantly exceeding the defined and defining boundaries of political categories and agendas. The poetics of transition throws everything into question, including, at least in its most extreme form, the comforting assurance that an unfolding transition is an instrument of morally sanctioned, politically progressive interests.

Pragmatists' concern with the marginal and transitional dynamics of consciousness, language, and action links them to Emerson's distinctly pragmatic Transcendentalism and to the experimental temper characteristic of American literary modernists. By joining all of these figures together here, my goal is not to describe a unified intellectual tradition so much as to illuminate the ways in which a poetics of transition informs and gives shape to shared attitudes toward the limits of meaning and identity. By foregrounding transitional or fringe experiences, these writers displace stable or coherent identities and meanings into the formal and linguistic processes that continuously negotiate identities and meanings. Instead of advocating the recovery of prior forms of belief or ritual practice — primitive or authentic forms which might redeem the apparent chaos and futility of modern life — they pursue habits of awareness that resist collapsing into positive beliefs. For these writers, everything turns on the quality of alertness to possibilities of meaning as they lurk in the always dynamic margins of experience.

This study will trace the history of these transitions at just the moment they begin to be named by American writers. This is necessarily a paradoxical moment, since, to adapt a line from Wallace Stevens's "Notes toward a Supreme Fiction," *transition* is "a name for something that never could be named." Transition is a figure for the process whereby the familiar is relentlessly exposed to the unfamiliar, incorporating an undefined, undefinable excess into a previously articulated system. Once that excess is incorporated, however, the system is modified—the unfamiliar familiarized, the dynamic stabilized —and so the transition itself is rendered illegible. *The Poetics of Transition* seeks to recover this illegible moment in American writing: to affirm the integrity of a passage that exceeds any available definition or meaning and to trace its distinct literary and intellectual history.

# Acknowledgments

IT GIVES ME great pleasure to acknowledge the many people who have helped make this book possible. My luckiest debt is to Richard Poirier, whose generosity, friendship, and instruction are a constant source of encouragement. Thanks also to Rick Blaha, Robert Weisbuch, and the late Joseph N. Riddel, extraordinary teachers who helped set my own work in motion.

I thank the many colleagues and friends who have read parts of the manuscript and offered criticism and encouragement along the way: Mark Bauerlein, Suzanne Becker, Martin Bickman, Annette Wheeler Cafarelli, Kenneth Dauber, Harriet Davidson, Kevin Dettmar, Ann Douglas, Kathy Eden, Art Efron, Andrew Epstein, Robert Ferguson, Jennifer Fleischner, Eileen Gillooly, James Guetti, Giles Gunn, Gordon Hutner, Marisa Januzzi, Edward Mendelson, Mark Scott, Joe Thomas, Priscilla Wald, and Deborah Elise White. Special thanks to Andrew Delbanco, who has followed the project from its early stages and helped both in framing larger questions and fine-tuning many details. David Scott Kastan, Michael Seidel, and David Damrosch have provided generous assistance and guidance as Chairs of Columbia's Department of English and Comparative Literature. Barbara Schwerdtfeger provided indispensable assistance in preparing the manuscript. Thanks also to Reynolds Smith, Miriam Angress, and my anonymous readers at Duke Press for their consistently wise and frequently challenging editorial advice. And especial thanks to Donald Pease, for helping bring this book into the world.

I have enjoyed the company and conversation of Marc Salm and Josh Aaronson for many years now, and it is a pleasure to acknowledge the impact of their friendship where I am sure they will least expect to find it. This book would never have been written without the unflagging love and support of my family: Lesley Siegel, Barry Levin, Jan Hale-Levin, Dustin, Sam, Ellie,

Emilia, and especially my parents, Milton and Rona Levin. Thanks, finally, to Halina Karachuk, whose inexhaustible "passion for yes" has often enriched these pages.

The research and writing of this book were supported by a Chamberlain Fellowship, a Junior Faculty Development Grant, and two summer grants from the Council on Research in the Humanities, all awarded by Columbia University. The project began as a dissertation at Rutgers University, which later awarded the book manuscript the David Kalstone Memorial Prize. It is a very special honor to receive an award so named. Thanks to Bridget Gellert Lyons, Chair of the Prize Committee. "The Mind's Limitations Are Its Freedom" is cited with the generous permission of the poet, William Bronk. Parts of the book have previously appeared elsewhere: an early version of chapter 2 appeared as "Life in the Transitions: Emerson, William James, Wallace Stevens" in *Arizona Quarterly* 48 (1992): 76–97, reprinted here by permission of the Regents of the University of Arizona; parts of chapter 3 appeared as "The Esthetics of Pragmatism" in *American Literary History* 6 (1994): 658–83, reprinted here by permission of Oxford University Press; an extended passage of chapter 4 appeared in "The Poetry of Ideas" in *Partisan Review* 62 (1995): 502–6; and a preliminary version of chapter 6 appeared as " 'Entering the modern composition': Gertrude Stein and the Patterns of Modernism" in *Rereading the New: A Backward Glance at Modernism,* edited by Kevin J. H. Dettmar (Ann Arbor: University of Michigan Press, 1992). I am grateful to the various editors for permission to reprint this material here.

# Abbreviations

## JOHN DEWEY

LW   *The Later Works, 1925–1953*, 17 vols., ed. Jo Ann Boydston
(Carbondale and Edwardsville: Southern Illinois UP, 1981–91).

MW  *The Middle Works, 1899–1924*, 15 vols., ed. Jo Ann Boydston
(Carbondale and Edwardsville: Southern Illinois UP, 1976–83).

## RALPH WALDO EMERSON

EL   *Essays and Lectures*, ed. Joel Porte (New York: Library of America,
1983).

JMN  *The Journals and Miscellaneous Notebooks of Ralph Waldo Emerson*,
ed. William H. Gilman (Cambridge: Harvard UP, 1960–82).

## HENRY JAMES

A   *The Ambassadors*, ed. S. P. Rosenbaum (1903; New York: Norton,
1964).

GB  *The Golden Bowl* (1904; New York: Penguin, 1985).

LC   *Literary Criticism*, 2 vols. (vol. 1: "Essays on Literature," vol. 2:
"French Writers"), ed. Leon Edel (New York: Library of America,
1984).

N   *Novels 1881–1886*, ed. William T. Stafford (New York: Library of
America, 1985).

## WILLIAM JAMES

LWJ  *The Letters of William James*, 2 vols., ed. Henry James (1920; Boston:
Little, 1926).

PP   *The Principles of Psychology*, 3 vols., ed. Frederick H. Burkhardt
(Cambridge: Harvard UP, 1981).

TC   *The Thought and Character of William James*, by Ralph Barton Perry,
2 vols. (Boston: Little, 1935).

W 1    *Writings 1878–1899*, ed. Gerald E. Myers (New York: Library of America, 1992).

W 2    *Writings 1902–1910*, ed. Bruce Kuklick (New York: Library of America, 1987).

WWJ    *The Writings of William James: A Comprehensive Edition*, ed. John J. McDermott (1967; Chicago: U of Chicago P, 1977).


GEORGE SANTAYANA

CO    *Character and Opinion in the United States* (1920; New York: Doubleday, 1956).

IC    *The Idea of Christ in the Gospels or God in Man* (New York: Scribner's, 1946).

GT    *The Genteel Tradition: Nine Essays by George Santayana*, ed. Douglas L. Wilson (Cambridge: Harvard UP, 1967).

PS    *Platonism and the Spiritual Life* (New York: Scribner's, 1927).

RA    *Reason in Art* (1905; New York: Dover, 1982).

RB    *The Realms of Being*, one-volume ed. (New York: Scribner's, 1942).

SAF    *Scepticism and Animal Faith* (1923; New York: Dover, 1955).

WGS    *The Works of George Santayana*, 4 vols., ed. Herman J. Saatkamp Jr. (Cambridge: MIT UP, 1986–94).


GERTRUDE STEIN

GSW    *Writings*, 2 vols. (vol. 1: 1903–1932, vol. 2: 1932–1946), ed. Catharine R. Stimpson and Harriet Chessman (New York: Library of America, 1998).


WALLACE STEVENS

CP    *Collected Poems* (1954; New York: Knopf, 1995).

CPP    *Collected Poetry and Prose*, ed. Frank Kermode and Joan Richardson (New York: Library of America, 1997).

LWS    *Letters of Wallace Stevens*, ed. Holly Stevens (New York: Knopf, 1966).

OP    *Opus Posthumous* (1957), rev. ed., ed. Milton J. Bates (New York: Vintage, 1989).

# Introduction:
# Life, Transition, the Energizing Spirit

"THE POEM REFRESHES life so that we share, / For a moment, the first idea . . .": so Wallace Stevens, writing near the outset of his "Notes toward a Supreme Fiction," restages the classic American drama of the return to origins (CP 382). "Why should not we also enjoy an original relation to the universe," Emerson asked in the introduction to his 1836 essay *Nature* (EL 7). Stevens's Emersonian dream of a return to origins might be regarded as an attempt (however unconscious) to evade contemporary social circumstances. But there is an important sense in which his mythic return undoes itself from within. Stevens's first idea proves to be so radically original that it even precedes its conceptualization as an idea or its representation as myth. The moment in which the first idea is realized is the paradoxical moment of its transition. The first idea, like the supreme fiction, lives not in its settled formal representations but rather in the informal gestures that bring it into being.

The strangeness of a poem like "Notes toward a Supreme Fiction" is in the poet's effort to imagine a supreme mythic ideal which is supreme only by virtue of its dramatically staged figurality. Stevens distinguishes between mythical forms and the imaginative processes that cultivate them. His first idea and supreme fiction become indistinguishable from the actual unfolding language of the poem. This accounts for what Stevens later describes as the inevitable "ennui" of the first idea, our impatience with it once it becomes formulated as a familiar, familiarizing idea. Before it is fixed in this way, the first idea is actualized *as* the poem itself, what is for Stevens an always elusive unfolding of language. This poetry makes the line between poem and world hard to draw because, as Stevens suggests later in the poem, its own "freshness of transformation is // The freshness of a world" (CP 397–98).

Stevens blurs the line between poem and world because he so thoroughly identifies the vital energies of writing with the cosmic forces that circulate through the world. "The world is a force, not a presence," he comments in one of his "Adagia" (*OP* 198). Writing does not reflect or correspond to a world of things, but rather contributes to and extends the active processes and energies that flow through and thereby constitute that world. Americans have not only written about energies, processes, movements, transitions, and transformations, but have also been subject to the recurring dream that they can make their writing the literal embodiment of these vital forces. To say that the world is a force, not a presence, is also a muted way of saying that one's writing has a certain force, that it draws on and extends the force that is always and everywhere coursing through the world of things.[1]

There is a rich background to this identification, one that begins most consequentially with Emerson. "But the quality of the imagination is to flow," Emerson comments in "The Poet," "and not to freeze" (*EL* 463). This aesthetic claim should be read alongside Emerson's prior epistemological and even ethical disclaimer in "Circles": "Do not set the least value on what I do, or the least discredit on what I do not, as if I pretended to settle any thing as true or false. I unsettle all things. No facts are to me sacred; none are profane; I simply experiment, an endless seeker, with no Past at my back" (*EL* 412). Emerson values processes but not necessarily their end products, which are in any event only instruments of further processes. So long as he keeps faith with these processes, at once cosmic and imaginative, Emerson can identify with the continuously emerging novelty of things. Emerson's process-oriented perspective allows him to distinguish mere form from what he invariably figures as the authentic life that infuses all form. Form is limited and limiting, whereas life is expansive, a never-ending process of vital transitions and transformations. "In nature every moment is new," he comments in "Circles," "the past is always swallowed and forgotten; the coming only is sacred. Nothing is secure but life, transition, the energizing spirit" (*EL* 413). If no fact is ever sacred in and of itself, it is because its sacredness is instead a function of its transitional unfolding.

Transition remains a slippery term in Emerson's prose. This is due, in part, to the way in which the term is used to stand for a process or event, not a thing. It is as if the term is itself "swallowed and forgotten" even as it is etched onto the page. The process inevitably outstrips what it names, as well as what names it. This links transition to what Emerson elsewhere calls abandonment. As he comments in "The Poet," "Beyond the energy of his possessed and conscious intellect," a man "is capable of a new energy (as of an intellect doubled on itself), by abandonment to the nature of things" (*EL* 459). The figure of abandonment more pointedly marks the shift of emphasis away from an agent of transition toward transition as an extra-human, even cosmic process. The intellect "doubled on itself" is a perfect figure for thought proceeding in full recognition of the limit of its present form. This doubled intellect identifies not with that limited and limiting form but instead with the encompassing processes or forces that suffuse and exceed that form. Emerson's "abandonment to the nature of things" serves less to indicate the possibility of arriving at an essential nature or core of being than to figure abandonment and transition as the nature of things.

Transition and abandonment figure a power that at once supports and shatters the self. This may seem odd, given the emphasis critics have traditionally placed on Emersonian self-reliance. Nevertheless, transition and abandonment mark the limit of the self's agency and self-control. As Emerson comments in an 1847 journal entry, "Every thing teaches transition, transference, metamorphosis: therein is human power, in transference, not in creation; & therein is human destiny, not in longevity but in removal. We dive & reappear in new places" (*JMN* 10:76). Creation, usually read as a figure for the self's originality and inventiveness, is synonymous here with mere transference. The originality of Emerson's poet and scholar is a function of their transference of prior energies. Transition thus locates human power in a fated destiny of perpetual removal.

Emerson also links creativity to transition in "Plato; or, the Philosopher." There, "the experience of poetic creativeness" is "not found in staying at home, nor yet in travelling, but in transitions from one to the other, which must therefore be adroitly managed to present as much transitional surface as possible" (*EL* 641). Staying at home appears to describe a state of complete familiarity; traveling, by contrast, suggests a pure exoticism. Emerson's brief against traveling is stated in "Self-Reliance," where he suggests that he who "travels to be amused, or to get somewhat which he does not carry, travels away from himself, and grows old even in youth among old things" (*EL* 278). Transition should instead bring the familiar into contact with the unknown, a process that extends knowledge further into the mysterious margin of things even as it defamiliarizes the very categories through which that movement is conducted. By maximizing the available "transitional surface," the great artist incessantly familiarizes the strange and, at the same time, estranges the familiar.

Pragmatism is in many ways an extension of this transitional dynamic. Pragmatists typically locate the functional processes of intelligence and belief within the realm of ongoing experience. Their concern is less with the accuracy of the content of a perception or intellectual formula — with how exactly or how adequately it corresponds to a reality — than with how it provisionally orients someone toward his or her world. Instead of troubling over how the various filters that mediate experience distort a reality, pragmatists emphasize the constant need to adjust and readjust knowledge and belief about the world. Instead of asking whether the content of a thought or perception is right, pragmatists typically ask how a thought or perception effects particular consequences in experience, and how those consequences lead to further adjustments in thought or perception. Hence Dewey's description, in *Democracy and Education,* of life as a perpetual development: "Our net conclusion is that life is development, and that developing, growing, is life. Translated into its educational equivalents, this means *(i)* that the educational process has no end beyond itself; it is its own end; and that *(ii)* the educational process is one of continual reorganizing, reconstructing, transforming" (*MW* 9:54). Democracy and education are both methods for Dewey: they do not rest on foundations, but rather provide methods for progressive development in the absence of any such foundations. Pragmatism never posits anything like critical self-consciousness, with its dream of revealing the truth to those who only look at things from the right angle or with an adequately historicized sensibility. Pragmatists' critique of truth is much more profound than that: there is no abstract truth, and so no possibility of getting the world "right" in thought or belief.[2]

The pragmatic emphasis on action and the contexts of action reflects the attempt to shift philosophers' focus from the correspondence between world and mind to the ways in which mind and world are always integrated in active experience. As Dewey comments in *Reconstruction in Philosophy,* "When the belief that knowledge is active and operative takes hold of men, the ideal realm is no longer something aloof and separate; it is rather that collection of imagined possibilities that stimulates men to new efforts and realizations" (*MW* 12:147). The pragmatist refuses to abstract the processes of knowing from the immediate and densely particular contexts of knowing. Just as an infant slowly learns by trial and error how to manipulate his or her environment, so a mind provides a way of experimenting with possibilities and adopting the options that most consistently lead to favorable consequences. Even our ideals of "favorable consequences" must evolve as the process unfolds, since they are never based on settled abstract truths. The task of human intelligence is to evolve, and to keep evolving, ideas of the world that meet constantly changing human needs, as well as shifting perceptions of those needs. Instead of seeking to understand the foundations or unchanging laws of all experience, intelligence should attempt, more modestly, to guide its consequences. Hence Dewey's claim that to the modern "an idea is a suggestion of something to be done or of a way of doing" (*MW* 12:148). Ideas point not back or above to fixed, immutable truths, but rather forward to their consequences in experience, on the basis of which we can further adjust our expectations and aspirations. As William James puts it in "What Pragmatism Means," pragmatism assumes the "attitude of looking away from first things, principles, 'categories,' supposed necessities; and of looking towards last things, fruits, consequences, facts" (*W* 2:510).

Richard Rorty has described pragmatism as a "de-divinizing" of the world, by which he means a coming to terms with the absence of any transcendent values or ideals to guide our human actions. Pragmatism, however, is only a further stage, even the logical development, of the religious reform set in motion by Emerson. Where Emerson rejects the rituals and dogma of his Unitarian Church while loosely retaining much of the vocabulary and even idealism of Christian tradition, the pragmatists reject all explicitly supernatural trappings while retaining and cultivating a naturalized, immanent idealism. The "coming only is sacred" still for the pragmatist who, like Dewey, emphasizes "continual reorganizing, reconstructing, transforming" or, like William James, insists that theories become "instruments, not answers to enigmas, in which we can rest" (*W* 2:509–10). Pragmatism's de-divinizing of the world follows the Emersonian pattern by which habitual and therefore degraded forms of spiritual and imaginative experience are rejected in order to open the space for a more authentic experience of spiritual and imaginative ideals. In a sense, the pragmatists are never more "spirited" than when insisting on the wholly secular dimension of the pragmatist project.

This is to offer a very different interpretation of pragmatism from most of what currently passes as neopragmatism. Richard Rorty's invaluable work on pragmatism is everywhere carried out under the sign of secular culture.[3] Cornel West has, by contrast, explicitly linked pragmatism with various prophetic traditions in American religious thought. According to West's genealogy of pragmatism, later religious thinkers find inspiration in pragmatism that they then bring to their religious traditions. West's religious thinkers espouse deeply pragmatic conceptions of the working of redemption in this world by means of specifically human agencies. West, however, echoes Rorty in his dismissal of what he describes as the latent Hegelianism and idealist aestheticism that occasionally surface in pragmatist writing. For both Rorty and West, aesthetics marks the less rigorous side of pragmatism, a sign of pragmatists' inability to move entirely beyond their Romantic origins.

This view, however, confuses different notions of aesthetic experience. For a pragmatist, art is neither an ornament to life nor a form of leisured indulgence. These are debasements of art. Instead, art is life. It is the process whereby humans devise and test the values, pleasures, and meanings that make life worth living. Sometimes this happens in what passes as high art, sometimes in what passes as popular art, and sometimes in other forms of experience that are not typically considered art at all: sports, romance, ritual, even experiences as mundane as playing with a pet or planning and cooking a meal. These become aesthetic experiences whenever we find meaningful drama in them. Critics, even those sympathetic with pragmatism, have often been dismissive of the occasional emphasis on "wholeness" and "unity" in such works as Dewey's *Art as Experience.* It is important, however, to view these terms within a larger transitional dynamic. Such terms never simply correspond to an external or ideal reality, but rather reflect the structure of an aesthetic experience. They have the same kind of meaning in relation to spiritual experience. What matters most to a pragmatist is not the object of that experience (be it Art, God, or Spirit), but rather the process the experience sets in motion. This process infuses life with deeper (but never definitive or absolute) meanings.

In *The Promise of Pragmatism,* John Patrick Diggins invokes Henry Adams as the significant dissenter to pragmatism. As Diggins tells the story of pragmatism and American modernism, both Dewey and Adams "set out to look for 'unity' without appealing to anything transcendent or supernatural," but for Adams, the "coherence, unity, and wholeness promised by pragmatism at the end of inquiry was nowhere to be found." Adams's rejection of pragmatism is, for Diggins, epitomized in his comment in *The Education of Henry Adams* that "experience ceases to educate." [4] Diggins's attempt to read pragmatism through the lens of Henry Adams is frequently helpful, but it falters through its misconception of just what Dewey and other pragmatists meant by "coherence, unity, and wholeness." It is the same misunderstanding that Henry James points to in his response to Adams's pessimistic and dismissive response to James's memoirs: "I still find my consciousness interesting," James wrote Adams, "under *cultivation* of the interest." [5] Interest, for James as for the pragmatists, is always made, not found. Adams was looking for coherence, unity, and wholeness in the world, in the facts of history and science alike. In their absence, he felt the ground slip treacherously beneath his feet. Adams was in search of something like absolute forms of certainty. His expectations were, as he acknowledges throughout the *Education,* perfectly classical.

Coherence, unity, and wholeness remain important to pragmatists not because they correspond to the structural features of the world or of some ideal form of the world—be it moral, intellectual, scientific, or mathematical—but because these qualities have always been and still remain psychologically and dramatically compelling. It is no coincidence that Emerson conceived his most dynamic essay around the geometry of the circle. The essay opens with the image of a series of ever-expanding circles: "The eye is the first circle; the horizon which it forms is the second; and throughout nature this primary figure is repeated without end" (*EL* 403). Thus Emerson sets up a dialectic interplay (his own frequent image is an "oscillation") between the internal coherence of every formulated system and the impulse to break through the limitations of that system and in so doing establish a new form of internal coherence. Each new horizon represents a newly emerging unity made available to experience and at the same time subject to reformation on the basis of further experience. The pragmatists adopt a similar transitional dynamic whereby the coherence of available rational forms runs up against the recognition of the limits of those forms and the impulse to reimagine them and so establish new intellectual and moral paradigms.

George Santayana, in many regards the apostate pragmatist, is a better guide to this dynamic than Henry Adams. Although he studied with James (as well as Josiah Royce), and although his books contain many echoes of James's *Principles of Psychology* and *Varieties of Religious Experience,* Santayana vigorously criticized James and his fellow pragmatists, especially on issues of what James dubbed "pragmatism's conception of truth." James and Dewey also liked to see their differences with Santayana writ large, just as later pragmatists have wanted to distinguish their project from that of the more "mandarin" Santayana. But Santayana's philosophy is more pragmatic than critics have generally acknowledged. His aesthetics, in particular, make explicit and loosely systematic attitudes that are implicit everywhere in pragmatist writings, and explicit in Dewey's *Art as Experience,* despite differences in tone.

William James was among the first to make much of Santayana's tone. His disparaging remarks in letters have been interpreted both as setting James's more worldly attitudes off from Santayana's vague otherworldliness and as deriving from James's own anxieties about Santayana's unconventional demeanor and personal style of being, even his sexuality. James's own attraction to intense forms of religious experience, to parapsychology, to mind-altering drugs — to just about any and all forms of marginal experience — should say something about his own vague otherworldliness. A number of critics have written very astutely about the psychological anxieties that underpin James's rough-and-tumble exterior. In a sense, James used his external demeanor to authorize — for himself first, as well as for his public — his investigations of intimations of immortality. Santayana caused a powerful reaction in James because Santayana had none of James's defenses, and apparently felt no need for them. The same could be said of William's brother Henry, though this relation must also depend on other sorts of anxiety toward a prodigiously productive younger brother.[6]

In fact, Santayana is himself not so otherworldly as his critics like to make him out to be. Santayana everywhere insists that he is a materialist. He does not, however, consider his materialism at odds with ideals. According to his pragmatic idealism, ideals are grounded in material experience and become meaningless when detached from that experience. There may not be much difference between this and the pragmatist account of how ideals operate in experience, but pragmatists would never follow Santayana in his emphatic valuation of ideals because that valuation would seem to them to reinforce an invidious dualism. Santayana, and pragmatists' nervous reactions to him, allow us to see just what is at stake in the unusual combination of skepticism and faith that shapes pragmatism and American literary modernism.

William James's response to his brother's late fictional style reveals the same anxiety. After he read *The Golden Bowl,* William reported in a letter to his brother that the novel put him "in a very puzzled state of mind." He complains in the letter that he does not enjoy "the kind of 'problem' " in the book, as well as the "method of narration by interminable elaboration of suggestive reference." He further comments that Henry's methods and his own ideals "seem the reverse, the one of the other," even though he claims "to admit your extreme success in this book." To cap it off, he asks Henry to "sit down and write a new book, with no twilight or mustiness in the plot, with great vigor and decisiveness in the action, no fencing in the dialogue, no psychological commentaries, and absolute straightness in the style," lightheartedly suggesting he publish it in William's name (*TC* 1:423–24).

Henry replies somewhat impatiently:

> I'm always sorry when I hear of your reading anything of mine, and always hope you won't—you seem to me so constitutionally unable to "enjoy" it, and so condemned to look at it from a point of view remotely alien to mine in writing it. . . . I see nowhere about me done or dreamed of the things that alone for me constitute the *interest* of the doing of the novel—and yet it is in a sacrifice of them on their very own ground that the thing you suggest to me evidently consists. It shows how far apart and to what different ends we have had to work out (very naturally and properly!) our respective intellectual lives. And yet I can read *you* with rapture. (*TC* 1:424–25)

Henry reiterates this last point in another letter to William from 1907, written after the appearance of *Pragmatism,* where he writes of being "lost in the wonder of the extent to which all my life I have (like M. Jourdain) unconsciously pragmatised" (*TC* 1:428). Ralph Barton Perry brushes aside this and other protestations of admiration by Henry for William's work, calling them "an extension of that admiring pride with which he had from childhood viewed all of William's superior attainments." Of philosophy generally, Perry says of Henry, "his mind was quite naive on that side" (*TC* 1:429).

In fact, it is William who appears naive on the side of literary language and form. Henry recognized the affinity between his brother's pragmatic reconception of the relation between truth and belief and his own literary method. Novels, which attempted both to report objective facts about the world and to record subjective impressions of those facts, were unusually well suited to explore the interrelations between subjective experience and objective environment. Language, Henry realized, was not transparent, as if words were somehow naturally suited to the things they describe. In his late fiction especially, James sets out to develop the densely layered verbal nuances that indicate the complex relationality inherent in any situation or scene. For William, who felt this method compromised dramatic immediacy, Henry's fiction seemed strangely removed from life. For Henry, by contrast, this method opened the way to life by conveying the richly and delicately textured web of relations that suffuses all experience.

Henry James seems to have recognized that his conception of character, as well as his understanding of the art of the novelist, is marked by the same transitional dynamic that runs through his brother's psychology and philosophy. The drama of James's fiction is built on accumulating transitions, a process whereby a character recognizes aspects of her world to which she had previously been blind, steadily modifying and refining her sense of her world. James typically uses a "center of consciousness" to stage the continuous appeal of peripheral relations and their transformational effect on the very consciousness that responds to them. The novelist, in James's view, is someone who is also on the lookout for every incipient transition: some element in the overall field of relations which, once brought into focus, will deepen and intensify the complex fabric of the fiction.

As an author, James wrote in the face of what in the first New York Edition preface (to *Roderick Hudson*) he calls a fear "of being unduly tempted and led on by 'developments.'" Such "developments" are "the very essence of the novelist's process," the "very condition of interest, which languishes and drops without them"; they alone allow the writer to approach his subject, "consisting ever, obviously, of the related state, to each other, of certain figures and things." But such relation could extend indefinitely: "Where, for the complete expression of one's subject, does a particular relation stop—giving

*Introduction*

way to some other not concerned in that expression?" (*LC* 2:1040–41). Every detail in the representation of character and scene suggests a further line of development, a constantly expanding margin that functions, for James, as a kind of eternal and exquisite temptation. This leads James to one of his central formulations about the art of the novel:

> Really, universally, relations stop nowhere, and the exquisite problem of the artist is eternally but to draw, by a geometry of his own, the circle within which they shall happily *appear* to do so. He is in the perpetual predicament that the continuity of things is the whole matter, for him, of comedy and tragedy; that this continuity is never, by the space of an instant or an inch, broken, and that, to do anything at all, he has at once intensely to consult and intensely to ignore it. All of which will perhaps pass but for a supersubtle way of pointing the plain moral that a young embroiderer of the canvas of life soon began to work in terror, fairly, of the vast expanse of that surface, of the boundless number of its distinct perforations for the needle, and of the tendency inherent in his many-coloured flowers and figures to cover and consume as many as possible of the little holes. The development of the flower, of the figure, involved thus an immense counting of holes and a careful selection among them. That would have been, it seemed to him, a brave enough process, were it not the very nature of the holes so to invite, to solicit, to persuade, to practise positively a thousand lures and deceits. The prime effect of so sustained a system, so prepared a surface, is to lead on and on; while the fascination of following resides, by the same token, in the presumability *somewhere* of a convenient, of a visibly-appointed stopping-place. (*LC* 2:1041)

James recognizes that the representation of any "figure" is to a large extent arbitrary: the artist imposes his own geometry on that figure's potentially infinite relations, thus obscuring most of those relations in order to create the appearance of a determinate form. Even as he is engaged in the construction of that form, James is constantly and quite intimately aware of other possible, unrealized forms. These are figured here as seducing him, leading him "on and on" and so distracting him from any definitive formal realization. Of course, what James describes here is not the impossibility of writing, but rather the conflicting impulses that constitute the art of writing. James enjoys the "perpetual predicament" of writing, the sense of grappling with the "thousand lures and deceits" that confront the writer at every turn. The drama of writing is, for James, an extension of the drama of all consciousness, and his greatest thrill is to watch that drama unfold in all its rich and demanding multiplicity.

No literary practice could seem more different on first glance than Gertrude Stein's experiments in language. In fact, as I will demonstrate in chapter 6, Stein saw herself as continuing a development in the history of English literature set in motion most influentially by Henry James. Stein also experiments with centers of consciousness, most notably in *Three Lives, The Making of Americans,* and the many portraits she produced during the early 1910s, but her experiments become increasingly abstract over time. Stein's interest in words and especially in the movement of words leads her to a more thoroughgoing rejection of the organizing center of consciousness than anything James had imagined. But the impetus for this shift is one she shares with James: the sense that literary language can foreground the potentially infinite play of meanings that precedes the formulation of any dominant meaning. If in James, psychological realism begins to collapse under the pressure of the dense verbal web cast over infinitely extending relations, in Stein, there is no longer any effort to reinforce the illusion of psychological realism. Stein uses words to represent character, emotion, even objects (as in *A Long Gay Book* and *Tender Buttons*) without the false and falsifying distortion imposed by the techniques of naturalistic illusion.

In "Portraits and Repetition," one of the 1934–35 lectures published in *Lectures in America,* Stein comments that "the strange thing about the realization of existence is that like a train moving there is no real realization of it moving if it does not move against something and so that is what a generation does it shows that moving is existing" (*GSW* 2:287). By seeing one generation against the background of another, one can see the relative progress of time. This progress, however, must in fact be going on all the time. The challenge, as Stein describes it in this talk, is to recognize this movement without the assistance of the relative block of time. "Moving is existing" suggests that being is as much in the energies of movement or change as in the settled states preceding or following after that movement or change. In William James's phrase, life "is in the transitions as much as in the terms connected" (*W* 2:1181). Stein describes her effort to realize movement in a single frame of time: "If the movement, that is any movement, is lively enough, perhaps it is possible to know that it is moving even if it is not moving against anything" (*GSW* 2:287). Language would then achieve "an intensity of movement so great that it has not to be seen against something else to be known" (*GSW* 2:287). Stein attempts to capture this "intensity of movement" not as centered in consciousness, or in any stable or coherent form, but instead as an open-ended play of connotation, implication, intonation, acoustic echo, and so on. Her use of language resists the conventions of representation in an effort to recover and foreground the more elusive and subtly suggestive play of language.

Stein's description in another 1934–35 talk, "Poetry and Grammar," of her return to the noun around the time of writing *Tender Buttons* should be linked to this effort to foreground the movement of words. Stein describes her early sense of the inadequacy of nouns: "A name is adequate or it is not. If it is adequate then why go on calling it, if it is not then calling it by its name does no good" (*GSW* 2:313). After trying to avoid nouns in her writing, she decides "not to get around them but to meet them, to handle in short to refuse them by using them and in that way my real acquaintance with poetry was begun" (*GSW* 2:325). Interestingly, Stein's description of the return to nouns is cast in terms of a series of gerunds, verbs made into nouns: "Poetry is concerned with using with abusing, with losing with wanting, with denying with avoiding with adoring with replacing the noun. . . . Poetry is doing nothing but using losing refusing and pleasing and betraying and caressing nouns" (*GSW* 2:327). All of these gerunds suggest the myriad ways in which we find ourselves emotionally engaged with the world and others in the world. Very much like Henry James, Stein is concerned here with the ways in which relationality is inscribed into objects. Poetry, as Stein defines it in this essay, seeks to draw this relationality out of the noun:

> I have said that a noun is a name of anything by definition that is what it is and a name of anything is not interesting because once you know its name the enjoyment of naming it is over and therefore in writing prose names that is nouns are completely uninteresting. But and that is a thing to be remembered you can love a name and if you love a name then saying that name any number of times only makes you love it more, more violently more persistently more tormentedly. Anybody knows how anybody calls out the name of anybody one loves. And so that is poetry really loving the name of anything and that is not prose. (*GSW* 2:327)

By loving a name, the name is infused with the entire range of emotional experience that characterizes an intimate relation to what is named. The name is no longer abstract, but belongs to the affective contexts in which it is invoked. Naming restores our sense of relation to and among things.

Stein's pursuit of the lively movement of language reflects her effort to foreground the transitional dynamic that is at the heart of all language. This dynamic is obscured when literary form becomes conventionalized or language becomes abstract. Wallace Stevens is also skeptical of formal conventions and language abstracted from the contexts that bring it to life. This is why in the

*The Poetics of Transition*

first canto of "Notes toward a Supreme Fiction" he insists that the sun "Must bear no name, gold flourisher, but be / In the difficulty of what it is to be" (*CP* 381). One name Stevens rejects here is "Phoebus": "Phoebus is dead, ephebe. But Phoebus was / A name for something that never could be named." In place of the mythological Phoebus, Stevens offers an "ephebe" who, in the first line of the poem, is invited to "Begin." Beginning—beginning the poem, or beginning any imaginative activity—is the latter-day Phoebus. Being is difficult because genuine "be-ing" is unnameable, and yet must nevertheless be realized in the language of the poem. The many plays on "being" in this canto — "Begin," "ephebe," "Phoebus," "to be" — suggest that being is not in any word, but is rather in the larger movement that at once evokes and resists the language that would name and contain it. This doubleness is apparent in the leap from "The sun / Must bear no name" to "gold flourisher." Here, the impulse to strip away layers of language is met head-on by the impulse to utter an original poetry.

There is a crucial paradox behind this effort to pare away accreted mythologies while at the same time recovering a kind of primordial myth. Stevens seeks to strip the sun of its layers of mythologized meanings, hoping to reach the "first idea" of the sun, but this "first idea" is nothing more than the unfolding language of the poem itself. Instead of getting behind or beyond the myths, Stevens attempts to recover the creative energies of the mythologizing activity. As this slippage between myth and mythologizing suggests, the real world and the mythologized or metaphoric world are inseparable for Stevens. A myth or metaphor may be inadequate, but the mythologizing and metaphor-generating imagination remains an essential component of any creative-intellectual life. We have as much need for this creative activity now, Stevens is suggesting, as we have ever had.

The second canto of "Notes" attributes this survival to endless cycles of desire. Just as "not to have is the beginning of desire," so "To have what is not" — to have the idol and not the authentic God — "is its ancient cycle":

It is desire at the end of winter, when

It observes the effortless weather turning blue
And sees the myosotis on its bush.
Being virile, it hears the calendar hymn.

It knows that what it has is what is not
And throws it away like a thing of another time,
As morning throws off stale moonlight and shabby sleep.
(*CP* 382)

*Introduction*

Poetry, for Stevens, is a constant throwing off, not only from one age to the next or one poem to another, but even from line to line and word to word. Stevens's metaphors here are of temporal change: winter becoming spring, night turning to day. But the desire he describes is a present desire that "sends us back to the first idea, the quick / Of this invention" (*CP* 381). This invention can only be this poem, realized in its every elusive turn of phrase. The change of season and dawn of day are metaphors, then, for how poems are written in present time. The first idea is not outside the poem, or before the poem, or behind it, but is instead lodged, paradoxically, in the very acts of turning that constitute the poem. As if to make matters still more elusive, Stevens's turnings are themselves often strangely disorienting: his "effortless weather," "calendar hymn," and "shabby sleep," just to cite the more obvious examples here, almost seem formulated to exceed our best interpretive ambitions.

Henry James, Gertrude Stein, and Wallace Stevens retain a strong conception of a sacred energizing spirit, even as they remain skeptical of the vocabularies, theological or otherwise, that would describe that spirit. Pragmatists share this attitude, though they also attempt to redescribe Emerson's dynamic energizing spirit in more rational terms, emphasizing its progressive contribution to moral and intellectual culture. There is a strong element of demystification in this project. Pragmatists are unwilling to accept any kind of transcendental, transexperiential force that guides or grounds moral and intellectual processes from without. All the guiding, for a pragmatist, is performed from within. Our moral and intellectual capacities are not in any way connected to higher powers or to purified reservoirs of abstract truths or moral ideals. This does not devalue our moral and intellectual powers but rather puts a higher premium on them, since they remain the only powers we can ever trust to direct our lives. They are imperfect and everywhere subject to the vagaries of time and place, mood and belief, confusion and error, but they are also the source of any impulse to rise above the worst effects of these limitations and biases. For all their effort to demystify religious superstition and metaphysical desire, the pragmatists remain strong believers in the human impulse to transcend limits. Their emphasis on dynamic, transitional processes becomes an expression of faith without the unlikely and inadequately imagined objects of that faith, a practice of belief that encourages skepticism of particular beliefs.

But where pragmatists have tended to emphasize the role of intelligence in directing these moral, intellectual, and even political processes, the literary modernists have had less to say about the sufficient virtues of intelligence. This is no doubt to some extent a reflection of professional disposition. They were not philosophers and so did not share the burden of justifying philosophy after the apparent demise of its foundational aspirations. Their characteristic poetics of transition instead allows for the satisfactions of coherence and intelligent design while at the same time cultivating the dislocations that break down and ultimately recast coherent designs. There is often no sense that the self guides this process. Dewey goes a long way toward deconstructing the self, but it is all in the interest of foregrounding the social and cultural forces that constitute selfhood. Dewey never displays the least skepticism toward his own vigorously sustained subjectivity. His sense of transition is comfortably projected onto external social processes.

The literary modernists' explorations into the transitional dynamics that rub away at the edges of self and world pose more of a challenge to the posture of intellectual authority. This challenge is posed also in Emerson and in pragmatist writing, but it is sometimes muted there by a willingness to settle into the role of professional lecturer or philosopher. While I hardly plan to suspend my own professional authority in what follows, I hope at least to recover the profound and often liberating sense of uncertainty located, in various ways and in varying degrees for all of these writers, at the leading edge of a transitional margin. This recovery will begin with Emerson, who characteristically said, "I cast away in this new moment all my once hoarded knowledge, as vacant and vain" (*EL* 413). This is a book about such castings-away, what in "The Auroras of Autumn" Stevens poignantly calls

> form gulping after formlessness,
> Skin flashing to wished-for disappearances
> And the serpent body flashing without the skin.
> (*CP* 411)

Emerson was the first American to bring his meditation on the relation between saying and unsaying to the center of his project, and it is to his prose that we must first turn to begin to trace the often surprising arc of these "wished-for disappearances."

# 1

## Divine Overflowings:
## Emerson's Pragmatic Idealism

EMERSON IS BEST known as a Transcendentalist and hence a philosophical idealist, but his Transcendentalism and idealism are inconsistent and full of tantalizing contradictions and paradoxes. Pragmatism itself has often been depicted as a critical rejoinder to philosophical idealism. There is, however, an abiding affinity between pragmatism and the idealism it would refute. Many neopragmatists are made uncomfortable by what they style the latent Hegelianism of some of the major works of pragmatism, and their adoption of the pragmatic method hinges on their separating that latent Hegelianism from what they characterize as pragmatism's genuine antifoundationalism. In what follows, I want instead to develop a way of understanding how pragmatism crucially depends on its latent idealism and to begin to approach this pragmatic idealism by disentangling a series of contradictions and paradoxes embedded in Emerson's writing.[1]

Every attentive reader already knows that Emerson, like Whitman, contradicts himself. Emerson justifies his many self-contradictions in his essay on Montaigne: "Why pretend that life is so simple a game, when we know how subtle and elusive the Proteus is? Why think to shut up all things in your narrow coop, when we know there are not one or two only, but ten, twenty, a thousand things, and unlike? Why fancy that you have all the truth in your keeping? There is much to say on all sides" (*EL* 694). Contradiction and multiplication of perspectives are Emerson's stock in trade. They are among the literary effects which make his writing distinctly modern. Stephen Whicher, linking Emerson with Whitman, Melville, and Henry Adams, notes that "we are dealing with a mind that makes any assertion of belief against the felt pull of its lurking opposite, the two forming together a total *truth of experience* larger than the opposing *truths of statement* of which it is composed."[2]

Henry James Sr. did not call Emerson a "man without a handle" for nothing, although it might be more apt to think of him as a man with all too many handles.

I am less interested, however, in the general, even marvelously self-contradictory texture of Emerson's prose than in a series of related contradictions and paradoxes that help shape Emerson's pragmatic idealism. These contradictions and paradoxes actually allow Emerson to balance, without exactly resolving, some of his deepest intellectual and spiritual conflicts. For one thing, Emerson's pragmatic idealism is grounded in a delicate balance of skepticism and faith. It is, for a certain kind of mind, unsettling to allow skepticism and faith to share the same psychological space. Emerson, however, thrives on his ability to make assertions that he will immediately reject or revise. He is a great believer, but he is also a careful skeptic, and he is more interested in the ways in which we believe and doubt, in the actual flow of experience, than in systems of belief or a systematically sustained skepticism. This dimension of his project has proven somewhat elusive to his critics. Emerson's prose is a little like the beautiful statue he describes in his essay "Love," which is beautiful "when it begins to be incomprehensible, when it is passing out of criticism" (*EL* 332). What could be more natural, given such elusiveness, than to try to hold him in place, to make him comprehensible by passing him into criticism: to play at Menelaus on the Egyptian strand, holding tight to a slippery Proteus in order to win the prophecy. But Emerson ever prefers the God to the critic. Skepticism and faith are both perfectly natural and vital attitudes, and Emerson attempts to cultivate both without reducing them to a petty consistency. As his Proteus analogy suggests, such contradictory energies, however incoherent and inconstant, actually constitute his idea of the sacred.

Emerson never defines what he means by the sacred. He decided very early that Christianity promoted notions of God and redemption as mediated through Jesus Christ that were simply too narrow and exclusive to encompass his own intuition of God. It is always unclear just what God means to Emerson. He certainly has no compunction about citing sources from every imaginable tradition or assimilating the latest scientific evidence to his conception of the sacred and ideal.[3] Nor does he hesitate to declare his own unimpeded impulses divine. Indeed, nothing could provide more certain access to the sacred. Emerson would neither limit his conception of God nor define a term like *the sacred* too narrowly. "The only sin," he comments in "Circles," "is limitation" (*EL* 406). Many spiritual and imaginative acts serve the interests of the sacred, and it would be a loss, by Emerson's calculations, to promote any one at the expense of so many others. Emerson's pragmatic idealism aims to cultivate the sacred without limiting it to any of its particular representations.

This is why Emerson is so dismissive of organization, even organization in the name of what is ostensibly good. Writing in his 1841 "Lecture on the Times" of what he calls the temptation of the young reformer to "lend himself to public movements," Emerson urges resistance to "the degradation of a man to a measure": "I must act with truth, though I should never come to act, as you call it, with effect. I must consent to inaction. A patience which is grand; a brave and cold neglect of the offices which prudence exacts, so it be done in a deep, upper piety; a consent to solitude and inaction, which proceeds out of an unwillingness to violate character, is the century which makes the gem" (*EL* 163). To consent to inaction, as Emerson puts it here, is actively to exercise restraint: a form of active passivity that locates agency precisely where it vanishes from the scene of its potentially visible triumph. Such "brave and cold neglect of the offices which prudence exacts" could easily devolve into a moral void, but it is redeemed — to the extent that it is redeemed — by the "deep, upper piety" in which this neglect is conceived and executed.[4]

But what distinguishes a morally bankrupt neglect from a "patience which is grand"? Surely, as stated in this passage, nothing that can be formulated as a code of prescribed behavior. The "deep, upper piety" in which Emerson's neglect is conceived is rather a state of mind governed by the effort, necessarily imperfect and inconclusive, to imagine our lives in light of our most profound aspirations and ideals. Anything that would put a definitive shape on those aspirations and ideals, that would define them, would also constrain the imaginative process whereby we envision and project those aspirations and ideals. By making our access to the sources of moral authority too assured, it would effectively limit the vital, ongoing cultivation of the sacred. Because our moral natures are always in the making, we must submit our most cherished ideals to a perpetual, demanding vigilance.[5]

It may seem odd to begin a study linking Emerson to pragmatism with a reference to one of Emerson's not infrequent calls to social inaction. William James conceived pragmatism as a form of intellectual activism: "A pragmatist turns his back resolutely and once for all upon a lot of inveterate habits dear to professional philosophers. He turns away from abstraction and insufficiency, from verbal solutions, from bad *a priori* reasons, from fixed principles, closed systems, and pretended absolutes and origins. He turns towards concreteness and adequacy, towards facts, towards action and towards power" (*W* 2:508–9). James's formulation suggests that we determine the nature of our truths and ideals by engaging our human problems just as they come to us, not by

*Emerson's Pragmatic Idealism*

the magic of metaphysical speculation. For James as well as for Dewey after him, metaphysics is a pale and inadequate substitute for the application of human intelligence to concrete social problems.

On the surface of things, Emerson appears to be bored by these human problems. He is bored by them, to the extent that they fail to engage his deepest imaginative sympathies. He writes of Transcendentalists in his 1842 address "The Transcendentalist" that "life and their faculty seem to them gifts too rich to be squandered on such trifles as you propose to them": "What you call your fundamental institutions, your great and holy causes, seem to them great abuses, and, when nearly seen, paltry matters. Each 'Cause,' as it is called, — say Abolition, Temperance, say Calvinism, or Unitarianism, — becomes speedily a little shop, where the article, let it have been at first never so subtle and ethereal, is now made up into portable and convenient cakes, and retailed in small quantities to suit purchasers. You make very free use of these words 'great' and 'holy,' but few things appear to them such" (*EL* 203). Long before mass media and celebrity combined to create a new way to package liberal causes, Emerson recognized that ideals are as easily commodified as other consumer goods, and that once commodified, they cease to engage our imaginative energies. Convenience and portability undermine Emerson's larger project of making human beings, the basis, for Emerson, of all genuine social reform.[6]

In fact, Emerson was all his life a champion of social reform. His first major address on slavery came not after Daniel Webster's infamous March 1, 1850, speech in support of the Compromise of 1850 and its Fugitive Slave Act (which outraged Emerson), nor in 1844 when he gave an Emancipation Day address in Concord, but as early as 1837, in a Concord address on "Slavery." This talk is largely unknown because it was never published and the manuscript has not survived, but the notes for the talk do appear in Emerson's journal. Although these notes reveal that Emerson held racist assumptions about Blacks, and that he did not see a larger role for white Northerners than voting their conscience — attitudes that would evolve over the next two decades — they also reveal his moral outrage at the institution of slavery and his support of its abolition.[7] Emerson is perfectly unambiguous on this score: "There is a little plain prose which has got I know to be somewhat tedious by often repetition which yet needs to be said again & again, until it has perforated the thick deaf ear, that no man can hold property in Man; that Reason is not chattel; cannot be bought & sold; and that every pretended traffic in such stock is invalid & criminal" (*JMN* 12:153–54). Emerson's language in the notes is sometimes quite passionate: "It is barbarism; it is amputation of so much of the moral & intellectual attributes of man" (*JMN* 12:158). The story of Emerson's involvement with the abolitionists has only slowly come to light, but it is unmistakable. Despite his early racial bigotry, Emerson opposed slavery from the first and considered it a moral duty to oppose it. Over time, he steadily demanded more of himself and of his fellow citizens.

Emerson supported many causes over the years, working with their various formal associations. He led an April 1838 effort to organize opposition to Van Buren's plan to relocate the Cherokee Nation and drafted an open letter to Van Buren protesting that "such a dereliction of all faith and virtue, such a denial of justice, and such deafness to screams for mercy were never heard of in times of peace and in the dealing of a nation with its own allies and wards, since the earth was made." He also served on committees, like the local Concord school committee, and gave addresses on various causes, like his 1838 address to the American Peace Society, "The Peace Principle," after which Garrison declared Emerson "a man of the new age." [8] The record of all of this activity has been slow to accumulate, in part because the earliest portraits of Emerson underplayed or altogether neglected this activity and in part because Emerson's major published essays — the essays Emerson himself chose to put before the reading public — relentlessly insist that social reform can only follow from self reform.

Emerson summarizes his dissatisfaction with the mania to reform in "New England Reformers," an address written and delivered early in 1844, just months before his emancipation address: "The criticism and attack on institutions which we have witnessed, has made one thing plain, that society gains nothing whilst a man, not himself renovated, attempts to renovate things around him: he has become tediously good in some particular, but negligent or narrow in the rest; and hypocrisy and vanity are often the disgusting result" (EL 596). "Disgusting" is a strong word, and one can only imagine that Emerson uses it to indicate his anger at his fellow citizens' capacity to support this or that cause without ever examining their more intimate obligations. His charge of hypocrisy reflects his sense that effective reform builds from within: "It is handsomer to remain in the establishment better than the establishment, and conduct that in the best manner, than to make a sally against evil by some single improvement, without supporting it by a total regeneration" (EL 596). Emerson holds his reformer to what may seem an impossibly high standard, but he does so to incite his audience, to make them recognize that so long as their rhetoric of reform refuses to acknowledge the interrelatedness of all institutions and their flaws — including institutions on which the reformer vitally depends — there can be no meaningful reform. This is precisely the sort of contradiction with which Emerson simply learned to live.

*Emerson's Pragmatic Idealism*

Emerson even insists that there is no position (or language) outside the present order of things from which to critique it:

All our things are right and wrong together. The wave of evil washes all our institutions alike. Do you complain of our Marriage? Our marriage is no worse than our education, our diet, our trade, our social customs. Do you complain of the laws of Property? It is a pedantry to give such importance to them. Can we not play the game of life with these counters, as well as with those; in the institution of property, as well as out of it. Let into it the new and renewing principle of love, and property will be universality. (*EL* 596)

This position on the danger of causes reflects Emerson's sense that such causes become a means of avoiding other obligations, assuaging the conscience without engaging it in the more demanding, uncertain struggle for renewal. Emerson never opposes social commitments, and in fact frequently encourages them, but he also insists that such commitments must flow from, and return to, a more profound, far-reaching concern. Above all, that commitment should not impede the continuing development of the individual, though of course this also means, however paradoxically, the continuing development of the myriad unfolding purposes that constitute the world. The sheer narrowness of devotion to a single cause struck Emerson as antithetical to the proper spirit of charity, which should recognize that the individual is defined not by any single purpose or ideal but by a complex web of purposes and ideals that together link individuals, with all their various needs and desires, to the world and to others in the world. Since every individual achieves meaning or purpose only within this complex web, every individual has a responsibility to the life of the whole.

It should be apparent that Emerson's discussion of reform turns on a subtle and pervasive paradox in his argument. The individual self has obligations only to itself ("Trust thyself: every heart vibrates to that iron string" — "Self-Reliance"), but those obligations at the same time reflect the individual's relatedness to the world as a whole ("Accept the place the divine providence has found for you, the society of your contemporaries, the connection of events" — the next sentence in "Self-Reliance" [*EL* 260]). The more individuated piety becomes, the less it is able to affect relations that extend in all directions; at the same time, if pious ideals are never individuated, they may never have any real effect in the world. This is the fundamental paradox at the heart of Emerson's writing: we only ever recognize the good as it is embodied in some particular circumstance, but any particular embodiment is a limitation of the good and so a hindrance to its further development. "Every spirit

*The Poetics of Transition*

makes its house," as he puts it in a passage cited earlier, "but afterwards the house confines the spirit" (*EL* 946).

This paradox informs Emerson's occasional habit of projecting a self that would be endlessly expansive, without constraining limits of any kind. Such a self would, in a sense, be selfless, since this self would have to be perfectly permeable to everything surrounding and sustaining it. Emerson likens this self, in "The Method of Nature," to an "ecstatical state": "It is pitiful to be an artist, when, by forbearing to be artists, we might be vessels filled with the divine overflowings, enriched by the circulations of omniscience and omnipresence" (*EL* 125). The dilemma Emerson is negotiating here is apparent in his very language. What could it mean to be a vessel "filled with the divine overflowings"? *Filled* implies a closed totality, whereas the *divine overflowings* imply an endless excess and superfluity. Is this self defined by the leavings of God, or is it undefined, rendered permeable by its participation in God's economy of excess? Or does this formulation imply something of both, a self at once defined by its limited participation in the divinity but still open to perpetual expansion by means of the unlimited potential of that participation?

The same contradiction is at play in Emerson's reference to the figure of the artist in this passage. The artist, it turns out, is too much himself, too personally present in the production of his art: "Are there not moments in the history of heaven when the human race was not counted by individuals, but was only the Influenced, was God in distribution, God rushing into multiform benefit? It is sublime to receive, sublime to love, but this lust of imparting as from *us,* this desire to be loved, the wish to be recognized as individuals, — is finite, comes of a lower strain" (*EL* 125). The prophet of self-reliance, then, is also, at least in one of his many famously shifting moods, skeptical of the individuated self. "God in distribution" appears to refer to the collection of selves constituting the human universe, working in all their combined distinctiveness and interrelatedness under, or rather as, God's influence. To separate one individual self out from this complex of selves is a kind of sacrilege, and not even the artist, generally a privileged figure for Emerson, is always free from the critical glare he casts at such failure of imagination.

For all the attention Emerson's notion of self-reliance has continuously attracted, the problem of Emerson's anxiety of individuation has never received adequate explanation. Emerson isolates the self as the authentic source of Being, but at the same time insists that the self is nothing in isolation. "Multiform benefit" belongs to the world as a whole, or to the world as a series of interrelated wholes, not to any individuated segment of it. Emerson will promote the isolated self only to the extent that by doing its own business, the self can forward the business of everything in the world that is not-self, or of all the world's energies-in-realization, which would include (without being limited to) the moral energies of humans. Emerson is committed to the sacred nature of the world's becoming, but he is at the same time skeptical of the vocabularies, institutions, causes, and rituals that claim to anchor the process of that becoming or to describe or delimit the nature of its sacredness. His skepticism and irony are characteristically directed toward these always imperfect systems, just as his faith and idealism are grounded in the ongoing processes of becoming that subsume those systems. But just as the self can only realize its divine purpose once it is individuated, so the sacred can only manifest itself within some coherent, particular system. Emerson needs the self and its sustaining systems, every bit as much as he needs to reject them.

Emerson first publicly grappled with this problem in deciding to leave the ministry in 1832, at the age of twenty-nine. Robert D. Richardson Jr. has noted that the dispute over the rite of communion is only a detail in what was a larger, long-simmering dispute with the central premise of Christian doctrine regarding sin and the role of Jesus in redemption. Emerson's wide reading in theology, natural philosophy, and science convinced him that revelation belonged not to any single theological practice or tradition, but to mind itself. "The Lord's Supper," his final sermon as minister of Boston's Second Church, reveals how central Emerson's concern with a constraining form is at the outset of his "secular" career. "Forms are as essential as bodies," he writes, "but to exalt particular forms, to adhere to one form a moment after it is out-grown, is unreasonable, and it is alien to the spirit of Christ" (*EL* 1138). Emerson would never entirely abandon a religious vocabulary, but, as his audiences changed, which is also to say as he sought different audiences, he would pursue other vocabularies that were less narrowly Christian. The "spirit of Christ" here is already indefinite enough, especially from an orthodox Christian point of view. Emerson rejects the rite of the sacrament because it belongs to another time and place, because it is, as he argues in the sermon, a secondary accretion to the religion rather than an essential and authentic practice. Christianity, he writes, "has for its object simply to make men good and wise": "Its institutions, then, should be as flexible as the wants of men. That form out of which the life and suitableness have departed, should be as worthless in its eyes as the dead leaves that are falling around us" (*EL* 1139).

"The Lord's Supper" is the result of what was surely one of Emerson's most significant spiritual struggles. The standard that Emerson applies in the sermon, and the one he was clearly applying in his own practice as minister, is one that is recognizably pragmatic. We must remember, he comments near the end of the talk, that "in the eye of God there is no other measure of the value of any one form than the measure of its use (*EL* 1139–40). Once a prac-

*The Poetics of Transition*

tice or rite has ceased to perform a useful function, it is time to abandon it, no matter how great its prestige among those who would preserve the form at all costs. This is obviously no narrow utilitarian measure. "Use" here suggests the way in which a value sets human energies, in all their potential, in motion. The sacred, for Emerson, is always a function of how human lives are inspired and provoked. Nothing is, in itself, so sacred that it can outlive this function. It is in this sense that his ideal is a pragmatic one. Emerson almost never envisions or even alludes to an eternal and perfect realm apart, but instead typically assumes that the ideal is a function of particular, imperfect, and immediately accessible actualities. Emerson's conception of the sacred and the ideal is thus tied to human experience in this world, a position that is bound to please neither the conventionally faithful, who will complain about his failure to comply with orthodox views, nor the conventionally skeptical, who will criticize his failure to follow his skepticism through to its logical conclusion.

Emerson's notorious 1838 address to the Harvard Divinity School expands the argument of "The Lord's Supper" by applying it not just to the rite of the sacrament but to the question of God's relationship to Jesus and to all humankind. Here again, Emerson combines skepticism and faith in equal parts. He faults the church for replacing Jesus' truly "provocative" teaching with institutions and rites: "The idioms of his language, and the figures of his rhetoric, have usurped the place of his truth; and churches are not built on his principles, but on his tropes" (*EL* 80). To read the Gospels correctly, one has to understand that Jesus spoke in symbols and parables. He did not intend to found permanent religious forms. By transmuting Jesus' parables and symbols into rites and institutions, we undermine the authentic power of his ministry, his ability to provoke and inspire us into new and newly enlightened postures of engagement with the world. Jesus' words do not describe a set of necessary forms, but rather encourage those with whom he had contact, and with whom he could continue to have contact via the Gospels, to reimagine their spiritual passage in this world. The church, according to Emerson, has obscured this ministry: "Historical Christianity has fallen into the error that corrupts all attempts to communicate religion. As it appears to us, and as it has appeared for ages, it is not the doctrine of the soul, but an exaggeration of the personal, the positive, the ritual. It has dwelt, it dwells, with noxious exaggeration about the *person* of Jesus. The soul knows no persons. It invites every man to expand to the full circle of the universe, and will have no preferences but those of spontaneous love" (*EL* 80–81).

Here one recognizes Emerson's characteristic geometry of the self: individuated selfhood collapses in favor of the self's expansion "to the full circle of the universe." Jesus is one of Emerson's great men, yet in correcting the

*Emerson's Pragmatic Idealism*

traditions that have accrued around him, and especially in seeking to reform the rites and institutions that have been founded on his rhetoric and tropes, Emerson insists that too much has been made of the person of Jesus. A great man, on this model, should teach us not to idolize his greatness, but rather to become great ourselves. This is why the introductory essay in *Representative Men* is titled "Uses of Great Men" instead of, more simply, "Great Men." "But *great men*," Emerson writes as he approaches the conclusion to that essay, "the word is injurious" (*EL* 629). Greatness brings with it the sort of "noxious exaggeration" that he had associated with the church's enshrinement of Jesus. Great men exist, he comments in "Uses of Great Men," "that there may be greater men" (*EL* 632).

So with Jesus: "Truly speaking," he writes in the Divinity School "Address," "it is not instruction, but provocation, that I can receive from another soul" (*EL* 79). Jesus inspires us to exercise our own divinity. The more he is appropriated and formalized by the church, the more "even virtue and truth [are] foreclosed and monopolized" (*EL* 81). Jesus should provoke us to constitute virtue and truth: "It is a low benefit to give me something; it is a high benefit to enable me to do somewhat of myself. The time is coming when all men will see, that the gift of God to the soul is not a vaunting, overpowering, excluding sanctity, but a sweet, natural goodness, a goodness like thine and mine, and that so invites thine and mine to be and to grow" (*EL* 82). Emerson suggests here that even goodness becomes an exclusive tool, allowing false and decadent ideals of sanctity to replace the concrete pursuit of good acts. Sanctity, in this regard, is a dangerous ideal, a path to God that is made all too easy: "We easily come up to the standard of goodness in society. Society's praise can be cheaply secured, and almost all men are content with those easy merits; but the instant effect of conversing with God, will be, to put them away. There are persons who are not actors, not speakers, but influences; persons too great for fame, for display; who disdain eloquence; to whom all we call art and artist, seems too nearly allied to show and by-ends, to the exaggeration of the finite and selfish, and loss of the universal" (*EL* 89–90).

Emerson makes no effort here to define what he means by "conversing with God." It is, effectively, coming under the influence of a strong provocation: the soul's response to such provocation. This provocation can come from any quarter. And not only are figures like Jesus subject to diminishment in this way, but even our own best, most inspired acts are subject to this same diminishment, as Emerson notes in his essay on Goethe: "Men's actions are too strong for them. Show me a man who has acted, and who has not been the victim and slave of his action. What they have done commits and enforces

*The Poetics of Transition*

them to do the same again. The first act, which was to be an experiment, becomes a sacrament" (*EL* 749).[9] What is good as an original action, as the spontaneous result of human feeling and desire engaged in some particular pursuit, becomes, almost by virtue of its success, an encumbrance. Our own spirits, then, must be as vigilant in their skepticism as they are pious in their faith. We have as much to fear from overestimation of a determined truth or ideal as from falsehood itself. "A man's wisdom," Emerson writes in "The Method of Nature," "is to know that all ends are momentary, that the best end must be superseded by a better. But there is a mischievous tendency in him to transfer his thought from the life to the ends, to quit his agency and rest in his acts: the tools run away with the workman, the human with the divine" (*EL* 124). What matters is onwardness, a perpetual development designed to resist the "mischievous tendency" to settle into a definitive form. Emerson would always favor the dynamic unfolding over any particular instance or phase of that unfolding.

This is the source of Emerson's skepticism regarding individuals. This skepticism will surprise readers used to taking Emerson's "self-reliance" as an end-in-itself, if not *the* Emersonian end-in-itself.[10] In fact, the individuated self elicits some of Emerson's most intricate and searching verbal maneuvering. The "blindness of the intellect begins," Emerson comments in "The Over-Soul," "when it would be something of itself. The weakness of the will begins, when the individual would be something of himself" (*EL* 387). Emerson rejects a conception of the self as isolated from its world. The strength of the individual is in its complex attachments, the relational matrix from which it derives its strength and to which it returns that strength. Emerson comments in "Uses of Great Men," "A man is a centre for nature, running out threads of relation through every thing, fluid and solid, material and elemental" (*EL* 618). Emerson's phrasing is telling: man is a center not *of* or *in* nature, but *for* nature, as if his being a center were a form of service in nature's interest.

Emerson's best critics have always recognized how slippery this self can be. For Richard Poirier, elusiveness is the defining feature of Emersonian self-hood: "Through his concept of 'genius' he manages to hold onto an idea of the self, even though it is a self far more shadowy than his rhetoric of individualism has led people to suppose. The self in Emerson is not an entity, not even a function; it is an intimation of presence, and it comes upon us out of the very act by which the self tries to elude definition." Referring to the way in which any available vocabulary becomes an obstacle even to conceiving the kind of self Emerson has in mind, Poirier cites the "dazzling complication of that moment in the essay 'Self-Reliance' when, in exasperation with his own title, Emerson asks, 'Why, then, do we prate of self-reliance? . . . To talk of reliance is a poor external way of speaking. Speak rather of that which relies, because it works and is.' "[11] This self-consuming gesture is like the one in "Uses of Great Men" cited earlier, in which Emerson calls the very phrasing *great men* "injurious." For Poirier, the self vanishes in the wake of Emerson's very act of writing—it is the movement of his tropes, not any detachable "power" responsible for that movement, that constitutes Emerson's, or any, genius. Indeed, this genius cannot even be Emerson's (let alone something like the "mind's" or "American Literature's"): it can belong only to the energies-in-realization, energies, for Poirier, of reading and writing.[12]

Donald Pease offers a similar, though more politically inflected reading of the Emersonian self: "The popular understanding of the doctrine [of self-reliance] consigns value to what Emerson himself denies is valuable—the individual's reliance upon his own person. The faculty of self-reliance permits the individual to discriminate the person's transitory interests from the unchanging principles upon which his person relies. An individual could then put those principles into practice, as Emerson did when he opposed the Fugitive Slave Law." Pease concludes that Emerson's "I" is never simply the individual subject, suggesting instead that the "spirit or the law of nature occupies the place of the subject in Emerson's essays, and each time Emerson writes, he impersonates this subjectivity." An individual can only impersonate subjectivity because that subjectivity is a manifestation of powers or, in Pease's analysis, laws that transcend individuation.[13]

Careful readers of Emerson have had to recognize that Emersonian self-reliance is never simply a matter of applying one's inner resources. Critics like Poirier and Pease instead read the term dialectically and self-reflexively. The self-reliant individual suspends even the available vocabularies of its own self-definition. But why, then, the constant and apparently defining emphasis on individuals throughout Emerson's prose? For all his sophisticated anti-humanism, Emerson remains as eloquent as any writer has ever been on the sanctity of the individual. In fact, the individual and its abiding genius exist for Emerson in a paradoxical relationship of mutual dependency and absolute incommensurability. The power of genius does not ultimately belong to a stable, coherent, rational agent, but rather derives from other powers that precede and subsume that agent and its agency. If anything, the more the rational agent controls the self, the less that self will actualize these powers. Ironically, the self remains the site at which this power circulates, even though it is in no way the source of that power.

This ambivalence toward the self is apparent everywhere in Emerson, as in the following description of the great man in "Uses of Great Men":

*The Poetics of Transition*

I like a master standing firm on legs of iron, well-born, rich, hand-some, eloquent, loaded with advantages, drawing all men by fascination into tributaries and supporters of his power. Sword and staff, or talents sword-like or staff-like, carry on the work of the world. But I find him greater, when he can abolish himself, and all heroes, by letting in this element of reason, irrespective of persons; this subtiliser, and irresistible upward force, into our thought, destroying individualism; the power so great, that the potentate is nothing. Then he is a monarch, who gives a constitution to his people; a pontiff, who preaches the equality of souls, and releases his servants from their barbarous homages; an emperor, who can spare his empire. (*EL* 625–26)

Greatness here is a form of self-consuming service. It operates not to its own personal ends but to ends of greater scope. It is one thing to be great and "carry on the work of the world," but another and still greater thing to abolish one's personal greatness in the broader interest. Paradoxically, this requires that one assume form as a great individual in order then to act as a channel for broader ends, "destroying individualism" in order to reap the benefits of individual genius.

Emerson sometimes figures this greatness in association not with a central, unified core of self, but instead with what always remains peripheral to that self. In an 1846 journal entry, he declares that "it is the largest part of a man that is not inventoried": for all the parts of the self that can be labeled, it is always the "remainder . . . which interests" (*JMN* 9:341). Emerson notes that the "preacher & poet & the musician" speak to this remainder, that "strong genius works upon" it, and that it constitutes "the region of destiny, of aspi-ration, of the unknown." Inchoate, full of contradictions and inconsistencies, the self's "remainder" is that part of the self which exceeds available defini-tion:

For the best part, I repeat, of every mind is not that which he knows, but that which hovers in gleams, suggestions, tantalizing unpossessed before him. His firm recorded knowledge soon loses all interest for him. But this dancing chorus of thoughts & hopes is the quarry of his future, is his possibility, & teaches him that his man's life is of a ridiculous brevity & meanness, but that it is his first age & trial only of his young wings, but that vast revolutions, migrations, & gyres on gyres in the celestial soci-eties invite him. (*JMN* 9:341)

What "hovers in gleams, suggestions" is the instrument of an always unfold-ing future. Such "unpossessed" knowledge drives genius to further realization, to the point even that, in Emerson's description, the human self becomes something of an angel, welcome at last in "the celestial societies." Genius "works upon" human responsiveness to pure possibility, and the Emersonian self is itself a figure for such possibility, a circle always expanding into broader circles by means of ceaseless crossings and transitions.

Another clue to the structuring paradoxes of Emerson's conception of self can be found in "The Method of Nature," an address delivered in August 1841, just months after the appearance of Emerson's first series of essays. Emerson's aunt, Mary Moody Emerson, one of Emerson's most esteemed correspondents, declared the volume, which includes "Self-Reliance," a "strange medley of atheism and false independence." There is nothing exactly new in "The Method of Nature," nothing to indicate a change in perspective, but the essay brings forward what is, elsewhere, more of an undercurrent in Emerson's argument. Whether or not Emerson felt compelled to write the essay as a response to characterizations, like his aunt's, that he could only feel were false to the spirit of his work, the essay stands almost as a reprimand of those who would confuse self-reliance with a spiritless individualism.

To begin, it is telling that Emerson chooses to emphasize not nature but its method. He emphasizes the laws that suffuse what otherwise would be a jumble of unrelated phenomena. Emerson never ceased to be awed by the fact that so many diverse facts could function as an integrated whole. In describing nature in this essay, Emerson has recourse to an analogy drawn from the sphere of human religious and psychological experience: "In short, the spirit and peculiarity of that impression nature makes on us, is this, that it does not exist to any one or to any number of particular ends, but to numberless and endless benefit; that there is in it no private will, no rebel leaf or limb, but the whole is oppressed by one superincumbent tendency, obeys that redundancy or excess of life which in conscious beings we call *ecstasy*" (*EL* 121). Ecstasy is Emerson's figure for the complex interrelatedness of all things, suggesting the quasi-mystical perception of manyness in oneness and oneness in manyness. In an ecstatic state, everything is related to everything else. The ecstatic self perceives no boundaries and so cannot separate one part of nature from another or distinguish the material world from the spiritual. Ecstasy is Emerson's figure for the self's fusion with nature's all-encompassing method. In our occasional experience of ecstasy, we intuit the active processes in nature that subsume us and our intuitions. Even in describing the relation of freedom and fate in "Fate" — "to see how fate slides into freedom, and freedom into fate" — Emerson utilizes the same model: "Our life is consentaneous and far-related. This knot of nature is so well tied, that nobody was ever cunning enough to find the two ends. Nature is intricate, overlapped, interweaved, and endless" (EL 961). Six wonder-filled paragraphs later, Emerson comments, "Life is an ecstasy" (EL 963).

This returns us to the problem of individuation: the difficulty in framing a conception of nature follows from the problem of framing it from an already individuated perspective. Nothing in nature is truly isolated, including individual selves, but at the same time, the intricate web of nature only works because individual selves accomplish their various, individuated functions. Emerson invokes this paradox in the passage from which the essay takes its title:

> The method of nature: who could ever analyze it? That rushing stream will not stop to be observed. We can never surprise nature in a corner; never find the end of a thread; never tell where to set the first stone. The bird hastens to lay her egg: the egg hastens to be a bird. The wholeness we admire in the order of the world, is the result of infinite distribution. Its smoothness is the smoothness of the pitch of the cataract. Its permanence is a perpetual inchoation. Every natural fact is an emanation, and that from which it emanates is an emanation also, and from every emanation is a new emanation. If anything could stand still, it would be crushed and dissipated by the torrent it resisted, and if it were a mind, would be crazed; as insane persons are those who hold fast to one thought, and do not flow with the course of nature. (EL 119)

According to Emerson's analogy of the rushing stream, the nature of individual objects is determined by their participation in encompassing processes. Nothing stands still on its own; everything is suffused by the surrounding stream. The doubleness of individual participants in the stream is reflected in the blunt paradoxes Emerson lists at the heart of this passage: wholeness as infinite distribution, permanence as perpetual inchoation, and emanations emanating from emanations, ad infinitum. Every part of the stream is most itself by virtue of its interdependence with the ongoing process of the whole. Identity is irreducibly relational. Any attempt to "stand still" is disastrous, a form of potentially destructive insanity.[14]

If nature exists as a complex, interrelated whole, always actively realizing itself, it is hard to know how the human mind can adequately comprehend that whole. Indeed, the passage begins in recognition of the limits of cognition: "The method of nature: who could ever analyze it?" Every cognition apparently isolates one element within the rushing stream and disengages it from the ecstatic, flowing whole. Nature will invariably resist any such effort to comprehend it: "Like an odor of incense, like a strain of music, like a sleep, it is inexact and boundless. It will not be dissected, nor unravelled, nor shown. Away profane philosopher! seekest thou in nature the cause? This refers to that, and that to the next, and the next to the third, and everything refers. Thou must ask in another mood, thou must feel it and love it, thou must behold it in a spirit as grand as that by which it exists, ere thou canst know the law. Known it will not be, but gladly beloved and enjoyed" (*EL* 119–20). There simply is no overcoming the gap between nature and the mind's cognition of it, so Emerson recommends that we approach nature in a different frame of mind, in the spirit of love and a perpetual self-overcoming. The spirit of knowing is too narrow and too static to open a passage into nature. Our intuition of nature's method should rather instill in us an attitude of awe.

Emerson does not worry that his sense of belonging to larger cosmic and social currents will undermine the authority he elsewhere invests in the individual self. These are phases of the same reality, and any overemphasis of one or the other would only distort the complex reality.[15] "Exaggeration," Emerson writes in the 1844 essay "Nature," "is in the course of things. Nature sends no creature, no man into the world, without adding a small excess of his proper quality" (*EL* 549). This excess guarantees that an individual will accomplish some particular function: "without this violence of direction, which men and women have, without a spice of bigot and fanatic, no excitement, no efficiency" (*EL* 549). Nature accomplishes its multiple and multiply interrelated ends, then, by generating individuals who believe in the significance of their own narrow, particular ends. This conviction is a distortion, but it is a happy distortion: "a *spice* of bigot and fanatic," Emerson hopefully hedges. Exaggeration helps sustain the health of all things. Human difference is formed by a self-deception built into the nature of things: "No man is quite sane; each has a vein of folly in his composition, a slight determination of blood to the head, to make sure of holding him hard to some one point which nature had taken to heart" (*EL* 550). In a sly turn on the figure of the over-soul, Emerson calls this the "overfaith of each man in the importance of what he has to do or say" (*EL* 550). The individuated self is a fantasy projected by a larger natural system that depends on such illusions to get its complex business done. It is telling that in a passage such as this, Emerson has made his peace with the sort of insanity he envisions in "The Method of Nature." A slight "vein of folly" is both necessary and healthy.

One does not have to go far to find Emerson contradicting this endorsement of the self's instinctive exaggerations. In "The Over-soul," as we have already seen, he equates the "blindness of the intellect" and "weakness of the will" with an overemphasis on the self and its narrow designs. So long as exaggeration serves nature's larger (and often, by this logic, incomprehensible) purposes, as in the later essay "Nature," it authorizes individuation. If exaggeration turns against this natural economy, however, it becomes an aberration and an obstacle. It will be recalled that in the Divinity School "Address," Emerson had related society's "cheaply secured" praise to "the exaggeration of the finite and selfish." When exaggeration can be pinned on mere will, it is a blindness or moral weakness, whereas when it can be viewed as a function of nature's larger, unwilled economy, it is not just indispensable but also the very basis of all particular genius.

Emerson's ambivalent authorization of the self's native exaggeration reflects another related ambivalence regarding the self's agency. In "Spiritual Laws," Emerson describes this agency in terms of the self's selective genius: "A man's genius, the quality that differences him from every other, the susceptibility to one class of influences, the selection of what is fit for him, the rejection of what is unfit, determines for him the character of the universe. A man is a method, a progressive arrangement; a selecting principle, gathering his like to him, wherever he goes. He takes only his own out of the multiplicity that sweeps and circles round him" (EL 311–12). Some of this language sounds active enough: a "selecting principle" has the ring of agency to it, and even seems to echo Kant's active, synthetic power. But is the self really the agent of selection here? The initial formulation, "the selection of what is fit for him," appears to attribute the agency of selection to some impersonal and mysterious force. So too the self's "susceptibility" to influence locates the agency of selection, so far as the self is concerned, in a condition of passivity and reception. Emerson's syntax here is telling: "A man's genius . . . determines for him. . . ." Emerson at once retains and undermines the self's agency by splitting a man's genius off from his actively thinking, willing self.

Selection is a key problem for Emerson, as it would be, however named, for all of the writers most deeply influenced by him. If the method of nature is process and relation-in-realization, then on what basis does individual selection occur? When is selection not a form of distortion? Emerson calls successful selection "the soul's emphasis": "What your heart thinks great is great. The soul's emphasis is always right" (EL 312). It is the "soul's emphasis" because anything less would cast suspicion on it. How else could selection, with all its implications of narrowing, limiting, constraining, ever be legitimized? So long as it comes from the regions of the soul—from the "deep, upper piety" that we noted earlier—it carries with it the authority of the whole, whose purposes and ends are simply hidden from mere discursive reason.

Emerson's metaphors throughout his description of the self as "a selecting principle" underscore the unconsciousness of the selective process:

*Emerson's Pragmatic Idealism*

He is like one of those booms which are set out from the shore on rivers to catch driftwood, or like the loadstone amongst splinters of steel. Those facts, words, persons, which dwell in his memory without his being able to say why, remain, because they have a relation to him not less real for being as yet unapprehended. They are symbols of value to him, as they can interpret parts of his consciousness which he would vainly seek words for in the conventional images of books and other minds. What attracts my attention shall have it, as I will go to the man who knocks at my door, whilst a thousand persons, as worthy, go by it, to whom I give no regard. It is enough that these particulars speak to me. (*EL* 312)

If the force of attraction were apprehended, it would cease to be a matter of soul and become instead a matter of understanding and narrow calculation, subject to all of the error characteristic of these more limited and instrumental forms of cognition. The boom, the loadstone, and the knock at the door all underscore the idea basic to Emerson's sense of authentic self-reliance, that it is never an affair of calculating advantages but is rather one of an inner depth intuitively and mysteriously answering an irresistible call from without. "What attracts my attention shall have it": the best we can do, apparently, is reason about choice after the fact, all the really vital factors having been determined and set in play without our active involvement anyway.

It will be obvious that this doesn't explain the vagaries of attention so much as it attributes the principle of selection to a higher power, or more specifically, to the self's unconscious or preconscious ability to act as a channel to that higher or encompassing power. If we think of this encompassing power as Spirit or God, this formulation will be satisfying so far as we already attribute this sort of role to something we call Spirit or God. But it is not altogether clear that Emerson simply thinks of this higher power as God, or just what it would mean to invoke God in such a context. Emerson never shies away from a religious vocabulary, but he also seems to view that vocabulary as itself limited, burdened by the baggage of its dogma, rites, and institutions. Even *soul* is a term that Emerson uses with a distinct nonchalance, if not exactly skepticism: it is not clear that the word *soul* is meant, by Emerson, to correspond to some definite reality, so much as to indicate a real force that is indefinite to its endlessly elusive core. This reality can be called God, Spirit, or Soul, but it can also be thought of as the broader currents of being in which the self becomes aware of itself as well as of its insubstantiality and insignificance in relation to those same currents of being.

In "The Method of Nature," Emerson figures these pervasive currents of being as "ecstasy" and "tendency," terms which tend to displace the super-natural Soul onto the world's natural processes. *Ecstasy* and *tendency* call to mind the active processes that encompass (and constitute) individuals. Emerson figures nature as one magnificent *tendency,* a vast ongoing process that suffuses everything. Every individual in nature is similarly a process-within-a-process. It is fascinating to watch Emerson juggling the language of philosophy to articulate this elusive perception: "Nature can only be conceived as existing to a universal and not to a particular end, to a universe of ends, and not to one, — a work of *ecstasy,* to be represented by a circular movement, as intention might be signified by a straight line of definite length" (*EL* 120). Emerson cannot quite be done with this sentence. It is as if every further clause would complete the thought, though completion here is still an illusion, the satisfaction of something definite ("a straight line of definite length") where all is, in reality, hazily indefinite ("circular movement"). A "universal end" is not necessarily the same thing as a "universe of ends," but Emerson's qualifying syntax suggests that they are very nearly the same. The One End of nature has become indistinguishable from its innumerable particular ends, each apparently going its own way. Emerson invokes *ecstasy* again here, almost as if to authorize the apparent illogic of the assertion. This effect is reinforced by his characteristic geometry, by which the straight lines of chronology and teleological purpose are replaced by the circles that indicate a multipurposeful, multi-intentional eternal return. Everything exists in relation, participating in larger systems, at once determined by these systems and actively determining them.

The interconnectedness of all things, including all things human, leads Emerson to associate nature with a state of mystical possession in which the usual boundaries separating self from world are suspended. Hence, the soul "can be appeased not by a deed but by a tendency" (*EL* 127). Every action must contribute to some larger current of unfolding forces that renders that same action irrelevant. The soul must project itself toward an ideal that destroys the soul in order to lead beyond it: "The imaginative faculty of the soul must be fed with objects immense and eternal. Your end should be one inapprehensible to the senses: then will it be a god always approached, — never touched; always giving health" (*EL* 128). In other words, the health of the self depends on its feeling of interrelatedness to everything that exceeds and so in some sense ruins the self and its limited inventions. The self must live in tendency. Its designs must be conceived in the spirit of reverence which recognizes the paltriness of all narrowly human designs. "What is Love," Emerson asks, "and why is it the chief good, but because it is an overpowering enthusiasm? Never self-possessed or prudent, it is all abandonment" (*EL* 128). Love and soul belong to the universe, not to the self. They are realized as an abandonment to energies that encompass the self. "The way of life is wonderful," Emerson comments in the conclusion of "Circles": "it is by abandonment" (*EL* 414). We live most authentically in loosing the grip of our personal attachments: "The one thing which we seek with insatiable desire is to forget ourselves, to be surprised out of our propriety, to lose our sempiternal memory, and to do something without knowing how or why; in short, to draw a new circle" (*EL* 414). Our desire to lose effective agency is insatiable because that is the only thing we cannot actually will into being. To do something "without knowing how or why" we find ourselves doing it is to have already released control to those energies that force us perpetually to abandon what we think of as our most authentic selves.[16]

By participating in the ecstatic tendency of things, the Emersonian self achieves a radically qualified will: "The poet must be a rhapsodist: his inspiration a sort of bright casualty: his will in it only the surrender of will to the Universal Power, which will not be seen face to face, but must be received and sympathetically known" (*EL* 126). Will and surrender of will are indistinguishable here. Passivity toward external things authorizes the self's active posture toward those things. "The only way into nature," Emerson comments, "is to enact our best insight. Instantly we are higher poets, and can speak a deeper law. Do what you know, and perception is converted into character, as islands and continents were built by invisible infusories, or, as these forest leaves absorb light, electricity, and volatile gases, and the gnarled oak to live a thousand years is the arrest and fixation of the most volatile and ethereal currents" (*EL* 131). Our "best insight" is not an ideal knowledge. It is irreducibly situated and particular, but at the same time, precisely because it is the realization of that situated particularity, it is also related to the universal processes that shape that insight.

Emerson's metaphors here are once again revealing. What we know as islands, leaves, and trees are in fact the manifestations of invisible or microscopic natural processes, about which Emerson actually had much of the latest scientific information.[17] We should learn to behave like nature, enacting our best (most hidden) insight in order to convert perception into character. In other moods, and indeed more often than not, Emerson laments "arrest and fixation." Here, however, they function to collect and focus the energies circulating through all things. As the natural imagery of this passage suggests, an individual is the fixed result of complex natural processes that constitute the conditions of its individuation. Humans are both of such processes, and particular foci within them, like the other forms of living energy described in the passage. When Emerson says in concluding "The Method of Nature" that the soul "goes out through universal love to universal power" (*EL* 132), he reminds his reader that the active soul's power depends on its complex relationality and on its sense of awe before the priority and sheer extent of these relations. Universal love—already described earlier in the essay as "all abandonment"—and universal power are mutually reinforcing terms for Emerson. One authorizes, even redeems the other. So long as power is exercised in a spirit of reverence, it is a service to the world. Of course, what constitutes the spirit of reverence must remain an open, even an endlessly troubling question.

This indeterminacy of the spirit of reverence can be linked to Emerson's description near the conclusion of "Compensation" of the soul as a site of perpetual reinvention:

> Every soul is by this intrinsic necessity quitting its whole system of things, its friends, and home, and laws, and faith, as the shell-fish crawls out of its beautiful but stony case, because it no longer admits of its growth, and slowly forms a new house. In proportion to the vigor of the individual, these revolutions are frequent, until in some happier mind they are incessant, and all worldly relations hang very loosely about him, becoming, as it were, a transparent fluid membrane through which the living form is seen, and not, as in most men, an indurated heterogeneous fabric of many dates, and of no settled character, in which the man is imprisoned. (*EL* 301–2)

What exactly is the soul here? For one thing, to the extent that the self remains content with its "whole system of things," it is not soul at all, but rather a complacent, dispirited individual. As "a transparent fluid membrane," Emerson's soul allows the self to retain some minimal identity, while giving that identity maximum flexibility to adjust and readjust even its most basic and defining characteristics ("its friends, and home, and laws, and faith"). Strength of soul is not a power to impose but instead a power of responsiveness. The more vigorous the individual, the more flexible the soul.

This "transparent fluid membrane" recalls the more famous "transparent eye-ball" of *Nature:* "Standing on the bare ground,—my head bathed by the blithe air, and uplifted into infinite space,—all mean egotism vanishes. I become a transparent eye-ball; I am nothing; I see all; the currents of the Universal Being circulate through me; I am part or particle of God" (*EL* 10). In order to see all, the transparent eyeball must first be nothing. This passage suggests that power derives from a vigorously cultivated passivity. The triumphant will is a matter of right reception. "In the tranquil landscape," Emerson writes in the same passage, "and especially in the distant line of the horizon, man beholds somewhat as beautiful as his own nature" (*EL* 10). By "his own nature,"

*Emerson's Pragmatic Idealism*

Emerson can only mean the human organism, in all its stunning complexity. Like the world around them, humans are natural phenomena, just as beautiful and mysterious, just as subject to natural law, and just as elusive as the "distant line of the horizon." It is this feeling of interrelation that the landscape and the horizon stir in Emerson. Even in the transparent eye-ball passage, Emerson is not suggesting that the self somehow replaces or displaces nature, but rather that the ecstatic experience in nature renders the boundary between self and nature permeable. We realize how complex our involvement in our environment really is, how far our relations extend, and perhaps too, as the remainder of *Nature* suggests, how far we are from realizing the potential of that relatedness. It is this always unrealized, infinitely extending relationality that keeps pushing the Emersonian self beyond its familiar bounds.

Emerson has myriad ways of indicating the overflow that is located both within and beyond the self. His descriptions frequently emphasize the impossibility of naming such "divine overflowings," as when he describes beauty in his essay "Love": "We cannot approach beauty. Its nature is like opaline doves'-neck lustres, hovering and evanescent. Herein it resembles the most excellent things, which all have this rainbow character, defying all attempts at appropriation and use" (*EL* 332). If we could define beauty, it would lose its appeal. Beauty instead hinges on its indefiniteness and inaccessibility: "The statue is then beautiful when it begins to be incomprehensible, when it is passing out of criticism, and can no longer be defined by compass and measuring-wand, but demands an active imagination to go with it, and to say what it is in the act of doing. The god or hero of the sculptor is always represented in a transition *from* that which is representable to the senses, *to* that which is not" (*EL* 332–33). The perception of beauty is a function of our critical, intellectual limitations. Just where the object is "passing out of criticism," it becomes the site of our interested, engaged attention. Beauty is invariably in transition. It belongs not to any realized form, but to those energies set in play by realized forms.

Although Emerson privileges the poet, the artist, and the thinker as figures who encourage this always expansive realization, he is everywhere careful to question the value of the works these figures produce. Even the most liberating works are dangerous to the extent that they become viewed as ends in themselves. The caution Emerson urges with respect to Swedenborg is perfectly characteristic: "These books should be used with caution. It is dangerous to sculpture these evanescing images of thought. True in transition, they become false if fixed. It requires, for his just apprehension, almost a genius equal to his own" (*EL* 682). Emerson admires Swedenborg's spiritual symbolism, but he is also skeptical of Swedenborg's literalizations, his habit of reading direct correspondences between the material and spiritual worlds. Emerson comments in an 1846 journal entry that "the world is enigmatical, every thing said & every thing known & done, & must not be taken literally, but genially. We must be at the top of our condition to understand any thing rightly" (*JMN* 9:351). To take the world genially, one must approach it not only with broad sympathy but also with a spark of genius. We resist dull literalizations by exercising our sympathetic imaginations toward the world.

Writing more generally (not to say less genially) in "The American Scholar," Emerson comments: "Books are the best of things, well used; abused, among the worst. What is the right use? What is the one end, which all means go to effect? They are for nothing but to inspire" (*EL* 57). The problem with books, like the problem with all ideas, is that they become exclusive: "The book, the college, the school of art, the institution of any kind, stop with some past utterance of genius" (*EL* 57). The point, for Emerson, is to extend beyond the past utterance, to become genius oneself. In a sense, genius has no past, no identity. It is always renewed in the present, as the word's roots in Latin and Greek verbs for "to beget" suggest. "The great poet," Emerson writes in "The Over-Soul," "makes us feel our own wealth, and then we think less of his compositions. His best communication to our mind is to teach us to despise all he has done" (*EL* 396). A book should teach us how to despise that same book. We will have learned from it to expect more, to turn our own energies toward whatever it aimed at but did not realize. The same will hold for any beautiful act, any moral fulfillment, any true statement: the very satisfaction they offer is bound up with something promised and not yet realized. "What is it men love in Genius," Emerson asks in "New England Reformers," "but its infinite hope, which degrades all it has done?" (*EL* 601).

Emerson describes the transitional dynamic of this infinite hope in "Circles." The circle provides him with the ideal form: it encloses, and so sets limits, but also expands, each horizon or circumference becoming the center of another circle. Emerson describes the "life of man" as "a self-evolving circle, which, from a ring imperceptibly small, rushes on all sides outwards to new and larger circles, and that without end." The circle is Emerson's figure of figures, collapsing the eye and its horizon, a life and the world that includes it, the forms of pleasure (the kitten chasing its tail, in one of Emerson's examples) and the forms of art and politics. It is a fundamentally dynamic figure:

> The extent to which this generation of circles, wheel without wheel, will go, depends on the force or truth of the individual soul. For it is the inert effort of each thought, having formed itself into a circular wave of cir-

cumstance, — as, for instance, an empire, rules of an art, a local usage, a religious rite, — to heap itself on that ridge, and to solidify and hem in the life. But if the soul is quick and strong, it bursts over that boundary on all sides, and expands another orbit on the great deep, which also runs up into a high wave, with attempt again to stop and to bind. (*EL* 404)

It is telling that Emerson could not write this last sentence without turning it back on itself, circling back, in its concluding clause. Every expansion thus implies another limitation. Just as telling, Emerson adds another qualifying sentence: "But the heart refuses to be imprisoned; in its first and narrowest pulses, it already tends outward with a vast force, and to immense and innumerable expansions" (*EL* 404–5). The circle, for Emerson, has dual connotations. It is both a limit and a dynamic force. At all times, circles enclose us, but their limits provide the basis for their own overcoming in the form of a new horizon. Every slightest pulse is already, at its very generation, tending "outward with a vast force." "Circles" is Emerson's testimony to the dynamic energies that outrun our best ideals, values, aspirations, or actions.

This preference for dynamic energies over the objects they produce suggests why Emerson celebrates the figure of the artist and the poet even while rejecting their productions as limited realizations of their initial promise. Every transition is ultimately judged on this sliding scale. Emerson comments, in "Art," that "there is higher work for Art than the arts" (*EL* 437). To the extent that art is an end in itself, it falls short of its full potential, its "higher work." That higher work belongs to the circulating energies that run through the creation and experience of art, not to the momentary foci of those energies. Art "should exhilarate, and throw down the walls of circumstance on every side, awakening in the beholder the same sense of universal relation and power which the work evinced in the artist, and its highest effect is to make new artists" (*EL* 437). To make new artists or to stimulate genius is to generate new and constantly renewing imaginative forms. Art is a privileged category for Emerson because of its stimulating power. No work of art is ever final or definitive. It claims no final truth outside its power to affect an audience. Art is the perpetual exercise of transitional imaginative energies.

The throwing down of walls echoes several key passages in "Circles." The poet, in that essay, "smites and arouses me with his shrill tones, breaks up my whole chain of habits, and I open my eye on my own possibilities" (*EL* 409). In great conversation, "all that we reckoned settled shakes and rattles; and literatures, cities, climates, religions, leave their foundations, and dance before our eyes" (*EL* 408). When "the great God lets loose a thinker on this planet," all things "are at risk": "It is as when a conflagration has broken out in a great city, and no man knows what is safe, or where it will end" (EL 407). Art, great conversation, great thoughts, all have the effect of breaking down former limits and opening up new possibilities. They are the pulses of transition. In one version of this scenario, Emerson acknowledges the implicit and inevitable tyranny even of the new possibility, but retains his faith that the process will subsume every tyranny in its turn: "When each new speaker strikes a new light, emancipates us from the oppression of the last speaker, to oppress us with the greatness and exclusiveness of his own thought, then yields us to another redeemer, we seem to recover our rights, to become men" (EL 408). The new emancipation, then, is also a form of oppression. As ever, Emerson learns to trust the larger process that includes and subsumes each particular redeeming light. Becoming men is a function not of any single idea, but of our ability to adopt and reject ideas (or prevailing metaphors, analogies, paradigms, systems of belief, and so on) over time. Emerson also calls this "recover[ing] our rights," as if our rights had somehow been diminished or we had diminished them by neglecting to cultivate them.[18]

To write about art and thought in this way is, however, also to cultivate a distinct risk: where art and thought become fetishized as ends-in-themselves, they are detached from the vital contexts of experience. They become idealized and abstract, objects of blind veneration and toys of luxury and idle leisure. This is antithetical to Emerson's understanding of authentic art and thought. Indeed, the transitions he describes in "Circles," "Art," and other essays and addresses are initiated by the failure of available art and thought to inspire or provoke an audience in meaningful ways. "Art must not be a superficial talent," Emerson insists in "Art," "but must begin farther back in man" (EL 439). Presently, he suggests, art and life are conceived as separate spheres: "They reject life as prosaic, and create a death which they call poetic. They despatch the day's weary chores, and fly to voluptuous reveries. They eat and drink, that they may afterwards execute the ideal" (EL 439). Execute, here, has a frightening double sense: not only do we accomplish our ideal in such art, but, separated thus from the affirmative contexts and activities of living, we also kill the ideal. Any ideal so imagined is also a dead and deadening ideal. What Emerson recommends by contrast would acknowledge life as poetic, and poetry as a necessary dimension of life: "Would it not be better to begin higher up,—to serve the ideal before they eat and drink; to serve the ideal in eating and drinking, in drawing the breath, and in the functions of life?" (EL 439). Art is in this sense the instrument of Emerson's pragmatic idealism. Such art is both less and more than the great works of art. It is the transitional agency that passes through works of art and serves to provoke or inspire new works of art. Art preserves the ideal, but only as an integrated dimension of lived experience.

Emerson concludes his essay on art by looking to the practical world and demanding that it be viewed with an eye to its "beauty and holiness": "Proceeding from a religious heart it will raise to a divine use the railroad, the insurance office, the joint-stock company, our law, our primary assemblies, our commerce, the galvanic battery, the electric jar, the prism, and the chemist's retort, in which we seek now only an economical use" (EL 440). This will seem naive to the extent that we see these technologies and economic arrangements as already co-opted by alienating and degrading social forces. But Emerson is challenging us to imagine how a "religious heart" might "raise" these forces "to a divine use." Near the conclusion of "Art," he associates this transitional agency with the power of love: "When science is learned in love, and its powers are wielded by love, they will appear the supplements and continuations of the material creation" (EL 440). According to most definitions, science does not depend on love. It is objective precisely because its empirical and experimental methods transcend human interests and emotions. But Emerson's point, made well before pragmatists and other post-Enlightenment theorists began to question the scientist ethos of objectivity, is precisely that science can and should be practiced with an eye to irreducible human interests and emotions. In this way, human ideals are embedded in the real conditions of experience, just as those conditions are continuously scrutinized and transformed by those same ideals.

It is hard to know exactly what this means, but this is not to say that it is meaningless. What is clear is that Emerson's divinity is indistinguishable from the "divine use" of technologies and other material conditions. To be any more explicit would simply be to apply some version of the available expectations and definitions. To suspend these expectations and definitions is unquestionably disorienting. Nothing Emerson says guarantees that our moral and social ideals will ultimately promote the interests of what we already recognize as good or true. In the absence of this kind of assurance, Emerson turns his focus to the transitional agencies themselves. These at least keep bringing new working definitions of the good (and the beautiful and true) into focus. As determined as we are by present conditions and the various institutional, cultural, and linguistic forms that support and reproduce them—what Emerson would simply call fate—there is always another force that effectively counters these settled determinations: "If Fate follows and limits power, power attends and antagonizes Fate" (EL 953). Power here is not simply the power of particular interests or individuals. It is not, in an important sense, human power at all and even depends on our ability to suspend our narrowly humanist aspirations. Power does not simply reinforce what presently passes as true or beautiful or good, but instead serves to carve out new ways of imagining and using such terms.

Emerson is constantly attempting to provoke his audience into assuming this inhuman power. This is the burden of his comment near the conclusion of "Experience": "In this our talking America, we are ruined by our good nature and listening on all sides. This compliance takes away the power of being greatly useful. A man should not be able to look other than directly and forthright. A preoccupied attention is the only answer to the importunate frivolity of other people: an attention, and to an aim which makes their wants frivolous" (*EL* 490). Our "talking America" is Emerson's figure for a nation that traffics in superficial moral values and social programs. Our "good nature" and "listening on all sides" is that part of us that looks to external definitions of the good as the basis of our own moral identifications. Emerson calls this compliance. To the extent that we form our ideals in this way, we remain cut off from the real sources of power. Such power may be located in an individual, but it serves unfolding purposes that are ultimately much larger than any individual and its narrow self-interests.

One can only begin to discover what it might mean to be greatly useful after suspending the prevailing and coercive definitions of usefulness. A "preoccupied attention"—utterly absorbed in its own demanding sense of what should count as useful, good, true, or beautiful—is necessary because nothing less could withstand the demands to conform imposed on the self from without. One simply has to cultivate that "brave and cold neglect of the offices which prudence exacts" in order to discover one's own divine use. Still, the problem of attention remains deep and perplexing. To return to the questions posed at the outset of this chapter, what guarantees that a "preoccupied attention" is not merely a self-centered one? Emerson never offers an easy answer to this question. Though some kind of answer would go far to boost our moral confidence, such confidence would probably only lead to moral arrogance and ineptitude. Emerson's own faith is sustained by his indefatigable trust in the larger processes or energies that at once rely on and subsume a preoccupied attention. He believes that so long as people continue to be imaginatively provoked by these energies, they will find the resources to exercise their own moral and intellectual energies. Paradoxically, these same moral and intellectual energies would serve the larger web of interests that constitutes the very conditions of subjectivity. Still, nothing in this faith protects against our inevitable failures of imagination. Emerson simply assumes that a genuinely preoccupied attention will do no serious wrong.

*Emerson's Pragmatic Idealism*

In their later elaborations of this transitional dynamic, pragmatists and literary modernists would variously address this problem. Since none of these writers appeal to any external, objective standard of truth or moral goodness, they typically emphasize that only the ongoing process of continuous imaginative activity can provide adequate protection against intellectual error and moral disaster. This process is designed to include mistakes—false beliefs and moral failures—from which both individuals and larger social communities learn. Mistakes contribute to the unfolding process by stimulating fresh adjustments and modifications in practice and belief. Such creative intelligence posits no definitive ideal or standard of truth, beauty, or goodness, but instead cultivates a transitional dynamic that at once assimilates and recasts available ideals and standards. Emerson's sacred unfolding of "life, transition, the energizing spirit" becomes, for William James and those he would influence, a dynamic principle of psychological, linguistic, and social organization, a principle predicated on James's own metaphorics of transition.

*The Poetics of Transition*

# 2

# William James and the
# Metaphorics of Transition

THE METAPHORICS OF transition is one of William James's most important, and neglected, Emersonian inheritances. "Life," James comments in a 1904 essay titled "A World of Pure Experience," "is in the transitions as much as in the terms connected." This is the sort of peculiar comment James was given to making, committed as he was to reversing the ways philosophers had of getting experience into language. He continues:

> Often, indeed, it seems to be there more emphatically, as if our spurts and sallies forward were the real firing-line of the battle, were like the thin line of flame advancing across the dry autumnal field which the farmer proceeds to burn. In this line we live prospectively as well as retrospectively. It is "of" the past, inasmuch as it comes expressly as the past's continuation; it is "of" the future in so far as the future, when it comes, will have continued *it*. (*W* 2:1181)

James's formulation here reflects his desire to place an active dynamic at the center of his conception of life. Life is not modeled on a thing or a condition, but rather on a dynamic process. We are most alive in the transitions that link past and future, in a continuation that is also a transformation.

Transition is the most basic unit (or event) of the pluralistic and heterogeneous tendency that James hoped to promote, in intellectual and scientific discourse as well as in social practice. The site of a transition figures for James the paradoxical spatial and temporal unfolding in which individual and pluralistic forces are not so much opposed as mutually constitutive. This means that, in transition, the individual is always being constituted relationally, as a function of a pluralistic heterogeneity. This dynamic is easily obscured by what typically passes as James's individualism, often described by

James's critics, admiring and otherwise, as a fundamental Jamesian ideal. In Cornel West's genealogy of pragmatism, James, who precedes the "coming-of-age of American pragmatism," is "first and foremost a moralist obsessed with heroic energies and reconciliatory strategies available to individuals."[1] For others, James's pluralistic individualism, couched in the capitalistic metaphors of a possessive individualism, masks even as it reproduces American laissez-faire market values, with all their defining structural exclusions.[2] By emphasizing James's market metaphors, these critics sometimes miss the broader dynamics of James's individualism, especially as that individualism is subsumed by his metaphorics of transition.

In "The Stream of Thought," the ninth chapter of *The Principles of Psychology,* James suggests that "feelings of tendency" are crucial to the working of mind.[3] Even the metaphor of the stream highlights the dynamic dimension of James's conception of thought. James is responding to the two dominant conceptions of mind of the day, what he calls the sensationalist account, which stresses the association of individual and disjointed sensations, and the intellectualist account, which stresses the rational ideas that bind sensations together. Both conceptions, according to James's fundamentally phenomenological view, ignore the basic experience of thought, which includes both discrete elements and their felt relations.[4] Even the experience of discontinuity is always an experience of a particular kind of discontinuity, which implies a continuity, latent or manifest, which the experience of discontinuity has broken. Abstract ideas, for all their sameness from context to context, are suffused in experience by what later phenomenologists would call the horizons of understanding that determine their meaning. Though logic holds that concepts are unchanging, in experience the same concept is subtly different every time it is evoked, depending on the shifting circumstances (in time, place, perspective, etc.) within which it is evoked.

"Thought," as James puts it in one chapter subheading, "is in Constant Change" (PP 1:224). James insists that nothing is identical in succeeding states of a thought: "When the identical fact recurs, we *must* think of it in a fresh manner, see it under a somewhat different angle, apprehend it in different relations from those in which it last appeared. And the thought by which we cognize it is the thought of it-in-those-relations, a thought suffused with the consciousness of all that dim context" (PP 1:227). Thoughts are always thoughts-in-relation, and no abstract form of those thoughts underlies or secures their shifting relations. The notion of a permanently existing idea is, according to James, "as mythological an entity as the Jack of Spades" (PP 1:230), a fantasy projected by our inveterate habit of confusing a mental process with its end product. Since we keep talking about a table, or justice, or the color blue, we imagine a permanent mental or ideal form that we think of as a Table, or Justice, or Blueness. But there is no Table, only tables, just as Justice is only the always unfinished product of many centuries of legal and political give and take and Blueness is an attempt to generalize from our individual and collective experience of all things blue. James suggests that inflected languages provide a better guide to the way our minds actually work: "Names did not appear in them inalterable, but changed their shape to suit the context in which they lay. It must have been easier then than now to conceive of the same object as being thought of at different times in non-identical conscious states" (*PP* 1:230).

Instead of conceiving thought in empirical-associationist or intellectualist terms, James proposes a dynamic model that depends on an interplay of continuities and transitions. He uses the example of a silence broken by a loud interruption or explosion to demonstrate that even a felt discontinuity is registered in relation to abiding feelings of continuity:

> A silence may be broken by a thunder-clap, and we may be so stunned and confused for a moment by the shock as to give no instant account to ourselves of what has happened. But that very confusion is a mental state, and a state that passes us straight over from the silence to the sound. The transition between the thought of one object and the thought of another is no more a break in the *thought* than a joint in a bamboo is a break in the wood. It is a part of the *consciousness* as much as the joint is a part of the *bamboo*. (*PP* 1:233–34)

An underlying continuity structures the perception of every particular discontinuity. There is, in James's description of the thunder clap, no purely separate instance that constitutes the essence of thunder: "Into the awareness of the thunder itself the awareness of the previous silence creeps and continues; for what we hear when the thunder crashes is not thunder *pure,* but thunder-breaking-upon-silence-and-contrasting-with-it" (*PP* 1:234). Consciousness is never reducible to any immediate perception or sensation. It always depends on what came before, as well as on the anticipation of what is to follow. James comments that language "works against our perception of the truth": "We name our thoughts simply, each after its thing, as if each knew its own thing and nothing else. What each really knows is clearly the thing it is named for, with dimly perhaps a thousand other things. It ought to be named after all of them, but it never is" (*PP* 1:234). Consciousness is a process in time, even if the language in which we become aware of it tends to isolate objects of consciousness as if they transcended the temporal structure of consciousness. Just as a long statement will be reduced to its gist, so mental processes get reduced to the apparent objects of those processes.

James analyzes sentences in order to illustrate these processes and approximate a mind at work. Commenting on the sentence "Columbus discovered America in 1492," James notes that most people will take either Columbus, America, or 1492 as the "topic" of the sentence, what it is "about." But he suggests that "it is a vicious use of speech to take out a substantive kernel from its content and call that its object," and just as vicious to "add a substantive kernel not articulately included in its content, and to call that its object" (*PP* 1:265). Only the entire sentence — "Columbus-discovered-America-in-1492" — is the unfolding object of the thought. Nothing but this hyphenated form, James comments, "can possibly name its delicate idiosyncrasy. And if we wish to *feel* that idiosyncrasy we must reproduce the thought as it was uttered, with every word fringed and the whole sentence bathed in that original halo of obscure relations, which, like an horizon, then spread about its meaning" (*PP* 1:266). The horizon of the sentence will depend on its running associations, some of them shared, others personally idiosyncratic. Meaning and communication depend on the relations established between the various parts of the sentence as it unfolds. As a thought, the sentence has no object that is not everywhere determined (and over time, constantly redetermined) by these relations.

James divides the stream of thought into two primary parts which he labels "substantive" and "transitive." The substantive parts he calls the "resting places" of thought — the nouns, or ideas, that stand in for the whole thought. The transitive parts are responsible for what we are aware of as "a passage, a relation, a transition *from* [the object of our thought], or *between* it and something else" (*PP* 1:236). James compares our thought to "a bird's life," made of "an alternation of flights and perchings" (*PP* 1:236). The resting places are occupied by "sensorial imaginations of some sort, whose peculiarity is that they can be held before the mind for an indefinite time, and contemplated without changing; the places of flight are filled with thoughts of relations, static or dynamic, that for the most part obtain between the matters contemplated in the periods of comparative rest" (*PP* 1:236). James notes how difficult it is to isolate and identify the transitive parts of the stream of thought: "If they are but flights to a conclusion, stopping them to look at them before the conclusion is reached is really annihilating them" (*PP* 1:236). James also compares the transitive part to a snowflake caught in a warm hand: "As a snowflake caught in the warm hand is no longer a flake but a drop, so, instead of catching the feeling of relation moving to its term, we find we have

*The Poetics of Transition*

caught some substantive thing, usually the last word we were pronouncing, statically taken, and with its function, tendency, and particular meaning in the sentence quite evaporated" (*PP* 1:237). The transitive parts of the stream of thought are delicate indeed, processes so elusive we can only recognize them by the traces they leave in their wake.

It is important to underscore the significant development achieved in James's new model of thinking.[5] For the sensationalists, the feelings of relation are simply not real: all that exist are the discontinuous sensations corresponding to particular things, objects, or states. For the intellectualists, feelings of relation correspond to a higher plane of understanding and are not sensations at all. The mind puts sensations, untrustworthy in and of themselves, in rational order. In James's modified empiricist view, feelings of relation are as real as other substantive sensations in the stream of thought, and with just the same kind of reality as the substantive parts of the stream. James resorts to the analogy of language to give form to these elusive shades of relation:

> There is not a conjunction or a preposition, and hardly an adverbial phrase, syntactic form, or inflection of voice, in human speech, that does not express some shading or other of relation which we at some moment actually feel to exist between the larger objects of our thought. If we speak objectively, it is the real relations that appear revealed; if we speak subjectively, it is the stream of consciousness that matches each of them by an inward coloring of its own. In either case the relations are numberless, and no existing language is capable of doing justice to all their shades. (*PP* 1:238)

James's phrasing here points to a problem he will return to in his later radical empiricism. By dividing his analysis into objective and subjective categories, he remains undecided about the reality of the transitive parts of the stream of thought. James will eventually make this ambivalence a specific feature of his thought. We can speak objectively or subjectively, but experience itself is not divided between subjective and objective realms. I will return to this point in discussing the significance of James's radical empiricism later in this chapter.

James claims that "no existing language is capable of doing justice" to all the shades of relation, but he repeatedly invokes language to describe mental processes, whether by pointing to declensional languages or by describing syntactic forms or inflections of voice. Indeed, James waxes rhapsodic about the many grammatical parts of speech that we typically ignore in our bias for substantives: "We ought to say a feeling of *and,* a feeling of *if,* a feeling of *but,* and a feeling of *by,* quite as readily as we say a feeling of *blue* or a feeling of *cold.* Yet we do not: so inveterate has our habit become of recognizing the existence of the substantive parts alone, that language almost refuses to lend itself to any other use" (*PP* 1:238). Feelings corresponding to relations-between-objects are as real for James as feelings corresponding to the objects themselves. The two types of feeling are mutually dependent, and one kind of feeling would be unrecognizable without the other. Without feelings of *and, if, but,* or *by,* we would never form a coherent, working sense of the world.

In James's description, the process of thinking revolves around a vaguely perceived center, drawing in every thought that feels related to that center and "tingeing with the feeling of tediousness or discord" any thought that is alien to it (*PP* 1:250). He calls the feeling of relatedness the "sentiment of rationality," the "transition from a state of puzzle and perplexity to rational comprehension" that is "full of lively relief and pleasure" (*W* 1:950). We would never know the peculiar satisfaction of rational comprehension if we did not first experience the transition from uncertainty or confusion to clarity, definition, and coherence. Rationality is not a matter of correspondence to antecedent truth, but rather of emotionally and aesthetically satisfying relations between the substantive and transitive parts of the stream of thought. When we are thinking, we do not hold a topic definitely and statically in mind, even if we have some general idea of what we are thinking about, but rather cycle through a series of variously associated terms, progressively building up our sense of the subject. The pragmatist conception of truth turns on this functional sentiment of rationality. James's antifoundationalism with regard to truth-claims is inseparable from his sense, developed very early in his writing about consciousness, that rational thought depends on psychological processes that include a prerational dimension.

Thinking, then, depends on constantly shifting affinities of feeling, even though James still insists that "the important thing about a train of thought is its conclusion" (*PP* 1:250). James makes a similar point in discussing an analogy between thought and algebra that he adapts from G. H. Lewes: "As the Algebrist, though the sequence of his terms is fixed by their relations rather than by their several values, must give a real value to the *final* one he reaches; so the thinker in words must let his concluding word or phrase be translated into its full sensible-image-value, under penalty of the thought being left unrealized and pale" (*PP* 1:261–62). Here is another significant indication in *The Principles of Psychology* of the direction James would later pursue under the name of pragmatism. The substantive conclusion of thought puts all the previous transition and relation in perspective: "Usually this conclusion is a word or phrase or particular image, or practical attitude or resolve, whether rising to answer a problem or fill a pre-existing gap that worried us, or whether accidentally stumbled on in revery. In either case it stands out from the other segments of the stream by reason of the peculiar interest attaching to it. This interest *arrests* it, makes a sort of crisis of it when it comes, induces attention upon it and makes us treat it in a substantive way" (*PP* 1:250–51). The transitive and relational parts of the stream of thought, then, are "but the means of the latter's attainment." As he will later suggest in describing the pragmatic method, the means do not particularly matter if the same consequences are achieved. James's formulation recalls Emerson's prior ambivalence about arrested or fixed form in "The Method of Nature": there is an irreducible tension between the conclusion or, as James would put it, "cash-value" of any thought and the heterogeneous, pluralistic relations and transitions that make that conclusion possible.

On the one hand, James's psychology seeks "the re-instatement of the vague to its proper place in our mental life" (*PP* 1:246), while on the other hand it underscores how dynamic mental processes issue in substantive, consequential ideas and acts. James explores how transitive parts work in the stream of thought, but he does not want simply to reverse the usual relationship between substantive and transitive parts. He suggests that our way of thinking about thinking is misleading, focusing too exclusively on substantive parts. By stressing the transitive and relational parts, James highlights the fundamentally dramatic structure of our thinking. The most important element of a felt fringe, James notes, is "the mere feeling of harmony or discord, of a right or wrong direction in the thought" (*PP* 1:251). This feeling is closely related to the satisfying feeling of "lively relief and pleasure" described in "The Sentiment of Rationality." As long as a thought process has a dramatic unity, as long as its tensions are being guided toward resolution, we can continue to follow it. James even calls the mind "at every stage a theatre of simultaneous possibilities" (*PP* 1:277), hinting that thinking has a dramatic structure. Many different productions can be staged at any time, but whatever gets staged will have to be dramatically persuasive. The mind's selection and emphasis are entirely a matter of dramatic effect: "Out of what is in itself an undistinguishable, swarming *continuum,* devoid of distinction or emphasis, our senses make for us, by attending to this motion and ignoring that, a world full of contrasts, of sharp accents, of abrupt changes, of picturesque light and shade" (*PP* 1:274). All of this drama is directed to thought's realization in action. Our absorption in the drama provides the mechanism that allows us to formulate particular interests and engage a course of action. The world could conceivably appear to us in any number of ways: "Other minds, other worlds from the same monotonous and inexpressive chaos!" (*PP* 1:277).

In James's description, the dramatic structure of thought guides the process of thought almost without our being aware of it. A thought has a functional beginning, middle, and end, even if, in the middle, we have lost clear sight of the beginning and cannot yet wholly guess the end. The dramatic structure of a thought keeps its whole form virtually present. James again has recourse to an analogy from art in describing this dramatic whole: "What is that shadowy scheme of the 'form' of an opera, play, or book, which remains in our mind and on which we pass judgment when the actual thing is done? What is our notion of a scientific or philosophical system? Great thinkers have vast premonitory glimpses of schemes of relation between terms, which hardly even as verbal images enter the mind, so rapid is the whole process. We all of us have this permanent consciousness of whither our thought is going" (PP 1:246-47). This is the horizon we always keep in sight, pointing simultaneously back and forward, establishing the relations that any present perception or cognition will dimly (but perfectly sufficiently) comprehend. Just as Mozart, according to a comment James cites in a footnote, could hear an entire symphony at once as he composed it, all thought proceeds with vast if also vague "premonitory glimpses" of its end as it works its way forward. Indeed, this unfolding toward an end-in-sight establishes the dramatic condition required to achieve that end by setting up a network of positive and negative associations that will encourage some kinds of terms and discourage others.

Having banished the ghost in the machine of consciousness—the intellectualists' transexperiential, rational ideas—James retains a sense of a "shadowy scheme" and of "vast premonitory glimpses" that guide our thinking. James's metaphors throughout "The Stream of Thought" reflect his effort to fuse his scientific empiricism with the sense of a pervading mystery. This is apparent in his description of what happens when we try to recall a forgotten name:

> The state of our consciousness is peculiar. There is a gap therein; but no mere gap. It is a gap that is intensely active. A sort of wraith of the name is in it, beckoning us in a given direction, making us at moments tingle with the sense of our closeness, and then letting us sink back without the longed-for term. If wrong names are proposed to us, this singularly definite gap acts immediately so as to negate them. They do not fit into its mould. And the gap of one word does not feel like the gap of another, all empty of content as both might seem necessarily to be when described as gaps. (PP 1:243)

This wraith is James's residuum of mystery. It is linked to the other wraiths that would so interest him and draw him to participate in psychical researches. James insists that the mystery is an integral, defining element in even the most rational of experiences.[6]

*The Poetics of Transition*

This residuum of mystery is apparent even in some of James's best-known descriptions of the stream of thought:

> The traditional psychology talks like one who should say a river consists of nothing but pailsful, spoonsful, quartpotsful, barrelsful, and other moulded forms of water. Even were the pails and the pots all actually standing in the stream, still between them the free water would continue to flow. It is just this free water of consciousness that psychologists resolutely overlook. Every definite image in the mind is steeped and dyed in the free water that flows round it. With it goes the sense of its relations, near and remote, the dying echo of whence it came to us, the dawning sense of whither it is to lead. The significance, the value, of the image is all in this halo or penumbra that surrounds and escorts it, — or rather that is fused into one with it and has become bone of its bone and flesh of its flesh; leaving it, it is true, an image of the same *thing* it was before, but making it an image of that thing newly taken and freshly understood. (*PP* 1:246)

James's metaphors are at first perfectly concrete, juxtaposing "moulded forms of waters" with the free-flowing stream. But with the "dying echo" and "dawning sense" of the image's past and future associations, James's metaphors begin to hint at the elusiveness of all thought. These terms, along with such tropes as "halo" and "penumbra," reinforce the sense of mystery at the heart of James's scientific investigation. The dim sense accompanying any definite mental image's relations, hinted at in its halo or penumbra, leaves it the same "*thing* it was before," but at the same time makes it "an image of that thing newly taken and freshly understood." The thing is itself-in-transition, its new form being created with reference to its past forms and in anticipation of its unfolding future forms.

James wrote his *Principles of Psychology* as a scientist writing for other scientists. His training at Harvard and in Germany made him a leading authority on the best scientific research of his day, and this, in addition to his considerable stylistic ease, surely accounts for the long popularity of the book and its abridgment, *Psychology: Briefer Course*. But James, who would give up the academic discipline of psychology almost immediately after the book appeared in 1890, already sensed the limits of the prevailing scientific discourse, even as he struggled to write his book within those limits. His interest in phenomena marginalized within the scientific establishment, an interest that would eventually issue in his opposition to the centralization of scientific authority as well as in his investigations of religious experience, psychical phenomena, and otherwise altered states of consciousness, is anticipated by the terms in which he formulates his description of the stream of thought. One thing James seems to have recognized from the start was the elusiveness of the self, even the strategic importance of that elusiveness as a phenomenon in itself. Having devised a middle path between the dominant sensationalist and intellectualist paradigms, James quickly sensed the limitations of his introspective approach. What guaranteed that the thinker's thoughts would bear any relation to the actual world? What if the dramatic unity of a thought is a strictly internal affair, bearing little if any relation to the external world? Having said so much about human feelings and the mystery at the core of rational processes, how could James bridge the gap between feelings and objective realities?

To deal with these problems, James would eventually posit a realm of "pure experience." Pure experience is neither subjective nor objective. These, for James, are classifications that we apply to experience after we have already undergone that experience. Looking back on experience, we can call some parts of it subjective, some objective, but the act of looking-back is different from the act of experiencing. James's focus is on the experience, the event, as it precedes the division into someone experiencing something. In the event, there is no such division. Only when we later describe the event do we invoke the division. By shifting his focus from the stream of thought to the stream of experience, James avoids the apparent subjectivity of his earliest investigations of self. The doctrine of pure experience no doubt struck James as perfectly unassailable, since to assail it one has to be looking back on experience, utilizing the language and categories with which human beings always have looked back on experience.[7]

James develops his idea of taking an event in more than one way in order to undermine the invidious dualism of body and mind. In "Does 'Consciousness' Exist?" (1904), he argues that a subjective perspective describes roughly the same set of facts as an objective perspective, only the facts are taken in a different context (my context, as opposed to the external world's context). When I think of this sheet of paper, there is only one kind of stuff, but that stuff can be taken in the context of other material objects (the desk, the pen, other objects that are white, etc.) or in the context of my own thoughts (I'd better get more paper soon, or I'll run out). Even "I" exist in this double register, both as an object-among-objects and as a set of recurring memories and impressions centered around my body. In his radical empiricism, James no longer depends on a dualism of mind and body, but rather views this dualism as a product of deeply ingrained habits of talking. Radical empiricism

*The Poetics of Transition*

locates the conjunctive relations between parts within experience itself and describes experience—what later phenomenologists would call prereflective experience—as preceding the subject-object division.

In his essay "A World of Pure Experience" (1904), James criticizes rationalism, with its constant impulse "to emphasize universals and to make wholes prior to parts," as well as empiricism, with its "stress upon the part, the element, the individual" (*W* 2:1160). One is too inclusive, the other too distributed. A radical empiricism would not "admit into its constructions any element that is not directly experienced, nor exclude from them any element that is directly experienced" (*W* 2:1160). Like the stream of thought as he describes it in the *Principles,* James's radical empiricism is designed to include elements and their implicit relations: "For such a philosophy, *the relations that connect experiences must themselves be experienced relations, and any kind of relation experienced must be accounted as 'real' as anything else in the system*" (*W* 2:1160). Ordinary empiricism, as James notes, tends to emphasize disjunctions while doing away "with the connections of things" (*W* 2:1160). Rationalism, by contrast, seeks to provide "trans-experiential agents of unification, substances, intellectual categories and powers, or Selves" (*W* 2:1161). For James, these connections come not from without, but from within the stream of experience. They are as real as the discrete elements of a traditional empiricism. Radical empiricism, then, "*does full justice to conjunctive relations,* without, however, treating them as rationalism always tends to treat them, as being true in some supernal way, as if the unity of things and their variety belonged to different orders of truth and vitality altogether" (*W* 2:1161).

According to this radical empiricism, our knowledge of the world is in fact a virtual knowledge that constantly changes as new experiences cause it to be revised. Just as the transitive parts of the stream of thought are vital to our thinking, so transitions are vital to experience. Since experience is not founded on anything transexperiential, the transitions between parts of experience provide all the conjunctive relation we ever experience:

In radical empiricism there is no bedding; it is as if the pieces clung together by their edges, the transitions experienced between them forming their cement. Of course such a metaphor is misleading, for in actual experience the more substantive and the more transitive parts run into each other continuously, there is in general no separateness needing to be overcome by an external cement; and whatever separateness is actually experienced is not overcome, it stays and counts as separateness to the end. (*W* 2:1180)

*James and the Metaphorics of Transition*

James insists that the heterogeneity of things is never unified by a common superstructure or overarching ideal. Our experience of the world is pluralistic all the way down.

As in the *Principles*, James again uses grammatical parts to illustrate his point: "Philosophy has always turned on grammatical particles. With, near, next, like, from, towards, against, because, for, through, my—these words designate types of conjunctive relation arranged in a roughly ascending order of intimacy and inclusiveness" (*W* 2:1161). James is being sly, but altogether serious, in suggesting that the noble institution of philosophy has "always turned on" such minute grammatical terms. Philosophy, in James's view, accomplishes more by means of these relational terms than by abstraction or system building. Whether or not some more absolute connection also holds remains a mystery. James always allows that such a connection is possible and in his psychical researches even seeks scientifically valid evidence of such broader relation. Still, he insists that enough connection attains within experience to provide all the coherence we ever need.

The sense of self, or of mind, is, for James, one kind of experienced transition. Mind and "personal consciousness" are, in James's description, "the name for a series of experiences run together by certain definite transitions, and an objective reality is a series of similar experiences knit by different transitions" (*W* 2:1177). The whole problem of objectivity to which James refers here arises because so much of our thinking is necessarily about realities that are not immediately present to the thinker. Most of our knowledge is what James calls "virtual knowing." Nothing external verifies the validity of our thinking, except that our thinking issues, eventually, in consequences we either approve or reject:

> To continue thinking unchallenged is, ninety-nine times out of a hundred, our practical substitute for knowing in the completed sense. As each experience runs by cognitive transition into the next one, and we nowhere feel a collision with what we elsewhere count as fact, we commit ourselves to the current as if the port were sure. We live, as it were, upon the front edge of an advancing wave-crest, and our sense of a determinate direction in falling forward is all we cover of the future of our path. It is as if a differential quotient should be conscious and treat itself as an adequate substitute for a traced-out curve. Our experience, *inter alia*, is of variations of rate and of direction, and lives in these transitions more than in the journey's end. The truncated experiences are sufficient to act upon—what more could we have *done* at those moments even if later verification were complete? (*W* 2:1172–73)

*The Poetics of Transition*

James later revised "truncated experiences" to read "experiences of tendency," recalling the section subheading "Feelings of Tendency" from the "Stream of Thought" chapter of the *Principles of Psychology*. Just as feelings of tendency determine what one experiences in the stream of thought, so these "experiences of tendency" determine how experience will hold together: as parts of a self, as parts of a landscape, as a historical or biological process, etc.[8]

By living "in these transitions more than in the journey's end," our "experiences of tendency" keep leading us into the "more." In this sense, James comments, "we at every moment can continue to believe in an existing *beyond*" (*W* 2:1181). This is the basis of James's defense of the will to believe, as well as his fascination with varieties of religious experience. Transitions always throw experience forward toward the beyond, whether or not one has faith in a beyond that is a heavenly paradise or a reservoir of the Absolute. The beyond remains a useful category for James, so long as it is "itself of an experiential nature." It is dramatically real, even if it has no transexperiential reality.

Since thought is always oriented toward the beyond, excess is the engine that drives transition: "Every smallest state of consciousness, concretely taken, overflows its own definition. Only concepts are self-identical; only 'reason' deals with closed equations; nature is but a name for excess; every point in her opens out and runs into the more; and the only question, with reference to any point we may be considering, is how far into the rest of nature we may have to go in order to get entirely beyond its overflow" (*W* 2:760). It is especially striking that even the "smallest state of consciousness" displays this propensity to excess. There is no basic unit of conscious experience that is simply itself. Every unit has a fringe that links it with innumerable other units. Everything is in relation. James captures the paradoxical implications of this relational excess in his 1909 essay "The Continuity of Experience":

My present field of consciousness is a centre surrounded by a fringe that shades insensibly into a subconscious more. I use three separate terms here to describe this fact; but I might as well use three hundred, for the fact is all shades and no boundaries. Which part of it properly is in my consciousness, which out? If I name what is out, it already has come in. The centre works in one way while the margins work in another, and presently overpower the centre and are central themselves. What we conceptually identify ourselves with and say we are thinking of at any time is the centre; but our *full* self is the whole field, with all those indefinitely radiating subconscious possibilities of increase that we can only feel without conceiving, and can hardly begin to analyze. (*W* 2:761)

*James and the Metaphorics of Transition*

The self undergoes (and is progressively redefined by) perpetual transitions between center and margins. The "indefinitely radiating subconscious possibilities of increase" keep these ceaseless transitions in perpetual motion.

James rejects all the available dualisms in favor of a conception of consciousness and world that is all shades and no boundaries, everywhere in transition. Despite his occasional references to the self's "self-possession," James's model for the self here is one of endlessly permeable boundaries. Transition, the constant play of these "possibilities of increase," dissolves any and all defined objects, subjective or objective. As James's language suggests, excess and possibilities of increase characterize experience as it unfolds beyond stable determinations of the subject and objects of experience. In experience, the beyond is situated at the always permeable margin between what we only later classify as subjective and objective realms or material and ideal realities. Though James does not name his excess *God,* he is endlessly fascinated with people who experience it as an influx of divinity.

It is important to recognize the relation between this perpetually unfolding *more* and James's much-maligned defense of the will or right to believe.[9] Where the "fact" is "all shades and no boundaries," there is no distinguishing what is a matter of fact from what is a matter of imagination, association, ideal, or desire. "The Will to Believe," first published in 1896 to immediately become one of the central essays in James's canon, traces the implications of this ambiguity. The basic position of the essay is that in the absence of definitive contradictory evidence, individuals have the right to assume the risk of belief. All cognitive postures entail particular risks, the only question being what kind and degree of risk one is willing to assume. James insists that the believing posture is not exclusive among religionists, but that it also functions as a necessary mechanism in all rational thinking. On the one hand, James defends the right to believe when there is no definitive evidence to contradict the belief; on the other hand, and more radically, James suggests that we have no choice but to adopt a believing posture, whether we will stake our belief in God or in the procedures and conclusions of rational, scientific methods. As James comments with regard to a narrowly intellectualist rejection of belief, "It is not intellect against all passions, then; it is only intellect with one passion laying down its law" (*W* 1:475). Our "passional natures" invariably play a role, not just in our beliefs but also in our general attitudes toward belief.

James's target in "The Will to Believe" is the scientific establishment that would insist on the strict separation of scientific method and passionate belief. James is not writing as an irrationalist but rather as a rationalist coming to terms with the limits of his rationalism. Just as every thought achieves its object by invoking more than its substantive parts alone, so science and philosophy will achieve their ends only once they have acknowledged their complicity with the kinds of ideals and beliefs they so often wish to banish. Belief, for James, is the mechanism that exposes the limits of rational thought and subjectivity. It allows us to imagine a deeper, more profound relatedness to the world than any made available by received science or philosophy. In James's formulation, belief is what allows us to question objective truth-claims: "Objective evidence and certitude are doubtless very fine ideals to play with, but where on this moonlit and dream-visited planet are they found? . . . I live, to be sure, by the practical faith that we must go on experiencing and thinking over our experience, for only thus can our opinions grow more true; but to hold any one of them — I absolutely do not care which — as if it never could be re-interpretable or corrigible, I believe to be a tremendously mistaken attitude" (*W* 1:466). "The Will to Believe" is more than just a defense of the right to believe in ideas that have not been positively disproven. It is also James's critique of what Dewey would later call "the quest for certainty," an instrument to guide thought beyond its rationalist status quo.

It is telling that James invokes a standard of truth — the idea that "our opinions [can] grow more true" — and at the same time undermines the possibility that any of our ideas can be absolutely true, "as if it never could be re-interpretable or corrigible." He seems to allow shades or degrees of truth while denying the possibility of certain truth. Pragmatism can be regarded as the attempt to provide philosophical authority to such relative degrees of truth. Instead of emphasizing the totalizing system within which certain truths attain, pragmatists emphasize the relational processes that favor some truths in certain circumstances instead of others. These processes are everywhere in transition, replacing old truths with new ones that serve newly emerging interests or capacities. The volatility of such a transitional dynamic is restrained by the already assimilated fund of past truths, which can never simply be ignored. This fund of truths is, however, constantly growing at its edges. As Emerson had insisted, no already adopted truth or ideal is more valuable than the unfolding process: "the coming only is sacred."

James's pragmatism also emphasizes these unfolding processes within which truths and ideals are continuously generated, modified, and reformulated. James still values truths and ideals, but he redescribes our relationship to them. His emphasis is never on what they are, but rather on how they get used. From a traditional perspective, this redescription will always seem inadequate, since it will seem to miss the absolute, unchanging dimension of anything worthy of being called a truth or ideal. From a pragmatic or "post-Philosophical" perspective, such redescription provides a way to continue talking about truths and ideals while acknowledging their contingent status.

*James and the Metaphorics of Transition*

This is why James is always of two minds with respect to classical philosophical terminology. He treats the received philosophical problems as so many terminological dead ends, by-products of a bad vocabulary. As we become enraptured by this vocabulary, our range of possible truths is limited and we fail to perceive newly emerging truths. But James never simply rejects this vocabulary, since to reject it would be to stop using it altogether. Instead, he hopes that by adopting the same terms in new ways, the classic philosophical problems will simply dissolve (they are only problems of bad vocabulary anyway) and the real issues that they have so long obscured will come into sharper focus. These issues typically concern the ongoing recognition and cultivation of marginalized, heterogeneous, pluralistic interests in a world that was classically conceived as monolithic, unified, and complete. James set out to devalue the available rationalistic philosophical vocabularies in order to redeploy those same vocabularies from a pragmatic, melioristic perspective.

James's conflicting imperatives are evident in a passage from a letter dated June 7, 1899, to Mrs. Henry Whitman in which James addresses the relationship between morality and social institutions. In this passage, James locates the source of our best moral energies in opposition to organized institutions.

> I am against bigness and greatness in all their forms, and with the invisible molecular moral forces that work from individual to individual, stealing in through the crannies of the world like so many soft rootlets, or like the capillary oozing of water, and yet rending the hardest monuments of man's pride, if you give them time. The bigger the unit you deal with, the hollower, the more brutal, the more mendacious is the life displayed. So I am against all big organizations as such, national ones first and foremost; against all big successes and big results; and in favor of the eternal forces of truth which always work in the individual and immediately unsuccessful way, under-dogs always, till history comes, after they are long dead, and puts them on the top. (*LWJ* 2:90)

This is a very Emersonian passage, especially in its impassioned identification with the individual as distinguished from all organized institutions. James identifies here with marginalized and unstructured forces of resistance, implying that the prevailing forms of organization either neglect or co-opt these vital human energies. By locating these moral energies at an invisible molecular level, James dissociates their power from any and all forms of associated or collective existence.

It is not hard to see the problems raised by this formulation. By emphasizing the molecular and invisible dimension of this pure moral energy, James

*The Poetics of Transition*

detaches that energy from the real conditions of human life. This is a problem that comes up repeatedly in James's discussions of the self, most notably in *The Principles of Psychology*, where it becomes clear that even the individual self is too vast an organization. James's treatment of the self can be summarized by his conclusion to his chapter on "The Self": "The thoughts themselves are the thinkers" (*W* 1:209).[10] James carefully distinguishes our thoughts from the experienced unities of self, which are many and which he arranges in what he calls a "hierarchy of the mes." To say that the thoughts themselves are the thinkers is to recognize that the various experiences of self are projected by individual thoughts that precede the formation of a self. There is no unified self in control of the process. Instead, there is only the unfolding process. As ever, James posits elemental units, each suffused by the fringe of relations described in "The Stream of Thought," antecedent to any collective formation of those units into a unified whole or series of unified wholes. The core of the Jamesian self is, paradoxical as it seems, "the thoughts themselves." Our moral energies therefore stem from a recovery of the "invisible molecular moral forces" that precede all later (and apparently secondary) formation into the functional unities of what we call the self.

This odd dissociation of moral force from the self becomes even clearer in the chapter on "Will," where James further separates the act of will from any antecedent willing agent. In effect, the agency of willing vanishes in James's description. This is especially odd because James puts so much emphasis on the heroic will. But the will turns out to be little more than what James calls "effort of attention," the "essential phenomenon of will" (*W* 1:418).[11] This effort is sustained in order "to keep affirming and adopting a thought which, if left to itself, would slip away" (*W* 1:421). This is a decidedly moral capacity for James: "*To sustain a representation, to think,* is, in short, the only moral act, for the impulsive and the obstructed, for sane and lunatics alike" (*W* 1:421). James later clarifies his sense that this effort of attention is a moral drama: "There are at all times *some* ideas from which we shy away like frightened horses the moment we get a glimpse of their forbidding profile upon the threshold of our thought. *The only resistance which our will can possibly experience is the resistance which such an idea offers to being attended to at all.* To attend to it is the volitional act, and the only inward volitional act which we ever perform" (*W* 1:422). To fail to attend to such thoughts is to lack moral fiber. Volition is only a word for this ability to attend to such frightening thoughts.

James even suggests that "the sense of the amount of effort which we can put forth" is the deepest measure by which we judge ourselves as individuals. The amount of effort we put out "seems to belong to an altogether different realm" from such measures as strength and intelligence, wealth and good luck, "as if it were the substantive thing which we *are,* and those were but externals which we *carry*" (*W* 1:424–25). Our deepest conviction of selfhood is thus a function of this effort of attention. Here James comes as close as he ever comes to defining a core of self: "If the 'searching of our heart and reins' be the purpose of this human drama, then what is sought seems to be what effort we can make. He who can make none is but a shadow; he who can make much is a hero" (*W* 1:425). A hero is someone who manages to attend to those thoughts that are most threatening to the self.

This is a very pragmatic analysis, reducing the will to what it is experienced as. It is not a mysterious faculty but only the sustained effort of attention that enables the self to push beyond its present limitations. This hardly seems much of a moral power, though, especially since there is nothing in it to allow the self to distinguish which ideas are worth attending to and which are not. It is explicitly a quantity, not a quality. Nothing in James's analysis tells us how we determine what is worth really attending to. James's descriptions even suggest that the process depends on a liberating blindness: "But the deepest question that is ever asked admits of no reply but the dumb turning of the will and the tightening of our heart-strings as we say, '*Yes, I will even have it so!*' " (*W* 1:425).[12] If the "turning of the will" is "dumb," it can hardly reflect the rational design of a willing agent. James reiterates his point at the conclusion of the chapter: " '*Will you or won't you have it so?*' is the most probing question we are ever asked; we are asked it every hour of the day, and about the largest as well as the smallest, the most theoretical as well as the most practical, things. We answer by *consents or non-consents* and not by words. What wonder that these dumb responses should seem our deepest organs of communication with the nature of things!" (*W* 1:426). Even as he sets out to describe the foundation of our heroic acts of will, James quietly erases the agency of will. Power, the heroic ability to "*stand* this universe," to assume risk and live "on the perilous edge," comes not from a faculty or innermost core of self, but from what can only be described as sheer transitional energy. Power belongs not to human designs but to transition itself.

James recognizes that transitional agencies unfold within biological and social processes, but his attempt to isolate and valorize transition leads him to posit a pure transitional agency antecedent to any socially formed self or externally trained will. Transition precedes the formation of human selves and their narrow purposes and designs. If the thoughts are the thinkers, then the actions are the men and women. What matters is not what particular men and women do, but the doing itself, action extrapolated from poor human actors. For all his emphasis on bold, heroic actions and the moral energies

*The Poetics of Transition*

they express, James is ultimately less interested in the self who imposes his or her will on the world than in the self that becomes a transparent transitional agency in the service of cultivating interests that subsume it. This becomes an explicit theme late in James's career, when he begins to speculate on forms of co-conscious experience.

When James began in the mid-1890s to write his essays in radical empiricism and pragmatism, as well as on psychical phenomena and religious experience, he was guided by his sense that human agency was one kind of transitional agency among other transitional agencies. In *The Varieties of Religious Experience,* ecstatic experience is figured as a means to access otherwise blocked energies: "Through prayer, religion insists, things which cannot be realized in any other manner come about: energy which but for prayer would be bound is by prayer set free and operates in some part, be it objective or subjective, of the world of facts" (*W* 2:417). After writing the *Varieties* (which appeared in 1902), James would develop his notion of a "pure experience" that precedes the division into subjective and objective. From that time forward James would increasingly allow the possibility of a level of being at which individuated identities are joined together. In the *Varieties,* James posits a region of personality with "unusually close relations to the transmarginal or, subliminal region." This level of being

is obviously the larger part of each of us, for it is the abode of everything that is latent and the reservoir of everything that passes unrecorded or unobserved. It contains, for example, such things as all our momentarily inactive memories, and it harbors the springs of all our obscurely motivated passions, impulses, likes, dislikes, and prejudices. Our intuitions, hypotheses, fancies, superstitions, persuasions, convictions, and in general all our non-rational operations, come from it. It is the source of our dreams, and apparently they may return to it. (*W* 2:433)

For those who experience religion deeply, "the door into this region seems unusually wide open" (*W* 2:434).

Later, in "The Continuity of Experience," James suggests that the irreducible feeling of the "more" is the basis of our sense of the possibility of the self's connection with a larger, more encompassing form of being:

Every bit of us at every moment is part and parcel of a wider self, it quivers along various radii like the wind-rose on a compass, and the actual in it is continuously one with possibles not yet in our present sight. And just as we are co-conscious with our own momentary margin, may not we ourselves form the margin of some more really central self

*James and the Metaphorics of Transition*

in things which is co-conscious with the whole of us? May not you and I be confluent in a higher consciousness, and confluently active there, tho we now know it not? (*W* 2:762)

This leads James to assert that "the absolute is not the impossible being I once thought it": "Mental facts do function both singly and together, at once, and we finite minds may simultaneously be co-conscious with one another in a superhuman intelligence. It is only the extravagant claims of coercive necessity on the absolute's part that have to be denied by *a priori* logic" (*W* 2:763). Citing the research of Janet, Freud, Prince, and Sidis, James declares in concluding this essay that the "abnormal or supernormal facts" revealed in this research provide "the strongest suggestions in favor of a superior co-consciousness being possible" (*W* 2:766). He supports Fechner's "conception of a great reservoir in which the memories of earth's inhabitants are pooled and preserved, and from which, when the threshold lowers or the valve opens, information ordinarily shut out leaks into the mind of exceptional individuals among us" (*W* 2:766). This, of course, is the path Jung, whom James met along with Freud at the 1909 Clark University symposium, would tread. James acknowledges that these "regions of inquiry are perhaps too spook-haunted to interest an academic audience," which is perhaps one of the reasons that, despite his impression of Freud as "a man obsessed with fixed ideas," he continued to hope that Freud, Jung, and their colleagues would continue to "push their ideas to their utmost limits" (*TC* 2:122). James concludes "The Continuity of Experience" by bringing the language of science to bear on religious experience: "I think it may be asserted that there *are* religious experiences of a specific nature, not deducible by analogy or psychological reasoning from our other sorts of experience. I think that they point with reasonable probability to the continuity of our consciousness with a wider spiritual environment from which the ordinary prudential man (who is the only man that scientific psychology, so called, takes cognizance of) is shut off" (*W* 2:766–67).

This final model of self in James depends on an ambiguity of agency similar to that noted previously in discussing Emerson. To access this realm of spiritual, co-conscious reality, the self has to relax its ordinary "prudential" posture. Once the threshold is lowered, or the valve opens, "information ordinarily shut out leaks in." The self has merely to allow that leaking-in in order to experience the enhanced power of the wider margin of being. At the same time, James never abandons his distinctly individualistic ethical model developed around his notion of the feeling of effort. In "The Energies of Men," a talk delivered in December 1906, he utilizes the same model of an unaccessed reservoir of energies: "*As a rule men habitually use only a small part of the*

*The Poetics of Transition*

*powers which they actually possess and which they might use under appropriate conditions*" (*WWJ* 674).[13] James refers here to powers which individuals "actually possess," but these powers appear to be made available to the self from some other dimension of being. Such power is, in effect, the power of transition, and so belongs to no one in particular. James discusses various disciplines that can awaken one's sleeping energies, from Yoga to "energy-releasing ideas" like "Fatherland," "the Flag," "the Union," etc. (*WWJ* 680–81). Conversions, James notes, provide another way "in which bound energies are let loose": "They unify us, and put a stop to ancient mental interferences. The result is freedom, and often a great enlargement of power" (*WWJ* 681). Interestingly, James never for a minute thinks that a conversion is a diminishment of power, as if one had to sacrifice one's independence or rational objectivity in order to experience the illusory power that accompanies belief. For James, the power of belief releases energy that can then be directed to whatever particular purposes one chooses to direct them. Toward the various pseudo-scientific phenomena of his day, James is surprisingly open-minded: "We are just now witnessing a very copious unlocking of energies by ideas in the persons of those converts to 'New Thought,' 'Christian Science,' 'Metaphysical Healing,' or other forms of spiritual philosophy, who are so numerous among us to-day. The ideas here are healthy-minded and optimistic; and it is quite obvious that a wave of religious activity, analogous in some respects to the spread of early Christianity, Buddhism, and Mohammedanism, is passing over our American world" (*WWJ* 682). For James, power results from giving oneself over to an intimation of some subsuming energy, thereby allowing the mind and body to rise to new levels of activity.

James's self is, in this sense, a purely transitional agency. The self's individuated identity is little more than an experienced unity. As such, it has a significant pragmatic function, but that function will only draw on a limited range of the self's "indefinitely radiating subconscious possibilities of increase." Realizing these possibilities of increase, the self can be reconfigured as an entirely new experiential unity. Any unified self is predicated on transitional processes and remains subject to further transitional processes that will issue in different, newly emerging kinds of unity.

This dynamic linking transitional processes and experienced unities is related to the broader aesthetics of pragmatism which I will take up in the following chapter. It is important to recognize that, to a pragmatist, aesthetics never means anything like an interest in art as a separate, separable realm of experience. Unity is key to the Jamesian imagination. It is, however, never a reflection or realization of an external unity, but is instead a projection of an imagination feeling its way through the world, searching for new efficiencies

*James and the Metaphorics of Transition*

of feeling. This is perhaps the source of greatest misunderstanding of pragmatism. The effort to sustain an anti-idealist, post-metaphysical perspective has led many astute critics to conclude that something goes wrong when pragmatists begin to talk about art and aesthetics. Nothing could be further from the truth. The aesthetics of pragmatism is essential to any pragmatic understanding of how mind puts truth, theories, and ideals to work. Art and literature, like science and rational thought, provide and cultivate dramatic experiences of unity. They do so not in order to isolate particular ideals but rather to extend our sense of the world and our possible relations to it. The aesthetics of pragmatism is not the lingering remains of a latent idealism, but is instead the basis of a pragmatic understanding of ideas and ideals.

# 3

# The Aesthetics of Pragmatism

AS A FIGURE for the agency that initiates change, transition is associated not with antecedent or eventual conditions, but rather with the unfolding processes that both suffuse and exceed any given condition. Transition, for Emerson and William James, figures power in its purest form. Such power does not serve already formulated interests but rather precedes those interests and ultimately remakes them. Transition is elusive because it unfolds at once within and beyond the social forms and intellectual categories by which we familiarize and, to some extent, control the world. Transition both draws on and challenges these forms and categories, cultivating the margin from within which novelty and innovation emerge.

Art is an agency of transition because, as Emerson suggests in "The Poet" and "Art," it also challenges familiar forms of perception and understanding and initiates processes that reconstitute them. But while aesthetic experience may be somewhat elusive, the materials of that experience are as concrete as the materials of any experience. For pragmatists, who would never endorse an aesthetic idealism that isolates art works from the social and historical conditions that make them possible, art is a very definite transitional agency. Proceeding from the conviction that truth and moral ideals have no absolute, rational foundation, pragmatists see art and aesthetic experience as processes that cultivate values without imposing or reifying them. So long as these processes remain responsive to shifting natural, social, and historical circumstances, they foster a deepened sense of the ways in which truths, values, and ideals emerge and evolve within the constantly expanding margin of material and cultural experience.

Still, pragmatists are always sensitive to the danger of a pragmatist aesthetics devolving into an aesthetic idealism. This is the basis of James's comment, in an 1894 review of Henry Rutgers Marshall's *Pain, Pleasure, and Aesthetics,* that "one's first impulse is to shy away from any book with the word 'Aesthetics' in its title, with the confident expectation that, if read, it could only emphasize once more the gaping contrast between the richness of life and the poverty of all possible formulas."[1] James is himself still provocative in part because of his deep-seated skepticism regarding the formulas used to organize and classify experience. Nowhere is the inadequacy of this intellectualist habit more glaring than in efforts to account for the experience of art.

That James was himself deeply responsive to art is evident from a comment to his brother in a letter of 1872, where he writes of envying "the world of Art" Henry inhabits: "Away from it, as we live, we sink into a flatter, blanker kind of consciousness, and indulge in an ostrich-like forgetfulness of all our richest potentialities—and they startle us now and then when by accident some rich human product, pictorial, literary or architectural, slaps us with its tail" (*TC* 2:254). Odd as it now seems, William had seriously pursued a career as a painter, studying in Europe with Léon Coigniet and then in America with William Morris Hunt. John Jay Chapman's reflections on the recently deceased James underscore the conflicts that virtually constituted his personality and intellect: "It has sometimes crossed my mind that James wanted to be a poet and an artist, and that there lay in him, beneath the ocean of metaphysics a lost Atlantis of the fine arts; that he really hated philosophy and all its works, and pursued them only as Hercules might spin or as a prince in a fairy tale might sort seeds for an evil dragon, or as anyone might patiently do some careful work for which he had no aptitude."[2] Chapman's conclusion regarding James's aptitude for philosophy aside, this comment captures one of the defining tensions of James's life and work. Noting the imbalance between James's work on religious and aesthetic experience, Ralph Barton Perry has suggested that James probably "shrank from any account of aesthetic experiences" because he "*had* the aesthetic experience, and borrowed the religious" (*TC* 2:257). James himself succinctly states his case against aesthetics in a letter to Marshall, whose book on aesthetics in fact earned his qualified praise: "Any abstract treatment of the 'Aesthetic Ideal' is inadequate to the innumerable different demands which different men (and the same man at different moments) are entitled to make upon the artist" (*TC* 2:256). Art is, almost absolutely for James, the antithesis of the formulaic and abstract.

George Santayana reveals the same misgivings when he notes at the outset of his earliest philosophical work, *The Sense of Beauty* (1896), that "to feel beauty is a better thing than to understand how we come to feel it" (*WGS* 2:11). It is as if Santayana were apologizing for writing a book about beauty, the subtitle of which is, prosaically enough, "Being the Outline of Aesthetic

Theory." Santayana further suggests in his introduction that for expression of "that incommunicable and illusive excellence that haunts every beautiful thing," we should "go to the poets, to the more inspired critics, and best of all to the immortal parables of Plato." But if what we desire "is to increase our knowledge rather than to cultivate our sensibility" — as one might expect from "the Outline of Aesthetic Theory" — "we should do well to close all those delightful books; for we shall not find any instruction there upon the questions which most press upon us" (*WGS* 2:11–12). *The Sense of Beauty* begins, then, by inviting the reader temporarily to suspend the affections that constitute life's higher value ("to feel beauty is a better thing"), in the interest of a more secure and objective knowledge about those same affections.

In beginning to foreground the aesthetics of pragmatism, the story of which has attracted surprisingly little attention, we should make note of this important divergence. James only grudgingly accepts Marshall's (and soon after, Santayana's) aesthetic theory, whereas Santayana far more aggressively insists that aesthetic experience be subjected to rigorous analysis. Indeed, Santayana had to look no further than James's own *Principles of Psychology* to recognize that there might be such a thing as a science of elusive phenomena, however subtle and complex that science would have to be. Santayana had fully absorbed his James. As he reports in his autobiography, he had in 1889 attended a weekly seminar in which James "read to us from the manuscript, chapter by chapter, his new *Principles of Psychology*." "Admirable stimulants," he calls this and Royce's concurrent seminar on Hegel's *Phenomenology of Spirit* (*WGS* 1:389). In the autobiographical essay "A General Confession," he attributes to James his own appreciation of "the unadulterated, unexplained, instant fact of experience." Distancing himself from James's later pragmatism, he concludes this warm tribute to James by declaring his pride at remaining "a disciple of his earlier unsophisticated self, when he was an agnostic about the universe, but in his diagnosis of the heart an impulsive poet: a master in the art of recording or divining the lyric quality of experience as it actually came to him or to me."[3] As Santayana's comments here suggest, James influenced Santayana most when his scientific, philosophic, and poetic inclinations were most fully integrated.

In *The Sense of Beauty,* Santayana draws on several of James's innovations in the contemporary understanding of mental life, most notably James's notion of the real existence of feelings of relation, developed in the "Stream of Thought" chapter of the *Principles.* Taking for granted James's claim that feelings of *and, if, but,* and *by* are as empirically real as feelings of *blue* and *cold,* Santayana comments that "right and left, before and after, good and bad, one and two, like and unlike, are irreducible feelings" (*WGS* 2:126). For

Santayana, as for James, thinking is not reducible to particular conceptions or abstractions, since a large part of the thinking process is the transitive relating of the different substantive elements of thought. Santayana's description of how "our ideas half emerge for a moment from the dim continuum of vital feeling and diffused sense, and are hardly fixed before they are changed and transformed" is very much the product of James's psychology (*WGS* 2:121). So too his reference to "a certain tendency and quality, not original to them, a meaning and a tone" recalls James's suffusing aura or fringe, which James also associates with feelings of tendency (*WGS* 2:121). For Santayana, "we not only construct visible unities and recognizable types, but remain aware of their affinities to what is not at the time perceived" (*WGS* 2:121). These unities and types are not existential, phenomenal realities, but are rather psychological projections, useful so long as the "objects and feelings" they connect lead to definite practical advantages. This would become the key to Santayana's aesthetic and religious attitudes: felt unities and harmonies are valuable not because they point to some overarching or trans-empirical unity or harmony (be it God's, Nature's, or Self's) but because they animate experience, render it meaningful and purposeful, and provide a concrete discipline for sustaining and cultivating its meanings and purposes.

Of course, like James, Santayana recognized the dangers that would attend any attempt to isolate this aesthetic function. This is apparent in the first chapter of *Reason in Art* (1905), the fourth volume of *The Life of Reason:*

> Productions in which an aesthetic value is or is supposed to be prominent take the name of fine art; but the work of fine art so defined is almost always an abstraction from the actual object, which has many non-aesthetic functions and values. To separate the aesthetic element . . . is more misleading than helpful; for neither in the history of art nor in a rational estimate of its value can the aesthetic function of things be divorced from the practical and moral. (*RA* 15–16)

This statement is characteristically pragmatic in a number of ways. First, Santayana blurs the boundary between fine and useful arts. The "actual object" still retains "many non-aesthetic functions and values," which is to say it must still function, and survive, as a material object in a material environment (*RA* 36). This assimilation of the fine and useful arts can be traced back to Emerson's insistence, in "Art," that "beauty must come back to the useful arts, and the distinction between the fine and the useful arts be forgotten" (*EL* 439). It can also be traced forward to Dewey's definition of the arts as the "immediate enhancements of the experience of living" (*LW* 10:36).

Santayana also suggests that to isolate an object's various elements from their mutually interacting functions is to misrepresent or misconstrue the object. Like James and other pragmatists, Santayana emphasizes the unfolding processes that encompass all individual forms or conditions of being. As Santayana puts it elsewhere in *Reason in Art,* "aesthetic and other interests are not separable units, to be compared externally; they are rather strands interwoven in the texture of everything" (*RA* 183). By emphasizing interaction and interrelation, Santayana implicitly locates the object of art in the larger field of its production and reception.

This is why "reason in art" must be viewed along with reason in common sense, in society, in religion, and in science—the subjects, respectively, of volumes 1–3 and 5 of Santayana's *Life of Reason.* Santayana sees human reason expressing itself equally, albeit differently, in all of these realms. His safeguard against aestheticizing experience rests on his pragmatic insistence that all of these functions operate together, indivisibly, in experience. Indeed, he would much later claim to recognize in philosophy "no separable thing called aesthetics" and refer to the course he taught at Harvard from 1892 to 1895 as his "sham course in 'aesthetics.'"[4] Even as early as 1904, Santayana had suggested that "aesthetic good is ... no separable value; it is not realizable by itself in a set of objects not otherwise interesting."[5]

James's gut distaste for abstract aesthetic theories derives from his sense that abstraction must in the end prove destructive of primary aesthetic feelings. Santayana obviously shared this anxiety, and increasingly over time, but he remained committed to finding a way to write about aesthetic experience that would be no more destructive than writing, as James had, about transitive, relational movements of thought. Where James, however, would remain skeptical about any attempt to provide a general account of aesthetic experience, Santayana could see no higher task for mind to attempt than just that. James distrusted theory and abstraction because he saw them as signs of metaphysical detachment. Santayana, distrusting theory and abstraction when they functioned to support metaphysical assumptions or claims, embraced them as the source of the "visible unities and recognizable types" with which the mind cultivates contingent meanings.

This gap between James and Santayana, like the one between Santayana and Dewey that I will describe in the next chapter, must be recognized as a gap *within* pragmatism, one made almost inevitable by the distinct set of intellectual habits and attitudes that pragmatism is. As Henry Samuel Levinson points out in *Santayana, Pragmatism, and the Spiritual Life,* it was as a pragmatist that Santayana was initially received. His disputes with James and Dewey, the latter characterized, as Levinson puts it, by "fairly weak misreadings on both sides," are significant, but they have too often served to

*The Aesthetics of Pragmatism*

open a chasm between Santayana and pragmatism.[6] This chasm is invoked to separate the temptations of withdrawal and contemplation, aligned with Santayana's alleged religious aestheticism, from the more compelling (and supposedly Deweyan) claims of active, instrumental engagement with the material and social world. The banishment of Santayana to the margins of the pragmatic project is, ironically, a way of keeping pragmatism pure, reinscribing the antipragmatic divisions between mind and body as well as nature and culture by diminishing our sense of how thoroughly each is implicated in the other.

Santayana himself recognized, and in 1905 reported to James, the affinities between his own and James's work. James responded gratefully but hesitantly, admitting in response, "Yours are still one of the secrets of the universe which it is one of my chief motives to live for the unveiling of" (*TC* 2:398). It would not have required much of Santayana to see through such a compliment. In a 1900 letter to his colleague G. H. Palmer, James had earlier allowed that "the great event in my life recently has been the reading of Santayana's book," *Interpretations of Poetry and Religion.* The same letter also claims, with more candor, to "absolutely reject the Platonism of it" (though he reports that he "squealed with delight at the imperturbable perfection with which the position is laid down on page after page" [*TC* 2:319]). It was in this context that James would comment, with characteristic ambivalence, "It is refreshing to see a representative of moribund Latinity rise up and administer such reproof to us barbarians in the hour of our triumph" (*TC* 2:319). He would later call *The Life of Reason* a "great" book, "Emerson's first rival and successor," but again resist what he felt was "something profoundly alienating in Santayana's unsympathetic tone, his 'preciousness' and superciliousness": "The same things in Emerson's mouth would sound entirely different. E. receptive, expansive, as if handling life through a wide funnel with a great indraught; S. as if through a pin-point orifice that emits his cooling spray outward over the universe like a nose-disinfectant from an 'atomizer' " (*TC* 2:399). As the imagery of this description suggests, Santayana epitomized for James a style of thought, perhaps even of personal comportment, that kept the world at too safe a distance, oversanitizing its vital and sustaining messiness.

Still, Santayana was no Platonist, at least not in any reductive sense of the term. Indeed, for Santayana, Plato was, if anything, the ultimate poet; his ideals make no claim on us as descriptions of metaphysical realities, but they still make every claim as persuasive poetry. As Santayana writes in *The Sense of Beauty,* "Those intuitions which we call Platonic are seldom scientific, they seldom explain the phenomena or hit upon the actual law of things, but they are often the highest expression of that activity which they fail to make comprehensible. . . . Platonism is a very refined and beautiful expression of our natural instincts, it embodies conscience and utters our inmost hopes" (*WGS* 2:9). Santayana removes the metaphysical pretensions from Platonism and leaves us with Plato as natural poet, one of the great masters of myth, narrative, and metaphor. One can only speculate how Plato, anxious as he was about the possible real-world effects of poetry, would have responded.[7]

James was even less a Platonist, but he must have followed Santayana's reasoning with some sense of recognition. He had also concluded that the feelings he associated with mental experience had a distinctly aesthetic component. This is made explicit in a note on "The Sentiment of Rationality," the essay in which he first argued that intellectual positions or conclusions fulfill psychological needs entirely apart from their appeal to principles of logic and reason. In the note, he comments that the essay might have been more appropriately titled "The Psychology of Philosophizing" because it "arose in the attempt to discover in an analysis of the motives which prompt men to philosophic activity, some facts which might help us to decide between the conflicting claims to authority of the different systems to which that activity gives birth" (*TC* 1:495).[8] This leads James to note the place of "aesthetic needs" in intellectual life: "In the following pages, then, I treat systems of truth as purely subjective creations, invented for the satisfaction of certain aesthetic needs." These aesthetic needs are tied to powerful psychological needs that must answer to prerational feelings of adequate continuity and orientation in the world. As James comments in the essay, looking forward to the argument he would later make in "The Will to Believe," "Our reasons are ludicrously incommensurate with the volume of our feeling, yet on the latter we unhesitatingly act" (*W* 1:528). We do not, and sometimes cannot, wait for evidence to enable rational decision-making. Instead, we typically trust our feelings to guide and orient our actions. While our philosophies may be designed to appear rational, they are in fact responsive to these same feelings. They are also formed to satisfy aesthetic needs, the "strong feeling of ease, peace, rest" and the "lively relief and pleasure" that we get when we make the transition from "a state of puzzle and perplexity to rational comprehension" (*W* 1:504).

John Dewey provides a telling commentary on the aesthetic implications of James's "sentiment of rationality." He writes to James in December 1903, proposing a piece tentatively titled "Truth As Stimulation and As Control," conceived as a commentary to "The Sentiment of Rationality." The essay will

> point out that in certain situations truth is that which liberates and sets agoing more experience, in others, that which limits and defines, which adjusts to definite ends. It seems to me this will straighten out some

*The Aesthetics of Pragmatism*

objections to pragmatism, its seeming over-utilitarianism (the "control" side), and provide a place for the aesthetic function *in* knowledge — "truth for its own sake," harmony, etc. (the liberation side). (*TC* 2:526)

The objections to which Dewey refers were not so easily dispelled, but it is revealing to see that Dewey resists the notion that pragmatism is excessively utilitarian. Pragmatic instrumentalism must be qualified by "the aesthetic function *in* knowledge." Dewey then criticizes F. C. S. Schiller, the British pragmatist, for overdoing "relatively the control side of truth, its utility for *specific* purposes, not making enough of the tremendous freedom, possibilities of new growth, etc., that come from developing an 'intelligence' that works along for a time according to its *own* technique, *in abstracto* from preconceived and preexperienced ends and results" (*TC* 2:526). The "tremendous freedom, possibilities of new growth, etc." represent the liberating function of transitional aesthetic agencies. Dewey believed that James was on to something in "The Sentiment of Rationality" which, given more precise formulation, could alter the way pragmatism was then being received. The "control side" had to be balanced by the "liberation side," instrumentalism by aesthetics.

James, however, remained resistant to theorizing aesthetic experience even in "The Sentiment of Rationality," where he comments at one point, "Why does the *Aesthetik* of every German philosopher appear to the artist an abomination of desolation?" (*W* 1:508). This characteristic dismissal hints at James's deep ambivalence toward his own work, for James is, after all, a scientist seeking to understand and explain natural and naturally elusive human phenomena. *The Principles of Psychology* sets out to explain a process not reducible to specific principles because always tending, in James's own formulations, *beyond* such principles, toward what we have already seen him call "all those indefinitely radiating subconscious possibilities of increase that we can only feel without conceiving, and can hardly begin to analyze" (*W* 2:761). James would always be attracted to what science had to struggle to account for: emotions, the feeling of effort, the will, parapsychology, mesmerism, religious mysticism, altered consciousness, and so on. As a writer, he was perpetually balancing his own conflicting impulses. He wanted to redirect philosophers away from what he thought of as merely verbal dilemmas (the classic problems of philosophy) toward the rough-and-tumble world in which a thought's only measure would be the particular consequences it wrought in the world. But he also felt the need to address an intelligent, reasoning community that necessarily traded in the sort of definitions, abstractions, and rational distinctions that generated these verbal dilemmas. If James's fluid

*The Poetics of Transition*

and engaging style is testimony to his best philosophical intentions, his characteristic and sometimes quite violent rejection of any idea that even hinted at a withdrawal from the world into the abstract or ideal testifies to his internal struggle with his philosophical inheritance. His ambivalence toward Santayana's writings, like his ambivalence toward his brother's novels—and no doubt toward both men's eccentric styles of being—is a product of this tension.[9]

It is instructive to trace James's response, over the years, to Italy, a country that came to epitomize for him an environment of aesthetic decadence.[10] In a letter to his father written from Italy in 1873, he compares the view from the train of villages "perched on hill spurs" with the experience of the same villages by those who built and inhabited them: "The 'picturesque'-ness that *we* now find there was the last thing present to the utilitarian minds of those who built them, and they make one realize how man's life is based historically on sheer force and will and fight, and how the inner ideal world only grows up inside and under the shelter of these brute tendencies" (*TC* 1:163). James specifically contrasts our detached experience of the picturesque with the "sheer force and will and fight" that characterize the growth of the "inner ideal world" within actual experience. He can only bear the thought of this "inner ideal world" so long as it is directly responsive to the "brute tendencies" of a violently impinging world.

As James traveled through Italy on this and other European excursions, he came to recognize the danger of eliding all concrete, historical context. The danger is not simply that of misunderstanding the actual facts of an aesthetic object's production but, more significantly, as he wrote from Rome to his sister in 1873, of "injuring all one's active powers." Italy is a "*delightful* place to dip into," but "the weight of the past world here is fatal,—one ends by becoming its mere parasite instead of its equivalent. This worship, this dependence on other men is abnormal. The ancients did things by doing the business of their own day, not by gaping at their grandfathers' tombs,—and the normal man today will do likewise. Better fifty years of Cambridge, than a cycle of Cathay!" (*TC* 2:258). This attitude to present "active powers" stems from an Emersonian desire to be the past's full equivalent. "Doing the business of their own day" has a much more athletic ring to it than any vocabulary seeking to account for the function of art in experience could possibly have. The suggestion that the "normal man today will do likewise"—with its not-so-subtle normative prescriptiveness—indicates that only our own "sheer force and will and fight" can *earn* us such delightfulness from our environment.[11]

In a letter written during another trip to Italy nine years later, James laments, "If anything can make one a fatalist it's the sight of the inevitable decay of each fine art after it reaches its maturity" (*TC* 1:385). While James feels a certain satisfaction in the pictures themselves (he calls them "the glorious pictures"), he is arrested by their crumbling environment. He compares modern Venice with the "old Venice":

> But the *canaille* character of the population of St. Mark's Square is something literally horrible when one thinks of what it once must have been. Cads of every race, and to the outward eye hardly anything but cads. I imagine some old patrician starting into indignant life again, merely to drive us away with his maledictions. I'm sure we should all flee conscience-stricken at the sight of him; for the energy of old Venice, as I've been reading it, must have been something prodigious and incessant. (*TC* 1:385–86)

It is striking that the decaying environment includes not only the buildings and other physical features of the city but the population of Venice itself. If the glorious paintings of Venice were once themselves full of energy, it was as part of this "energy of old Venice," a living culture of an active population that found its truest expression in its daily labor. Yet James finds modern Venice overrun by a canaille population, among whom, in a telling grammatical shift mid-passage, he includes himself. As long as artistic production is the outgrowth of a living culture, it too is prodigious and incessant. Once the sustaining culture has died—and James takes Italy's ever-present tokens of decay as signs of such cultural death—the people become, at best, dependent worshippers of the past, at worst, cads.

Perhaps the most revealing of these letters is one of 1892, written to Charles Ritter, in which James compares Italy with Switzerland, admiring the former's attractions but preferring something more "solid" in the latter. Florence is "even more attractive" than before, yet Switzerland is "sovereignly *good*": "It meets all the major needs of body and soul as no other country does, in summer time. After the aesthetics, the morbidness, the corruptions of Italy, how I shall want again in *ihrem Thau gesund mich zu baden!*" (*TC* 2:252). This preference for "good" (solid) Switzerland over morbid and corrupt (diaphanous) Italy leads James without transition into the recent death of the French historian and critic Joseph Ernest Renan. James considers Renan a disappointment for his failure to recognize that moral ideals are *of* the world, responsive to the pressures and constraints of social and material environments. This is why Renan's writing serves, for James, a "merely *musical* function." Like Italy, Renan represents aesthetic experience divorced from the physical needs of a living culture, art that invokes "the vocabulary of the moral and religious life too sweetly and freely" for refusing "to be *bound* by those ideals," that is, to integrate them into the lived, physical experience of self or culture.[12] Such art is not earned by "sheer force and will and fight" within and against a constraining environment. This, for James, encapsulates the seductive danger that art and aesthetic perception pose: that they might establish a world that, however beautiful, could have nothing to do with the concrete, unforgiving world in which we are daily called on to act. Despite the attraction that brought him back again and again, Italy was never the place for James because it always suggested art at too great a remove from the conditions of life.

James recognized the aesthetic needs with which thought was ultimately entangled, but could not help but feel that any overt treatment of the aesthetic and the ideal removed these from their real-world basis. Santayana, who shared James's initial recognition, was at least for a time convinced that this overt treatment was necessary because otherwise the aesthetic and the ideal were destined to be misunderstood and either attributed to a metaphysical cause or altogether ignored or denied. James was happy enough to have an experience of beauty, but associated any effort to dwell on or rationally account for such an experience as idealist. Santayana, a persistent critic of idealism, saw this very dwelling as the higher ideal of life, so long as this ideal was understood as an affective, not a metaphysical ideal.

In this sense, Santayana is only taking James's own psychological method a step beyond where James was himself willing to take it, into the feeling or sense of beauty. It is impossible not to hear echoes of James in the background even when Santayana invokes the ideal in *The Sense of Beauty:* "If in referring to the ideal we were not thus analysing the real, the ideal would be an irrelevant and unmeaning thing. We know what the ideal is because we observe what pleases us in the reality" (*WGS* 2:80). Santayana emphasizes the different attitudes people adopt toward this ideal:

> The pathetic part of our situation appears only when we so attach ourselves to those necessary but imperfect fictions, as to reject the facts from which they spring and of which they seek to be prophetic. We are then guilty of that substitution of means for ends, which is called idolatry in religion, absurdity in logic, and folly in morals. In aesthetics the thing has no name, but is nevertheless very common; for it is found whenever we speak of what ought to please, rather than of what actually pleases. (*WGS* 2:81)

Santayana carefully distinguishes in this comment between the descriptive and prescriptive aspects of any aesthetic theory. What actually pleases is a function of historically and environmentally specific experience, whereas

*The Aesthetics of Pragmatism*

what ought to please is an empty ideal, usually put forward in the service of some supposed value that has no basis in actual experience.

James's anxious resistances to the philosophy of aesthetics underscore his sense that lived experience depends on aesthetic feelings to interweave self and environment, orienting the self toward action in the world. This crucial aesthetic dimension of experience is, for James, just as it was for Emerson, a perfectly natural human function, integral to how we creatively position ourselves within the world and orient our present and future actions there. Alluding to the philosopher Hermann Lotze in his essay "Pragmatism and Humanism," James speaks of our previous descriptions of reality as existing not for themselves but for the more important purpose "of stimulating our minds to such additions as shall enhance the universe's total value." He continues, "In our cognitive as well as in our active life we are creative. We *add*, both to the subject and to the predicate part of reality. The world stands really malleable, waiting to receive its final touches at our hands. Like the kingdom of heaven, it suffers human violence willingly. Man *engenders* truths upon it" (*W* 2:599). Whereas scientific rationalism encourages us to see our cognitive activity much as the traditional psychology had—as a passive registering of external data, most reliable when most objectively performed—James insists that our cognitive lives are first and foremost creative. It is because James felt so strongly about this primary aesthetic function that he became agitated by what he saw as secondary, and therefore quite diminished, forms of aesthetic seduction, including the cultivation of any aesthetic theory.

There is, then, something thoroughly Jamesian about the distinction Santayana draws in *The Sense of Beauty* between good and bad theory:

> If when a theory is bad it narrows our capacity for observation and makes all appreciation vicarious and formal, when it is good it reacts favourably upon our powers, guides the attention to what is really capable of affording entertainment, and increases, by force of new analogies, the range of our interests. Speculation is an evil if it imposes a foreign organization on our mental life; it is a good if it only brings to light, and makes more perfect by training, the organization already inherent in it. (*WGS* 2:8)

This bit of reasoning is worth a good deal more than any argument for or against theory, simply because it plainly dismisses theory's most grandiose and idealized pretensions. James would no doubt embrace the notion of increasing the range of our interests, though he would probably begin to shuffle restlessly at the mention of making "more perfect" any "inherent" organization. But Santayana frankly acknowledges that organization is "already inherent" only to the extent that it has been made so by prior "training." Santayana characteristically refuses to shy away from the sense of perfection, or the sense of beauty, just because the intimation will never entirely square with the manifestation.

Santayana's "necessary but imperfect fictions" grow up, in James's terms, "inside and under the shelter of [the] brute tendencies" of the material, contingent world. If Santayana could endorse contemplative retreat from the world, he still understood that no product of the mind's contemplation could survive that did not acknowledge and engage that world. As he comments in *Reason in Art,* "A living art does not produce curiosities to be collected but spiritual necessaries to be diffused" (*RA* 209). Art's vital fictions are, in this light, products of a mind that is, itself, a function of the world, not something that operates in its own separate, ethereal realm of being. Indeed, pragmatic aesthetics depends on the crucial remodeling of mind implicit, and sometimes explicit, in pragmatism. Mind is not active *over and against* nature, but *within* it, a natural force like all the rest, shaped by and within its natural and cultural environment. As this formulation suggests, pragmatists reject the polarity of subjective and objective realms. Mind is an active, creative force, but it is not a force that can be separated from the world on which it acts.

In "Does 'Consciousness' Exist?", James goes so far as to suggest that there is no distinct stuff that we can label consciousness. Consciousness is instead an abstraction with no distinct, immaterial being of its own. Dewey, who saw this as a position James developed to revise his prior conception of the stream of thought, suggests in his 1934 volume *Art as Experience* that

> the idiomatic use of the word "mind" gives a much more truly scientific, and philosophic, approach to the actual facts of the case than does the technical one. For in its non-technical use, "mind" denotes every mode and variety of interest in, and concern for, things: practical, intellectual, and emotional. It never denotes anything self-contained, isolated from the world of persons and things, but is always used with respect to situations, events, objects, persons and groups. (*LW* 10:267–68)

This determined unwillingness to separate mind from the world by means of the usual binary opposition is commonplace among pragmatists. Like Santayana, Dewey sees the "practical, intellectual, and emotional" functions of mind as evidence of an irreducible and interlocking pluralism. We "mind" the world, but we do not have minds that look on it from without.[13]

Dewey even criticizes our culturally ingrained habit of taking the word *mind* as a noun: "Mind is primarily a verb. It denotes all the ways in which we deal consciously and expressly with the situations in which we find ourselves. Unfortunately, an influential manner of thinking has changed modes of action into an underlying substance that performs the activities in question" (*LW* 10:268). This "influential manner of thinking" is the philosophical tradition and style that Richard Rorty would later describe in *Philosophy and the Mirror of Nature,* a tradition that figures mind according to a visual paradigm, derived from the metaphor of the mind as a type of eye. Because the eye is a material substance adapted to record impressions of the external world, we think of the mind itself, on this model, as a spiritual substance, similarly adapted to record mental impressions of external phenomena.

According to Dewey, this misconception of mind underwrites aesthetic theories that promote detached contemplation: "This conception of mind as an isolated being underlies the conception that esthetic experience is merely something 'in mind,' and strengthens the conception which isolates the esthetic from those modes of experience in which the body is actively engaged with the things of nature and life. It takes art out of the province of the live creature" (*LW* 10:268). For Dewey, as for the later James, the philosophical emphasis on mind too often leads to a subjectivism indistinguishable from solipsism. Both James and Dewey view mind instead as an active function linking humans to their natural and social environments. One effect of this shift is to undermine neatly demarcated categories like mind and matter, subject and object. Experience is always affective because we are always actively combining what we have "in mind" with "things of nature and life," thereby channeling interest and attention to specific objects. Art belongs within the "province of the live creature," in Dewey's phrase, because it helps us synchronize our bodies with their immediate environments. Without the feelings of vital attachment and involvement that this pragmatically grounded aesthetic sensibility fosters, we could never even begin to formulate or execute rational designs.[14]

This is the argument of *Art as Experience,* announced both in the volume's title and in its first chapter, "The Live Creature." If the aesthetics of pragmatism has been generally ignored or misconstrued, this has been nowhere more apparent than in the renewal of interest in Dewey, which has for the most part skirted (and sometimes misrepresented) Dewey's understanding of art as experience. In *The American Evasion of Philosophy,* for example, Cornel West dismisses Dewey's *Art as Experience,* claiming that it is marred by "an organic idealism unbecoming a card-carrying pragmatist."[15] As the title of Dewey's first chapter indicates, organicism, or at least some sort of naturalism, is indeed at the heart of Dewey's aesthetics. His idealism, however, is a much more complicated affair than West acknowledges.

*Art as Experience* has to be reexamined, both in terms of the argument

Dewey puts forward in the book and for its place in Dewey's larger philosophical project. This place is far more central than most critics, with a few notable exceptions, have allowed.[16] As Dewey notes as early as 1920 in *Reconstruction in Philosophy*, the "material out of which philosophy finally emerges is irrelevant to science and to explanation. It is figurative, symbolic of fears and hopes, made of imaginations and suggestions, not significant of a world of objective fact intellectually confronted. It is poetry and drama, rather than science" (*MW* 12:83). However much this material is transformed by human intelligence, its source, in both individual and cultural life, is always at base aesthetic. In his Carus lectures of 1925, published as *Experience and Nature,* Dewey comments, "the history of human experience is a history of the development of arts": art is "a continuation, by means of intelligent selection and arrangement, of natural tendencies of natural events" (*LW* 1:290–91). Knowledge and intelligence, throughout Dewey's career, are inextricably bound up with the various interests and passions that animate life: "The view which isolates knowledge, contemplation, liking, interest, value, or whatever from action is itself a survival of the notion that there are things which can exist and be known apart from active connection with other things" (*LW* 1:324).[17]

Richard Rorty criticizes *Experience and Nature* in his essay "Dewey's Metaphysics," arguing that Dewey's effort in that volume to determine the "generic traits" of experience reflects a decidedly unpragmatic metaphysical yearning on Dewey's part. Rorty distinguishes this nostalgic yearning from the "polemical critique of the tradition offered in *Reconstruction in Philosophy* and *The Quest for Certainty,*" both works that epitomize the proper function of philosophy in a "post-Philosophical culture." West agrees with Rorty's specific criticism, associating the metaphysical project of *Experience and Nature* with the idealist *Art as Experience.* He then distinguishes what he more favorably calls the role of "critical intelligence" in Dewey: "to overcome obstacles, resolve problems, and project realizable possibilities in pressing predicaments."[18] West cites other works by Dewey to describe this project, even though critical intelligence of this sort is precisely the subject of the concluding chapter of *Experience and Nature,* "Existence, Value, Criticism." This critical intelligence is integrally related to aesthetic experience, as suggested in the previous chapter, "Experience, Nature, and Art." Neither Rorty nor West reads *Experience and Nature* with an eye to this fundamental relationship between critical intelligence and aesthetic experience, and so both are left to distinguish between what is authentically pragmatic and what is latently idealist in Dewey's work.

In effect, both Rorty and West criticize the notion that philosophy should provide a general description of things or of the nature of knowledge. Phi-

*The Aesthetics of Pragmatism*

losophers should be less concerned with the discovery of truth than with what Rorty has eloquently called the "slow and painful choice between alternative self-images." [19] Rorty's "liberal ironists," like West's "prophetic pragmatists," are concerned only with what the world might possibly become, not with what past descriptions have made it out to be or even with what it presumably is. [20] Both also seek to resituate pragmatic hopes and tendencies within what they take to be a specifically cultural context. Both emphasize Dewey over James, focusing on Dewey's cultural materialism and critique as opposed to what West takes to be his occasional organicism and idealism and what Rorty takes to be his latent metaphysical ambitions.

Of course differences also abound. Rorty's post-Philosophical conversation bears a very different accent from West's, which can draw equally from Emerson, especially in his mood of provocation, and from African American oral tradition. Rorty, a determined secularist, rigorously avoids religious vocabularies and contexts, whereas West embraces emancipatory Christian traditions. West is also critical of Rorty's avowed liberalism, noting that Rorty's neopragmatism "requires no change in our cultural and political practices." [21] Still, both Rorty and West are similarly invested in a version of pragmatism that has, at best, seen no reason to acknowledge such a thing as an aesthetics of pragmatism, and has at worst seen pragmatism's occasional brush with aesthetics as a positive obstruction to the development of freer, more inclusive social and intellectual practices. Indeed, one of West's criticisms of Rorty is that his "neopragmatism is implicitly of an Emersonian sort in that poetic activity tends to regulate his conception of human redescription and constitute the most noble of human practices." [22] This is true insofar as it goes, right down to the qualifying "implicitly," since Rorty's explicit engagement with Emerson has been minimal. Rorty's understanding of poetic activity has largely been shaped by his reading of Harold Bloom's brilliant but idiosyncratic theory of poetic influence, of strong poets struggling to define their own poetic fates in what would be their own exclusive, hard-won poetic terms. Almost completely silent on Emerson and the poets and other writers he actually influenced, Rorty ignores Emerson's poetics of transition and the aesthetics of pragmatism that extends that poetics into a broader range of social and cultural experience.

For a critic such as Giles Gunn, by contrast, the "redefinition of experience as a form of art and the reformulation of the purpose of art as life's continuous revaluation of itself—and thus as the formal realization of its own possibilities" constitute the central motive of "the pragmatist turn." Pragmatism's vital cultural force, for Gunn, is linked to what it promises by way of possible aesthetic realizations, not in works of art but in life lived as a con-

*The Poetics of Transition*

tinuous creative adventure. It is in this spirit that Richard Poirier describes the "superfluous Emerson" in *Poetry and Pragmatism:* "The superfluous has to do with excess and luxury and exuberance and uselessness and desire, none of which are usually thought necessary to the rational and moral conduct of life."[23] That they are necessary in precisely this sense is the lesson of any pragmatic aesthetics. This was also Santayana's frank conclusion: "Sportive self-expression can be prized because human nature contains a certain elasticity and margin for experiment, in which waste activity is inevitable and may be precious: for this license may lead, amid a thousand failures, to some real discovery and advance. Art, like life, should be free, since both are experimental" (*RA* 178). Even Rorty's slow and painful pursuit of alternative self-images must ultimately depend on our delight in this "waste activity," the exuberant production of that which we as yet have no standards to assimilate or judge.

West's specific charge of organic idealism has a particular history of its own that requires further consideration. He cites Stephen C. Pepper's classic "Some Questions on Dewey's Esthetics" in a footnote to his passing dismissal of *Art as Experience.* Pepper criticizes an undercurrent of organic idealism in Dewey's aesthetics, although he finds a powerfully pragmatic strain running through the book as well and acknowledges the strength of "its plea to break down the separation between art and life, to realize that there is beauty in the commonest and meanest things."[24] Still, Pepper concludes that *Art as Experience* is divided between its proper (and approved) pragmatic aesthetics and its organic idealism. He is troubled by Dewey's assimilation of values and terms that are conventionally associated with organic idealism. In fact, however, Dewey's aesthetics resists this organic ideal. Whereas Pepper takes terms like *wholeness, organic,* and *universal* to imply Dewey's confused trafficking in idealist aesthetic principles, these terms, inflected by Dewey's pragmatism, echo in a double register that at once invokes and disturbs their organic meanings. Dewey himself makes this point in "Experience, Knowledge, and Value: A Rejoinder," where he responds to Pepper by insisting that words such as "*coherence, whole, integration, etc.*" have "a meaning consistent with naturalistic and pragmatic empiricism" (*LW* 14:34–35). He turns the table on Pepper by associating Pepper's criticism with the tendency among ancient Greek philosophers, as well as among contemporary objective idealists, to take "categories which *are* applicable to works of art and to their enjoyed perception" and then extend them "illegitimately" until they become "categories of the universe at large, endowed with cosmic import" (*LW* 14:35, 38).

Dewey's reference here to Greek philosophy offers an important clue to any reconstruction of the aesthetics of pragmatism. In a number of previous books, Dewey had argued that philosophy's first significant error had been to hypostatize what had been the properly aesthetic satisfactions and pleasures of ancient Greek culture. Philosophy establishes itself as the sole foundation and source of adequate knowledge precisely when poetry and mythology cease to acknowledge their ritual and dramatic functions. Aesthetic satisfaction thus paves the way for knowledge of the immutable characteristics of the cosmos or the nature of being. In *The Quest for Certainty* (1929), Dewey suggests that the Greek love of harmony and order in form led Greek philosophers to posit such harmony and order as "static properties" of the universe itself: "They aimed at constructing out of nature, as observed, an artistic whole for the eye of the soul to behold" (*LW* 4:73). On this model, as Dewey notes, scientific progress was left to depend on more rational observation of the inherently harmonious (and beautiful) properties of Being.[25] Santayana's analysis of pre-Socratic Greek culture is strikingly similar to Dewey's: "Before making statistics of her [Nature's] movements," he writes of the Homeric hymns in *Interpretations of Poetry and Religion,* "they made dramatisations of her life. The imagination enveloped the material world, as yet imperfectly studied, and produced the cosmos of mythology" (*WGS* 3:19). Like Dewey, Santayana conceives philosophy's proper function—the proper function of any human intelligence—on the model of such imaginative activity. The unity common to philosophy and art is only "momentarily attained" and is never immune from "recurring conflicts with hostile forces" (*WGS* 3:33). Like myth, philosophy can only offer a temporary foothold on the world, what Robert Frost aptly called a "momentary stay against confusion."

The unities about which Dewey writes are also felt, aesthetic unities. They are not unified wholes embedded in the world, as if awaiting human discovery, but human projections onto the world. So too organic processes always include, for Dewey, cultural experience: nature and culture together provide the material from which and onto which the self projects these unities. In *Art as Experience,* Dewey foregrounds aesthetic activity in order to isolate the mechanism by which individuals and cultures engage their surrounding environments. He argues, like James, that the arts, when they were most thriving and compelling, "were part of the significant life of an organized community" (*LW* 10:13). Artistically based rituals provide the glue that not only holds a community together but also makes an individual life meaningful within that community: "Each of these communal modes of activity united the practical, the social, and the educative in an integrated whole having esthetic form. . . . Art was *in* them, for these activities conformed to the needs and conditions of the most intense, most readily grasped and longest remembered experience. But they were more than just art, although the esthetic strand was ubiquitous" (*LW* 10:330–31). Pepper and West ignore

*The Poetics of Transition*

84

the development from Dewey's first chapter in *Art as Experience,* "The Live Creature," to its last, "Art and Civilization," from which the above passage is taken—a development implicit from the book's very beginning. For Dewey, the biological rhythms of life remain a significant force behind the power of art, yet these are never entirely separable from the rhythms of "the substantial life of community." Both together constitute "life."

The process of art's perpetual renewal both reflects and sustains the biological and cultural rhythms of living itself. Having already described the rhythms of the "basic vital functions" humans share with other animals, Dewey treats the "rhythm of loss of integration with environment and recovery of union" as the basis of aesthetic experience (*LW* 10:20–21). Such union is neither empirically nor metaphysically grounded, given its dramatic and imaginative function. Indeed, Dewey focuses not on phenomenal unity but rather on the integrated process that includes the rhythm of loss and recovery, dissociation and union. The artist cultivates "moments of resistance and tension" because of their potential for "bringing to living consciousness an experience that is unified and total." An experience can be "unified and total," as *an* experience, precisely because it is limited in scope and duration.[26] Neither resistance nor unity tells the whole story, since the rhythm of life and of art requires both together, in all their experienced tension. Dewey comments that "the moment of passage from disturbance into harmony is that of intensest life," a formulation that recalls James's claim in "The Sentiment of Rationality" that we move from "a state of puzzle or perplexity to rational comprehension" with a charge of "lively relief and pleasure" (*LW* 10:21–22). Art stems from and further cultivates this transitional rhythm. An achieved harmony is only one moment or phase in this larger rhythm.

Dewey's discussion of art should be recognized as another variation of the Emersonian poetics of transition. Instead of focusing on the aesthetic finality or autonomy of the work of art, Dewey looks to art as an agency of continuous re-creation and renewal. Art is situated at "the junction of the new and old," a site of "re-creation" where "the present impulse gets form and solidity while the old, the 'stored,' material is literally revived, given new life and soul through having to meet a new situation" (*LW* 10:66). Life and soul, tropes for the exercise of creative human energy, do not die out once spent, but rather seek new forms that will channel and sustain this energy: "Things in the environment that would otherwise be mere smooth channels or else blind obstructions become means, media. At the same time, things retained from past experience that would grow stale from routine or inert from lack of use, become coefficients in new adventures and put on a raiment of fresh meaning" (*LW* 10:66–67). Such conversion—with its dimly retained spiritual connotations—is the fate of all experience. This is the dynamic described in Emerson's "Circles," in which "every ultimate fact is only the first of a new series" and "nothing is secure but life, transition, the energizing spirit" (*EL* 405, 413). So for Dewey, nothing is secure from this process of incessant transition. Art is the ongoing conversion of all that has grown "stale from routine and inert from lack of use" into some new, vital form that reanimates experience and thereby restructures the world.

Because his attention is directed toward "the delight of experiencing the world about us in its varied qualities and forms," a process that would issue in "a new experience of life" (*LW* 10:110), Dewey is especially skeptical about the value of any single ideal of art: "The value of experience is not only in the ideals it reveals, but in its power to disclose many ideals, a power more germinal and more significant than any revealed ideal, since it includes them in its stride, shatters and remakes them. One may even reverse the statement and say the value of ideals lies in the experiences to which they lead" (*LW* 10:325). Like ideals, art is judged by the further experience to which it leads. Art must ultimately serve "the promotion of th[e] active process" of living, shattering and remaking ideals in the service of further experience.

Dewey's conception of imagination registers the paradoxical double status of artistic productions:

> The artist is driven to submit himself in humility to the discipline of the objective vision. But the inner vision is not cast out. It remains as the organ by which the outer vision is controlled, and it takes on structure as the latter is absorbed within it. The interaction of the two modes of vision is imagination; as imagination takes form the work of art is born. It is the same with the philosophic thinker. There are moments when he feels that his ideas and ideals are finer than anything in existence. But he finds himself obliged to go back to objects if his speculations are to have body, weight, and perspective. Yet in surrendering himself to objective material he does not surrender his vision; the object just as an object is not his concern. It is placed in the context of ideas and, as it is thus placed, the latter acquire solidity and partake of the nature of the object. (*LW* 10:273)

Pepper cites parts of this passage as proof of Dewey's organic idealism. Yet Dewey's emphasis here on "body, weight, and perspective" and on the "solidity" of thought reflects his effort to turn thought out into the world. Imagination is "the interaction of the two modes of vision," not one mode set over and against the other. Though the philosopher may at times feel his "ideas and ideals are finer than anything in existence," he must "surrender" himself

*The Poetics of Transition*

to a world of objects: "The artist is driven to submit himself in humility to the discipline of the objective vision." This disciplined submission constitutes a victory for neither the subjective ideal nor the physical world, since the aesthetic process makes each responsible and responsive to the other.

It is precisely here, where Dewey formulates a response to his critics within the pragmatist fold by defending his organicism and idealism on pragmatist grounds, that the literary modernists can help shed light on the aesthetics of pragmatism. The mutual inherence and interdependence of subjective and objective realms is the burden of Wallace Stevens's essays and lectures, all of them written between the mid-1930s and Stevens's death in 1955. In his 1942 address "The Noble Rider and the Sound of Words," Stevens comments on the poet's impossible choice between imagination and reality: "He will find that it is not a choice of one over the other and not a decision that divides them, but something subtler, a recognition that here, too, as between these poles, the universal interdependence exists, and hence his choice and his decision must be that they are equal and inseparable" (*CPP* 657). Imagination and reality are "equal and inseparable" because they are mutually determining. The "something subtler" to which Stevens refers here reflects the choice of both an imagination responsive to real conditions and a reality revealed through an attentiveness and responsiveness shaped by imagination. Stevens's poet occupies the always unfolding margin within which these poles meet. Confronted by the "pressure of reality," the poet draws on his own power to return pressure. This is the "violence from within that protects us from a violence without" that Stevens describes at the end of the essay, the "imagination pressing back against the pressure of reality" (*CPP* 665). Stevens's play here on "pressing back" and "the pressure of reality" suggests that the pressure in question cannot simply be located in the self or its external environment. This pressure rather figures the medium of exchange between them, a medium of exchange that constitutes them as such. Dewey offers a similar wordplay when he examines the etymology of "expression," a "squeezing out, a pressing forth": "The thing expressed is wrung from the producer by the pressure exercised by objective things upon the natural impulses and tendencies — so far is expression from being the direct and immaculate issue of the latter" (*LW* 10:70). Expression, as the exercise of imagination, belongs both to the objective world which exerts its pressure on us and the human impulses and tendencies that press back against that pressure.

The pragmatist imagination is not a miraculous, godlike power that enters into the world on the wings of intuition, free of the taint of contingency and history. Imagination is rather a form of human power (not unlike muscular power, though it is significantly encultured) in a world that limits and constrains and, ultimately, defeats any merely human power. Imagination responds to material conditions — natural, social, and cultural — and has no possible existence apart from them. Always nurtured from within and sustained by these material conditions, imagination seeks to transform them. Imagination learns its necessary discipline from these forces, where it also acquires, in defeat, and in the record of past defeats, its posture of humility.

This humility is apparent in Stevens's claim in "Imagination as Value" that no product of imagination will ever be permanently satisfying: "It would be the merest improvisation to say of any image of the world, even though it was an image with which a vast accumulation of imaginations had been content, that it was the chief image. The imagination itself would not remain content with it nor allow us to do so. It is the irrepressible revolutionist" (*CPP* 736). No matter how powerful a "metaphoric redescription" (to echo Rorty) proves to be, no matter how many imaginations are for a time content with it, there is no possible end to the perpetual rhythms of disjunction and harmony. Hence we seek not one ultimately satisfying image of harmony but an endless dance to the fluctuating rhythms of form and formal rupture. This dynamic issues in what Stevens describes as a proliferation of imaginative values: "The imagination is the power of the mind over the possibilities of things; but if this constitutes a certain single characteristic, it is the source not of a certain single value but of as many values as reside in the possibilities of things" (*CPP* 726). This perfectly Santayanan multiplication of values is essential to any pragmatist aesthetics, even Dewey's, pointing not to the power of any single value to become dominant but rather to the power to generate as many values as human imaginations — differently situated, differently endowed — can generate. Even an individual imagination cannot rest content with any single value or metaphoric resemblance.

This is why Stevens puts so much emphasis in his essays and poems on the power of metaphor and analogy. Metaphor is not, for Stevens, the source of ultimate, intuitive truths, but is rather a perpetual and perpetually self-revising activity. In "Three Academic Pieces," Stevens distinguishes resemblance-in-nature from identity-in-nature: "Nature is not mechanical to that extent for all its mornings and evenings, for all its inhabitants of China or India or Russia, for all its waves, or its leaves, or its hands. Its prodigy is not identity but resemblance and its universe of reproduction is not an assembly line but an incessant creation. Because this is so in nature, it is so in metaphor" (*CPP* 687). Like Emerson, Stevens claims to find the basis for the "incessant creation" of metaphor in nature itself, which is always producing differences in its constant flux, even when its objects appear to be infinitely repeated (as in waves, leaves, and hands, as well as in Chinese, Indian, and Russian masses as seen from Hartford, Connecticut). On this model, metaphor conveys not an inherent and necessary link between objects, the sort of link that would render such objects aspects of a single (metaphysical) reality, but rather resemblances between objects that retain their differences to the end.

Nor does metaphor merely imitate an object, as Stevens insists in the same essay: "An imitation may be described as an identity manqué. It is artificial. It is not fortuitous as a true metaphor is" (*CPP* 687). By "identity manqué," Stevens appears to mean a failed attempt to describe an object as it truly is. A "true metaphor" makes no effort to capture or convey an object's identity. It rather generates, fortuitously, previously unimagined resemblances that become part of our experience of a world which we have always understood, whether we realized it or not, on the basis of such resemblances. Stevens's claims for poetry derive from his suggestion that "poetry is a satisfying of the desire for resemblance. . . . Its singularity is that in the act of satisfying the desire for resemblance it touches the sense of reality, it enhances the sense of reality, heightens it, intensifies it" (*CPP* 690). It is hard to say what Stevens means by "the sense of reality," let alone what it might mean to "touch" or "enhance," "heighten" or "intensify" it. Indeed, such language makes it hard to distinguish the reality from our imaginative engagement with it. Fact and desire become one in the imaginative unfolding of the poem. A pragmatist aesthetics turns on the recognition of this interdependence. This is the background of Stevens's claim that "poetry is a part of the structure of reality" (*CPP* 692).

In his 1936 address "The Irrational Element in Poetry," Stevens encourages his readers to "live by literature, because literature is the better part of life, provided it is based on life itself" (*CPP* 786). That "provided" is the catch, of course, and precisely what keeps Stevens, at his best, from reposing in easy symbolisms or idealizations. For Stevens, as for Emerson and the pragmatists, living by literature is a means of cultivating life's possibilities, in full view of the contingent, historical conditions that shape those possibilities. The literary and aesthetic imagination depends on its own built-in vigilance, a wariness of the laziness by which tentatively posed literary or aesthetic values get promoted as ultimate, redemptive values. Stevens's conception of imagination is no doubt Romantic, as many of his critics have suggested, but his Romanticism is inflected by his pragmatism. He is acutely sensitive to the way in which imaginative forms become inadequate to the experience of things that initially give rise to them. As I will demonstrate later, his formulations and reformulations of the relations between reality and imagination reflect

*The Aesthetics of Pragmatism*

an Emersonian poetics of transition in the service of a Deweyan rhythm that defines art as experience. Poetry is at once the product and the instrument of our evolving individual and communal sense of things.

Before turning to the literary modernists, however, we need first to face the problem posed by my pairing of Dewey and Santayana. I have been suggesting throughout this chapter that Dewey and Santayana share a similar conception of the place of art in experience, but this underplays what both they and their later commentators recognized as their significant differences. Dewey called Santayana's philosophy a "broken-backed naturalism," while Santayana complained about pragmatism's narrow instrumentalism and muddled conception of truth. Much as Emerson's prose is marked by contradiction and paradox, Dewey and Santayana stage some of the key, even defining contradictions and paradoxes that are latent in the aesthetics of pragmatism. For all their differences, Dewey and Santayana are linked by more than just their notions of art as experience. Their similar poetics of transition also links their social and cultural thought, despite obvious differences of temperament and political affiliation. Neither the aesthetics of pragmatism nor the poetics of transition implies a particular politics or moral code, but each encourages and reinforces certain attitudes toward the moral and intellectual processes that ultimately issue in social and political commitments. By retracing the lines that Dewey and Santayana drew between themselves, we can clarify the relationship between the aesthetics of pragmatism and its social and political consequences.

# 4

## Santayana, Dewey, and the
## Politics of Transition

DESPITE THEIR MUTUAL interest in the role of art in experience, John Dewey and George Santayana pursued their respective philosophical projects largely without reference to one another's work. To all appearances, they epitomize antithetical philosophical allegiances. Roughly speaking, Dewey situates intelligence in the world, both natural and social, while Santayana locates intelligence at the permeable margins of this world, a position from which it can better contemplate the ideal forms cultivated by the human imagination. Dewey is typically represented as the standard-bearer for a socially and politically engaged intelligence, Santayana for a disengaged, aristocratic imagination.

Historians emphasize Dewey's steady involvement with the affairs of his day, his sense that the philosopher's task is to guide the public in its effort to secure and expand the benefits of democracy. The prevalent picture of Santayana, by contrast, highlights his steady retreat from the world of affairs. Santayana was always on the margins, even at Harvard, whose president, Charles W. Eliot, considered him "abnormal," a "withdrawn, contemplative man who takes no part in the everyday work of the institution, or of the world."[1] Santayana's departure from Harvard and the United States is often taken as confirmation of this retreat. For many, these facts make explicit what had been implicit in Santayana's philosophy from the start: a studied unworldliness that could only lead to withdrawal from social responsibilities. Whereas Dewey would come to stand as the philosopher of American democracy, Santayana would epitomize at best an illiberal withdrawal from social issues, at worst a misguided and deluded retreat from the duties of mind.[2]

To some extent, Santayana's present relative obscurity is a consequence of his refusal to adopt the progressive metaphors so characteristic of late-nineteenth- and twentieth-century American social and political thought. His rejection of the basic framework of American intellectual and political culture should, however, be distinguished from other claims about his political views. John McCormick usefully discusses Santayana's politics, as well as his anti-Semitism, in his 1987 biography, *George Santayana.* While acknowledging that Santayana's social and political views, especially as he grew older, reveal "an astonishing failure of imagination, and either wilful disregard of fact or wilful ignorance," McCormick demonstrates that Santayana's politics should not be conflated with those of Ezra Pound, with whom Santayana had had contact during the period of Pound's notorious radio broadcasts in Italy and with whom he corresponded while Pound was at St. Elizabeths.[3] Santayana found Pound disturbingly confused and actually considered him insane. Scholars and critics have often ignored the facts of the relationship, as well as the complex, often skeptical substance and tone of much of what Santayana actually had to say about Mussolini and his regime. Santayana's vague otherworldliness, his resistance to the strenuous moralism of turn-of-the-century Harvard as epitomized by William James, his criticism of American democracy, and his permanent return to Europe, all combine with the hastily formed generalizations about Santayana's politics to keep Santayana at the margins of almost every discussion of American intellectual and literary culture.

I do not mean to minimize or ignore Santayana's frequent failures of imagination. They are all the more disturbing since it is Santayana who so insisted on the power of the imaginative arts. I do, however, aim to recover the relation between Santayana's thought and the pragmatist project, a relation that was apparent in the early decades of the twentieth century and that faded from view as particular constructions both of Santayana and of pragmatism came to dominate the intellectual and cultural horizon. The reductive dichotomy between Santayana and Dewey has obscured the affinity between their philosophical and even their social projects. While it is beyond the scope of this book to summarize and analyze these projects comprehensively, I hope to establish the affinity between them and to assess, through the filter of that affinity, their mutual misunderstanding of one another's work. The basic affinity I will demonstrate can be stated very simply: each rejects a metaphysical idealism, along with all the intellectual and spiritual trappings of that idealism, in favor of a pragmatic conception of the ideal as a transitional agency in experience.

To begin, Santayana and Dewey share an abiding (and perfectly Jamesian) skepticism toward any and all fantasies of the absolute: "Whatever interpretations we offer for experience will become impertinent and worthless if the experience we work upon is no longer at hand. Nor will any construction, however broadly based, have an *absolute* authority; the indomitable freedom of life to be more, to be new, to be what it has not entered into the heart of man as yet to conceive, must always remain standing." Though this sounds like Dewey, it is in fact Santayana, writing in the conclusion to *Three Philosophical Poets,* his 1910 lectures on Lucretius, Dante, and Goethe.[4] Dewey strikes a similar note in his 1920 *Reconstruction in Philosophy:* "Philosophy which surrenders its somewhat barren monopoly of dealings with Ultimate and Absolute Reality will find a compensation in enlightening the moral forces which move mankind and in contributing to the aspirations of men to attain to a more ordered and intelligent happiness" (*MW* 12:94). For both Dewey and Santayana, the only meaningful ideal is a "more ordered and intelligent happiness," a happiness which depends on its perpetual embrace of novelty and change.

Both Santayana and Dewey consider themselves post-Darwinian naturalists. They reject correspondence models of truth and representation in favor of models of symbolic intelligence that highlight the perpetual revisability of all conception, both imaginative and scientific. Like the world itself, human intelligence is in constant transition. Because of this deep if often neglected affinity, Santayana and Dewey provide an unusual opportunity to compare two versions of pragmatic naturalism. They also provide an opportunity to isolate some of the abiding tensions within pragmatism. Pragmatism is often defined in its most narrow, instrumental sense, to the point that anything not in line with a Deweyan instrumentalism is not held to be properly pragmatic. But pragmatists have from the start struggled with the narrowness of such nuts-and-bolts instrumentalism. The contrast between Dewey and Santayana should illuminate that struggle. For both, moral, spiritual, and aesthetic satisfactions are grounded in natural, biological phenomena. If moral and spiritual authority do not come from a realm beyond, then what serves to legitimate that authority? The more Enlightenment-minded Dewey would focus on the potential for ongoing social progress, while the more skeptical and ironic Santayana would focus on the appreciation of finite satisfactions.

Dewey shares Santayana's sense that all experience is finite, but would hold that any particular experience must be related to a larger series of experiences. A finite satisfaction is only one moment in a larger rhythm of satisfaction, a rhythm directed ultimately toward broader, more expansive satisfactions. Emerson had described this dynamic in "Circles": "Every ultimate fact is only the first of a new series. Every general law only a particular fact of some more general law presently to disclose itself. There is no outside, no inclosing wall, no circumference to us" (*EL* 405). For Dewey as for Emerson, the emphasis is decidedly on this dynamic unfolding. Santayana, by contrast, sees the finite

*The Politics of Transition*

satisfaction as an end in itself, something to pause over and appreciate in its own terms, not as a prelude to other, more expansive (hence, not so decidedly finite) terms.

Dewey is committed to a rigorous program of perpetual reconstruction, whereas the more sensually inclined Santayana seeks to amass finite satisfactions, experiencing as many of them as possible, as fully as possible. Dewey's effort to resist all forms of dualism also stems from a rigorous sense of duty. Dualisms introduce a certain laziness in thought, whereby the values and ideals for which we must be humanly responsible are attributed to external forces. This attitude is apparent in *A Common Faith*, where Dewey comments that "dependence upon an external power is the counterpart of surrender of human endeavor" (*LW* 9:31–32). Santayana also rejected a common sense dualism, but did not believe, like Dewey, that it was the social sphere that ultimately unified the world and our ideals about it. Santayana instead posits the imminence of the spiritual in this world: "There is only one world, the natural world, and only one truth about it; but this world has a spiritual life possible in it, which looks not to another world but to the beauty and perfection that this world suggests, approaches, and misses" (*RB* 833). This view, cited from the late *Realms of Being,* is the basis of Santayana's insistence on the ultimate value of definite sensuous appreciations, as well as his constant awareness of the limited value of all particular appreciations in relation to the unlimited variety of appreciations possible in the world.

Eventually, Santayana and Dewey did everything in their power to underscore their differences. In their one major exchange, Santayana's review of *Experience and Nature* and Dewey's response to that review, each sets out to demonstrate the inadequacy of the other's naturalism. In an earlier review, Dewey had called *The Life of Reason* "the most adequate contribution America has yet made—always excepting Emerson—to moral philosophy" (*MW* 4:241). In another review of earlier volumes in *The Life of Reason,* Dewey had commented that they "afford more than the promise, they afford the potency, of the most significant contribution, made in this generation, to philosophic revision" (*MW* 3:319). Philosophic revision is Dewey's own ideal, as his praise of Santayana's accomplishment makes clear: "But, with whatever criticism and qualification, those who think, as does the present writer, that the really vital problem of present philosophy is the union of naturalism and idealism, must gratefully acknowledge the extraordinary force and simplicity with which Dr. Santayana has grasped this problem, and the rich and sure way in which he has interpreted, in its light, the intricacies and depth of our common experiences" (*MW* 3:322). As Henry Samuel Levinson has noted, *The Life of Reason* was greeted by many as a contribution to the literature of pragmatism, a remarkable fact subsequently lost sight of, especially after the later polemical exchange between Dewey and Santayana.[5]

Before turning to that exchange, it is worth examining how deep the affinity actually runs. To do so, I will examine the rhetoric of the ideal in the work of both philosophers, their sense of the mutual inherence of the actual and the ideal. Both Dewey and Santayana seek to complicate the conventional opposition between such paired terms as *actual* and *ideal* or *reality* and *imagination*. Such crude opposition is misleading, since each term in the opposition dynamically conditions and shapes the other. The ideal, if it is to have any consequential meaning, must be an expression of the real, just as the real, if it is to attract and sustain our attention, must appeal to our imaginations. Dewey and Santayana often invoke the ideal while at the same time insisting that no ideal ever exists apart from the natural and social conditions of its possibility.

Dewey discusses ideality in the second chapter of his 1925 volume *Experience and Nature*, "Existence as Precarious and as Stable." Because all experience involves what Dewey describes as the "union of the hazardous and the stable, of the incomplete and the recurrent," we define as "good" whatever satisfaction is necessarily in jeopardy: "When a fulfillment comes and is pronounced good, it is *judged* good, distinguished and asserted, simply because it is in jeopardy, because it occurs amid indifferent and divergent things" (*LW* 1:57). A "good object," then, "once experienced acquires ideal quality and attracts demand and effort to itself." This ideal quality is perfectly real: "A particular ideal may be an illusion, but having ideals is no illusion. It embodies features of existence. Although imagination is often fantastic it is also an organ of nature; for it is the appropriate phase of indeterminate events moving toward eventualities that are now but possibilities. A purely stable world permits of no illusions, but neither is it clothed with ideals. It just exists" (*LW* 1:57). Ideality, then, is not lodged in the nature of things, but is rather a quality associated with things so long as they indicate a better state of existence. Dewey offers water as an example: as long as we are thirsty, water has an ideal quality, but once that thirst is slaked, it is only "brute" water.

Santayana's analysis of the good in his 1927 *Platonism and the Spiritual Life* follows the same pattern, showing that the good has no meaning apart from its reference to the contexts in which something is experienced as good: "Values presuppose living beings having a direction of development, and exerting themselves in it, so that good and evil may exist in reference to them. That the good should be relative to actual natures and simply their innate ideal, latent or realized, is essential to its being truly a good. Otherwise the term 'good' would be an empty title applied to some existing object or force for no assignable reason" (*PS* 13–14). Even in establishing the special senses

*The Politics of Transition*

in which this good can be called absolute, Santayana retains a strong sense of the relativity of what is experienced as absolute: "Moreover, their natural good may be absolute in the sense of being fixed and unalterable, so long as the living beings concerned and the circumstances in which they flourish remain constant in type" (PS 14). Santayana parts company with Dewey simply by seeking the special senses in which the good can count as absolute, but his understanding of the good is, in its essential features, remarkably similar to Dewey's pragmatic understanding of the good. The ideal is not, for Santayana, something separate from, or supplementary to, the real, a point Santayana underscores in *The Idea of Christ in the Gospels*, published in 1946 after he had completed his charting of the realms of being: "For the ideal would lose its moral ideality were it not, for some real person, the ideal of some natural demand. Nothing can be good unless something real aspires after it" (IC 231).

Of course, the differences between Santayana's and Dewey's conceptions of the ideal remain significant. Santayana's very willingness to posit the absolute value of the ideal indicates a very different sense of the value of a value. For Dewey, a value or ideal exists to a specific end, such as the satisfaction of a thirst. For Santayana, a value can be contemplated and appreciated as an end in itself, despite its ultimate contingent status. Santayana's last justification in *Platonism and the Spiritual Life* for regarding the good as absolute is telling in this regard: "Finally, the good may be called absolute in the sense of being single and all-sufficient, filling the whole heart, and leaving nothing in the rest of the universe in the least tempting, interesting, or worth distinguishing. It is in this sense that lovers and mystics proclaim the absoluteness of the good with which they are united, and when the thing is true as a confession it would be frivolous and ungracious to quarrel with it as a dogma" (PS 14). Such satisfaction may prove to be temporary, subject to the many vicissitudes of our radically imperfect existence, but, for as long as it lasts, it will still be all-sufficing. Lovers and mystics provide Santayana with a model for what everyone experiences in varying degrees. However one defines the good, that definition will be functionally absolute as long as it provides the background to one's specific patterns of commitment, thought, belief, and concern.

Santayana also underscores the ultimate value of the experience of the ideal, despite its contingency, in the passage from *The Idea of Christ in the Gospels* cited above: "And such an ideal good, like a visual or musical harmony, though it is a pure essence and static in itself, appears to the spirit by virtue of a myriad material vibrations, approaches, and conjunctions. These the spirit overleaps, and rests ecstatically in suspended animation before the transfiguring apparition" (IC 231). The spirit, in its transport, pays no heed to the material conditions of its realization. It only knows its ideal, and knows it fully: "Facts thus culminate for the spirit in ideal revelations, in attainments or perfections of form: that is the only ultimate function that passing existence can have. The theme of such a revelation is not a further coming and vanishing fact, but simply that idea in its eternal essence, like the idea of Christ on which this book is a meditation" (*IC* 231). Dewey, in describing such an ideal, would place his emphasis precisely on the further coming and vanishing facts. Santayana, by contrast, pauses in the experience of a realized ideal, recognizing this experience, and the impassioned meditation on it, as a good-in-itself.

Despite his stated unwillingness to quarrel with an experience of the ideal as dogma, Santayana is not fond of dogma. He is as critical of idealism in its dogmatic forms as Dewey. The supernatural, Santayana suggests in *The Idea of Christ,* is "the ideal hypostasised," which in effect kills the ideal: "To quicken it again you must revert to the plane of nature, reincarnate the spirit there, and let circumstances awaken in that spirit once more some eternal image of the real become an ideal" (*IC* 232). The problem, for Santayana as for Dewey, begins when the ideal is externalized, removed from the vital currents of natural existence. The "mistake" of "positing the supernatural," however, is not entirely gratuitous: "It arises in the effort to do justice at once to nature and to the ideal, and to vindicate the superiority, or rather the exclusive ultimate value, of the latter" (*IC* 232–33). Still, this is a process that even Santayana believes can be carried too far:

> Illusion comes in, however, when the ingrained habit of speaking metaphorically congeals into an incapacity not to think mythically. People then feel they would be dishonouring the ideal, did they not materialise or personify it: not considering that an actual thing or person would have no excellence unless it approached an ideal demanded of it by itself or by some other person. Thus the ideal is really something *super*natural and divinely authoritative over the natural; but only because the natural, when it has life and thought, posits that ideal as its intimate need and perfection. (*IC* 233)

For Santayana as for Dewey, the consequences of this error are both ethical and political: supernaturalism in theology and ideology is the source of religious and political persecution. Illusion is the breeding ground of social disaster. As he puts it in *The Realms of Being,* "The supernatural is nothing but an extension of the natural into the unknown, and there is infinite room for it; but when these deeper or remoter parts of nature are described in myths evidently designed for the edification or easier government of human society, I distrust the fiction" (*RB* 155).

Both Santayana and Dewey reject supernatural illusion without rejecting the psychological and social dynamics of belief, a pattern that recalls William James. Whenever James writes about religious experience or the will to believe, his emphasis falls not on the metaphysical reality of a spiritual dimension of being, but rather on how human energies are mobilized by spiritual ideals. James would eventually offer a tentative defense of the possibility of broader realities, drawing largely on recent psychological and psychical research. Still, even when in the late essay "The Continuity of Experience" he allows the possibility of "a superior co-consciousness," his primary interest remains in how human access to its "great reservoir" of memories and perceptions affects those "exceptional individuals among us" who experience them (W 2:766). As he makes clear in another late essay, "The Energies of Men," what ultimately matters about our relation to any higher ideal is what happens when the "potential forms of activity that actually are shunted out from use" are finally released (WWJ 683). James is always pragmatic about the daily consequences of spiritual, aesthetic, and other marginal psychic phenomena.

Dewey describes religious beliefs in A Common Faith as "attitudes that lend deep and enduring support to the processes of living" (LW 9:12). He also comments there that "all endeavor for the better is moved by faith in what is possible, not by adherence to the actual" (LW 9:17). Like James, Dewey's emphasis is not on the content of belief, nor on the metaphysical status of a divine being or moral ideals, but rather on how belief motivates forms of behavior. He comments that the "inherent vice of all intellectual schemes of idealism" is the conversion of "idealism of action into a system of beliefs about antecedent reality" (LW 9:17). Religion, for Dewey, is, or at least should be, less about any such antecedent reality than about habits of thought and belief that make possible particular patterns of action. More positively, Dewey allows in A Common Faith that "the ideal itself has its roots in natural conditions; it emerges when the imagination idealizes existence by laying hold of the possibilities offered to thought and action" (LW 9:33). God, in Dewey's formulation, is not a divine being, but rather "denotes the unity of all ideal ends arousing us to desire and actions" (LW 9:29). Shorn of its metaphysical claims, religion for Dewey becomes the will to progress.[6]

As for broader realities, however, Dewey does retain a strong sense of the unity implicit in shared social and historical contexts. In Experience and Nature, he comments that "everything that exists in as far as it is known and knowable is in interaction with other things. It is associated, as well as solitary, single" (LW 1:138). Significance is a function of "the consequences that flow from the distinctive patterns of human association" (LW 1:138). Though we may ignore the many ways in which our lives are determined by our manifold relations, we could not be who we take ourselves to be without those relations, past, present, and future. When we associate ourselves with our experience of innerness, we forget for the time how that innerness is itself a product of complex external relations. In his essay on "The Vanishing Subject in the Psychology of James," Dewey criticizes James's introspective subject as that subject is developed in *The Principles of Psychology*. He continues, however, to advocate what he describes as James's "general doctrine of the function of the nervous system as an instrumentality of effective interaction of organism and environment" (*LW* 14:161). Dewey thus isolates a conflict between James's introspective psychology, which he rejects, and James's psychological behaviorism, which he approves and seeks to expand. He rejects what he calls James's "spiritual" self in favor of what James describes in *The Principles of Psychology* as "the permanent core of turnings-towards and turnings-from, of yieldings and arrests, which naturally seem central and interior" (qtd. in *LW* 14:165). There must be a shared reality toward and from which the self is constantly turning, and it is this reality that becomes the real object of Dewey's quasi-religious aspiration.[7]

Communication, as Dewey suggests in *Experience and Nature,* is the capacity to use signs in a participatory, not an ego-centric, way: to comprehend how signs function in relation to others, and not just as they have an impact on (or within) the self. To understand, Dewey says, "is to anticipate together, it is to make a cross-reference which, when acted upon, brings about a partaking in a common, inclusive, undertaking" (*LW* 1:141). The "heart of language," Dewey says, "is not 'expression' of something antecedent, much less expression of antecedent thought. It is communication; the establishment of cooperation in an activity in which there are partners, and in which the activity of each is modified and regulated by partnership" (*LW* 1:141). This is a, if not *the* characteristic Deweyan move, pointing to processes of relation and cooperation without which the self's feeling of innerness and uniqueness could not even occur. Dewey describes language as "specifically a mode of interaction of at least two beings, a speaker and a hearer; it presupposes an organized group to which these creatures belong, and from whom they have acquired their habits of speech" (*LW* 1:145). Language, like aesthetic and ritual experience, inscribes us in a social environment without which we would have no available sense of self, let alone of value or purpose.[8]

According to Dewey, when we name a thing, we typically ignore the network of events and consequences for which the name stands. His example is fire:

> Fire burns and the burning is of moment. It enters experience; it is fascinating to watch swirling flames; it is important to avoid its dangers and

*The Politics of Transition*

to utilize its beneficial potencies. When we name an event, calling it fire, we speak proleptically; we do not name an immediate event; that is impossible. We employ a term of discourse; we invoke a meaning, namely, the potential consequences of the existence. . . . The ultimate meaning, or essence, denominated fire, is the consequences of certain natural events within the scheme of human activities, in the experience of social intercourse, the hearth and domestic altar, shared comfort, working of metals, rapid transit, and other such affairs. (*LW* 1:149–50)

The meaning of *fire,* in other words, includes all the social and natural consequences associated with fire that necessarily go unnamed in our shorthand discourse. Just as James had said of the stream of thought that our language names one thing and ignores the thousand others that are dimly associated with it, so for Dewey language only dimly evokes the manifold relations, social and natural, that constitute the meaning of any named object in the first place. We ignore these dimensions of meaning because it is efficient to do so: "To ascertain and state meanings in abstraction from social or shared situations is the only way in which the latter can be intelligently modified, extended and varied" (*LW* 1:150). This abstraction is useful because it so effectively enables us to satisfy our needs and desires, opening the way "to new uses and consequences," that is, to new kinds of shared experience (*LW* 1:151). James's "fringe" and his "feelings of tendency" play the same role in "The Stream of Thought," but Dewey's emphasis is more emphatically on scientific and social consequences.

Communication, abstraction, and science all imply relational being. Even when signs are utilized without apparent reference to the shared dimensions of experience, as in mathematics, they function to enable and expand the shared, social dimensions of experience. We typically ignore this social dimension, thinking that a sign simply corresponds to a thing. The notion, however, that anything has a being or essence outside its matrix of relations is a mistaken extrapolation from this confusion of reference. Any thing's being is inextricable from its interrelations and interactions with everything else around it. The key to Dewey, early and late, is that everything that appears private turns out to be a function of public conditions, the inner a result of external relations, the individual a matter of extensive relations to larger, encompassing wholes. Language and art are the building blocks of these relations, for language and art posit the shared, social ground of all human experience. To put anything in language or to make it the material of a ritual enactment, it must already belong to the public domain, even when it represents or expresses the most intimate content. Science and mathematics are public languages as well. Even when they seem most abstract and so most removed from all social context, they still refer, both retrospectively and prospectively, to a world of irreducibly shared experience.[9]

Santayana has a very different understanding of how social contexts function, but those contexts are just as central to his philosophical system. If Dewey's philosophical project is devoted to analyzing the natural and social ground of ideal values and appreciations, Santayana's is devoted to cultivating the ideal values and appreciations that humans project from within their natural and social contexts. Dewey and Santayana agree that human life is an affair of contingencies. Like James, both reject narrow sensationalist accounts and absolute idealist accounts of experience. For both, ideals are real, but not as a kind of metaphysical stuff designed to provide a transexperiential bedding for our material lives. As Santayana would repeatedly say, this is mere superstition, the projection of a fantasy of a permanent, universal ideal onto the cosmos. As noted in the previous chapter, Dewey and Santayana agree that this kind of superstitious thinking began with the Greeks, and with Plato most vividly and consequentially, when aesthetic values were projected as metaphysical, cosmic principles.

Dewey, however, would see ideals (and aesthetic appreciations) as transitional agencies, extending or otherwise developing material circumstances. Language does not correspond to things for Dewey, but it does project a shared world, and our ideals, like other imaginative or scientific symbols we employ, serve to shape that world. Santayana, in his critical review of *Experience and Nature*, would call this the "dominance of the foreground," suggesting that Dewey confuses our accidental discourse about the world with the world itself. Santayana would also have us recognize the contingent contexts of any ideal appreciation, or what Dewey would often call consummation, but at the same time Santayana would insist that the consummation is itself the fundamental aim of civilization. His criticism of pragmatism in "The Genteel Tradition in American Philosophy" underscores this difference, and with characteristic vividness: "This may seem a very utilitarian view of the mind; and I confess I think it a partial one, since the logical force of beliefs and ideas, their truth or falsehood as assertions, has been overlooked altogether, or confused with the vital force of the material processes which these ideas express. It is an external view only, which marks the place and conditions of the mind in nature, but neglects its specific essence; as if a jewel were defined as a round hole in a ring" (*GT* 57). Santayana agrees that the jewel is a product of contingent conditions, but he thinks instrumentalists are mistaken when they focus so exclusively on the jewel's setting—"the dominance of the foreground"— that they neglect to notice the jewel at all.

*The Politics of Transition*

Santayana's discussion of language, symbols, and communication reflects these differences. For Dewey, language and communication everywhere imply the relational contexts and shared ground of experience. In an early discussion of language in *Reason in Art,* Santayana suggests that because language is originally a form of pure music and only secondarily a medium of communication, it is never merely an instrument to convey meanings. Words do not correspond to things, but act as a portable "medium of intellectual exchange" (*RA* 73). Hence language is always divided between two impulses: the poetic, a "primitive" aspect which always exceeds its merely representational function, and the prosaic, a later, more mature aspect which aspires to a perfect transparency in the communication of meanings. Though language is "essentially significant viewed in its function," it is also "indefinitely wasteful, being mechanical and tentative in its origin": "It overloads itself, and being primarily music, and a labyrinth of sounds, it develops an articulation and method of its own, which only in the end, and with much inexactness, reverts to its function of expression" (*RA* 80–81). While this "function of expression" implies the Deweyan shared social ground, the musical dimension of sound exceeds and, in Santayana's formulation, even precedes the positing of that ground. The social constitutes the shared world implicit in the symbolic function of words, but because Santayana locates the origins of language in something other than this symbolic function, he refuses to reduce humans to their merely social function.

In his later work, Santayana further underscores the gap between language and world that Dewey had bridged by means of the social dimension of language. Santayana insists on the "illusory" dimension of all communication. Our mental images of things, and the languages and representations we form of them, both poetic and scientific, are never the things themselves, and so always require a degree of "faith" on our part that they do provide us with "messages," as Santayana calls them, from the world. In *Scepticism and Animal Faith,* the 1923 introductory volume to Santayana's major philosophical sequence on the realms of being, he describes myth as "a relevant fancy, and genuinely expressive." Despite its illusory dimension, it provides a significant understanding of the nature of things and of human involvement with them. A myth will be "built upon principles internal to human discourse, as are grammar, rhyme, music, and morals," and so even if it proves to be "egregiously false if asserted of the object," it will still be "admirable as an expression of these principles" (*SAF* 178). In other words, a myth may be false as a description of the world but true and altogether profound as an expression of a coherent system of human practices and the beliefs that support them. Thus, after declaring, in the passage cited earlier from *The Realms of Being,* his dis-

*The Poetics of Transition*

trust of any supernatural fiction, Santayana allows his potential appreciation of that same fiction: "I distrust it, I mean, as a piece of physics, or information about matters of fact; but it may be a genuine and beautiful expression of the moral experience and the moral interests which have prompted it" (*RB* 155).

For Santayana, all discourse, including science, shares this mythical quality. In *Scepticism and Animal Faith,* he compares an astronomical description of the moon with the Greek myth of Diana: "This, too, is no added object, but only a new image for the moon known even to the child and me. The space, matter, gravitation, time, and laws of motion conceived by astronomers are essences only, and mere symbols for the use of animal faith, when very enlightened: I mean in so far as they are alleged to constitute knowledge of a world which I must bow to and encounter in action" (*SAF* 178). In this description, the untutored child knows the same moon that the astronomer knows. They simply have different images of the moon, which empower them differently in relation to it.

The astronomer's scientific laws are "essences" in Santayana's special sense of the term, so central to his late philosophical writing. It is a term almost universally misunderstood, because it is commonly associated with a quality inherent in an object, the essence of a thing. For Santayana, essence does not inhere in an object in this way. The symbols of scientific understanding no more correspond to reality than those of an openly mythical imagination. What distinguishes the scientific from the mythical imagination is scientists' commitment to methods of investigation and experimentation that lead them continuously to revise their understanding of things. Scientists' essences are "the fruit of a better focussed, more chastened, and more prolonged attention turned upon what actually occurs" (*SAF* 177). The symbol, like an essence, derives its significance and its effectiveness from its appeal to human imagination. Because the mind does not record realities, it always requires the exercise of "animal faith": we have faith in essences or symbols which in no way correspond to reality, but prove advantageous or useful, in an essentially Darwinian sense, as beliefs about reality.[10]

Knowledge, Santayana suggests, is always a form of belief: "belief in a world of events, and especially of those parts of it which are near the self, tempting or threatening it. This belief is native to animals, and precedes all deliberate use of intuitions as signs or descriptions of things; as I turn my head to see who is there, before I see who it is" (*SAF* 179). Such belief precedes mere knowledge. By turning my head, I may confirm that someone is there, and even discover details leading me to identify the person, but I only turn my head in the first place because of a nagging intuition that someone is in fact there. As it is experienced, the intuition requires no confirmation;

*The Politics of Transition*

none is even possible. Such intuition always clears the way for later "knowledge about" things. Santayana further insists that intuition constitutes "true belief": "It is such an enlightening of the self by intuitions arising there, that what the self imagines and asserts of the collateral thing, with which it wrestles in action, is actually true of that thing. Truth in such presumptions or conceptions does not imply adequacy, nor a pictorial identity between the essence in intuition and the constitution of the object. Discourse is a language, not a mirror" (*SAF* 179). Like Dewey, Santayana did not suppose that language simply corresponded to an external reality.

Santayana's analysis, however, focuses on the status of what intuition puts before the mind before discourse (language or science) ever names it:

> The images in sense are parts of discourse, not parts of nature: they are the babble of our innocent organs under the stimulus of things; but these spontaneous images, like the sounds of the voice, may acquire the function of names; they may become signs, if discourse is intelligent and can recapitulate its phases, for the things sought or encountered in the world. The truth which discourse can achieve is truth in its own terms, appropriate description: it is no incorporation or reproduction of the object in the mind. (*SAF* 179)

If our intuitions were not valid, we simply would not survive, animals defeated in the harsh arena of natural selection. In fact, our intuitions prove remarkably effective, and all the more so as they are guided by rational intelligence. The mind intuits essences as "messages, signs, or emanations sent forth to it from those objects of animal faith; and they become its evidences and its description for those objects" (*SAF* 180). Knowledge of the world, based on the scientific method of observation and experimentation, is built up from intuition of the world, which for Santayana is a necessary fact of animal life.

For Santayana, science is one kind of truth pursued by human imagination. It is not, however, the only available truth. Intuition is equally at home in other symbolic forms, and it is only human arrogance that would place one symbolic form ahead of all others. Santayana's only caveat is that the symbolic form not be mistaken for a cosmic reality. There is a reality "out there" for Santayana, but we only ever know it by intuiting essences in which we simply have "animal faith." Our symbolic languages name that reality, but do so with always a touch of poetry and myth. Dewey would also recognize that the results of science are always subject to modification based on new experimentation, but he did not consider those results poetic and mythical in Santayana's sense. Indeed, although he would recognize the role of aesthetic experience in all dimensions of thought and life, he would still distinguish science from

*The Poetics of Transition*

myth, since, in his view, an experimental method provided a better, more effective transitional agency than a nonexperimental one. For Dewey, science was a privileged instrument for expanding democratic values. Santayana, by contrast, explicitly sought to place science on an equal footing with the other imaginative arts, seeking to dispel what in *The Realms of Being* he called the illusion "that scientific ideas reveal the literal and intimate essence of reality" in favor of the simple recognition that "both sense and science are relatively and virtually true" (*RB* 829). Santayana is finally uninterested in the relative effectiveness of transitional agencies, especially since he views the standard of effectiveness as a mechanism to limit the range of cultivated values.

In his review of *Experience and Nature*, Santayana complained that Dewey took "accidental" discourses and opinions that invariably mediate our relationship to the world as perfectly natural expressions of the world. It is Dewey, in Santayana's assessment, who falls into the classic metaphysical trap of taking an illusory understanding to be the full reality. For Santayana, this criticism of Deweyan pragmatism is synonymous with a criticism of American intellectual and cultural life. In a young nation anxious about its international cultural, social, and political status, material appearances, however thin, come to count for everything. As traditional sources of meaning lose their authority, Americans are quick to replace them with sheer material progress, what for many was the visible sign of America's exceptional status. American notions of duty, trained by a deeply ingrained Puritan legacy, are quickly transferred to these narrowly material ends.

The line, of course, had always been fine between the spiritual life of Puritan Americans and the material ends that they were often so successful at pursuing. By the mid–nineteenth century, writers like Hawthorne and Melville perceived the sharp double edge of this inheritance. Americans' remarkable genius for material progress was at once the survival and the inversion of the New World's spiritual vocation. Melville brilliantly dramatizes this tension in "The Ship" chapter of *Moby-Dick* when Queequeg and Ishmael first arrive at the *Pequod* as the ship's primary owners, Captains Peleg and Bildad, blatantly (and uproariously) mix Christian rhetoric with hard-headed capitalist self-interest in order to minimize the new arrivals' share in the venture. In Santayana's often trenchantly unsympathetic view of Protestant America, Americans had sacrificed all genuine spirituality in this compromise and could no longer appreciate either a simple sensual pleasure or a profound moral or spiritual ideal.

The chief criticism of pragmatism has always been that it has no spiritual, or moral, basis, that it simply reinforces a standard of expediency, never a particularly moral or spiritual standard. James had defined truth as that which is expedient in the way of belief. He did not, in fact, mean by that whatever best serves narrow self-interest, but it is not hard to see why someone might view such a statement in that light. James highlights the crucial distinction in a letter to Thomas Sargeant Perry: "When *I say* that, *other things being equal,* the view of things that seems more satisfactory morally will legitimately be treated by men as truer than the view that seems less so, *they quote me as saying* that anything morally satisfactory can be treated as true, no matter how unsatisfactory it may be from the point of view of its consistency with what we already know or believe to be true about physical or natural facts. Which is rot!!" (*TC* 2:468). James's critics, in other words, ignore the role of rational intelligence in determining what it is possible to believe. This criticism could be called the reductionist account of pragmatism, of which Santayana was an early, though hardly a crude, proponent.

Indeed, Santayana's criticism of the pragmatist conception of truth is remarkably sophisticated. In *Character and Opinion in the United States,* Santayana suggests that the pragmatist retains the notion of truth as "correctness" because of "his idealism, which identifies ideas with their objects; and he asks himself how an idea can ever come to be correct or incorrect, as if it referred to something beyond itself" (*CO* 96). This is a telling criticism, especially in its indication of Santayana's effort starting in *Scepticism and Animal Faith* and running through the *Realms of Being* to conceive ideas (and discourse more generally) symbolically. According to Santayana, ideas never refer beyond themselves in this way. Ideas simply do not correspond to the structure of the real. Pragmatists attempted to avoid this problem by insisting that the mind creates its truths, but Santayana responds that the mind's ideas are never truths in this sense. But he never concludes from this that there is no stable truth about the world. Truth, as Santayana suggests in *Character and Opinion in the United States,* still means "the sum of all true propositions, what omniscience would assert, the whole ideal system of qualities and relations which the world has exemplified or will exemplify" (*CO* 95). Invoking the language that would soon appear in his discussions of the realms of being, he comments that the truth "is all things seen under the form of eternity" (*CO* 95). The truth is not "human," but belongs instead to the world of fact. Santayana is very close to Charles Peirce in his understanding of truth. For both, human ideas never correspond to things, but rather provide symbolic representations of them. These representations are not, strictly speaking, truths. Peirce compared the scientific pursuit of truth to the "operation of destiny," insisting that for all the give and take of experimental methods, there is only one truth to reveal: "The opinion which is fated to be ultimately agreed to by all who investigate, is what we mean by the truth, and the object represented in this

*The Poetics of Transition*

opinion is the real."[11] Santayana's omniscience, like Peirce's fate, exceeds any individual perspective, which suggests why Santayana always objected to the pragmatist conception of truth, which associated truth with an irreducible human perspective.[12]

According to Santayana, pragmatists, by working from the individual (and psychological) perspective, confuse what is true and real for an individual with what is true and real of the world in general. Pragmatists rightly recognize that there may be no general test of the validity of an idea, but then proceed to conclude that ideas in general are true not because they correspond in any way to the world, but rather because they work, and do so better — more effectively and more consistently — than other possible ideas. As Santayana suggests in *Character and Opinion,* we may only believe an idea to be true by something like animal faith: "In the end we may be reduced to believing on instinct that our fundamental opinions are true; for instance, that we are living through time, and that the past and future are not, as a consistent idealism would assert, mere notions in the present" (*CO* 96). Such beliefs are not less valid for being adopted on the model of instinctual faith, since their validity would still be a matter of fact, not of our present or even eventual (Peircian) confirmation of their truth. If I believe that I will get flattened by an automobile if I leap into oncoming traffic, my belief can be characterized as true even if nothing I "know" can guarantee that I am right. My ideas about the physics of fast-moving automobiles and the physiology of the body are certainly true, though they in no way "correspond" to the facts of the situation. Their truth has nothing to do with my own belief in them.

These differences in conception of truth reflect larger assumptions about the nature of human intelligence and its relation to moral and ideal realities. Dewey deeply believed that material progress could bring with it moral and spiritual progress: we only have to be scientific, which is to say experimental, about our moral ideals. Santayana, by contrast, believed that material progress, in America especially, was driven by narrowly Protestant values, and that these values were distinctly inhospitable to other possible values, not least his own. Dewey's Enlightenment sensibility convinced him that pragmatism served progressive, democratic ideals on a naturalistic basis, whereas Santayana, with his divided loyalties to Europe and America, saw nothing liberating about moral or material progress in America. Santayana's status as a Spanish-born, lapsed Catholic in Protestant New England sensitized him to the very local socio-cultural basis of pragmatism. His complaint about the dominance of the foreground in Dewey is, in effect, a complaint about the central but unacknowledged role of the Protestant-American work and success ethic within pragmatism.

*The Politics of Transition*

In their critical exchange, Dewey seems content to establish that his own naturalism is the more radically antidualistic of the two. Hence, when Santayana complains of the dominance of the foreground, Dewey responds that the foreground is "nature's own foreground," thereby underscoring the extent to which what Santayana tends to think of as "accidental" is in fact nature's own way of becoming manifest to human intelligence. Dewey is following the lead James had established in his notion of pure experience, whereby the dualisms of subject and object, and by extension nature and culture, are dissolved. For Dewey, writing in his response to Santayana's review of *Experience and Nature,* culture must be considered an extension of nature: " 'Convention' is not conventional, or specious, but is the interaction of natural things when that interaction becomes communication. A 'sign' may be conventional, as when a sound or a mark on a piece of paper—themselves physical existences—symbolizes other things; but *being* a sign, the sign-function, has its roots in natural existences; human association is the fruit of those roots" (*LW* 3:79). Here again, echoing the language of *Experience and Nature,* Dewey insists that social reality grounds our use of language and symbols and so guarantees their relevance to "natural existences." Social conventions cannot be treated as artificial or specious, because they derive from interactions with nature. The distinction between nature and artifice is itself invalid. Dewey concludes, "I can understand Santayana's idea that the social medium is conventional in a prejudicial sense only as another illustration of that structural dislocation of non-human and human existence which I have called a broken-backed naturalism" (*LW* 3:79).

Behind the "foreground" of the "social medium" for Santayana are the truths and ideals that make experience meaningful and compelling in the first place. These, as Dewey and Santayana would agree, are not metaphysical realities. Santayana makes this clear everywhere in his work, and does so with characteristic clarity in his review of *Experience and Nature,* "Dewey's Naturalistic Metaphysics":

Naturalism may, accordingly, find room for every sort of psychology, poetry, logic, and theology, if only they are content with their natural places. Naturalism will break down, however, so soon as words, ideas, or spirits are taken to be substantial on their own account, and powers at work prior to the existence of their organs, or independent of them. Now it is precisely such disembodied powers and immaterial functions prior to matter that are called metaphysical. Transcendentalism is not metaphysical if it remains a mere method, because then it might express the natural fact that any animal mind is its own center and must awake in order to know anything: it becomes metaphysical when this mind is said to be absolute, single, and without material conditions. (*LW* 3:368–69)

For Santayana, Dewey himself becomes metaphysical insofar as he projects his characteristically American attitude to the foreground as an unconditioned philosophical truth. Santayana sees his own perspective, by contrast, as "justifying moral diversity." Seeing fictions and mythologies

> should enlighten our sympathies, since we should all have lived in the society of those images, if we had had the same surroundings and passions; and if in their turn the ideas prevalent in our own day can be traced back to the material conditions that bred them, our judgment should be enlightened also. Controversy, when naturalism is granted, can yield to interpretation, reconciling the critical mind to convention, justifying moral diversity, and carrying the sap of life to every top-most intellectual flower. (*LW* 3:383)

In Santayana's view, Dewey is hostile to ideals, seeking everywhere to reduce them to the social conditions that produced them. In *Experience and Nature,* he comments, one finds "a rude blow dealt at dogma of every sort: God, matter, Platonic ideas, active spirits, and creative logics all seem to totter on their thrones; and if the blow could be effective, the endless battle of metaphysics would have to end for lack of combatants" (*LW* 3:369).

Santayana would replace this reductive attitude with a more sympathetic, and at the same time more detached, attitude toward possible ideals:

> God and matter are not any or all the definitions which philosophers may give of them: they are the realities confronted in action, the mysterious but momentous background, which philosophers and other men mean to describe by their definitions or myths or sensible images. To hypostatize these symbols, and identify them with matter or with God, is idolatry: but the remedy for idolatry is not iconoclasm, because the sense, too, or the heart or the pragmatic intellect, can breed only symbols. The remedy is rather to employ the symbols pragmatically, with detachment and humor, trusting in the steady dispensations of the substance beyond. (*LW* 3:384)

For Santayana, the sense, the heart, even the pragmatic intellect "can breed only symbols." The "remedy" is not to ignore the symbols in the interest of their inevitable social foreground, but rather to exercise "detachment and humor" in the use of such symbols, recognizing their limitations while at the same time appreciating the life they make possible. Santayana's appropriation of the term *pragmatic* in his phrase "to employ the symbols pragmatically" is particularly telling. Pragmatism should not make us hostile to our symbolic activity, but should foster a more enlightened attitude to the contexts and pleasures of that activity, as well as to the diversity of ends it makes possible.

Dewey leaves the impression that intelligence follows a single, necessary path of development. If intelligence would only recognize its genuine destiny, the cause of freedom and democracy would be definitely advanced. Over time, intellect should look much the same everywhere. Science should weed out false conceptions, preparing the ground for genuinely democratic values and institutions. Santayana never had such faith in science or democracy, and so he characteristically sets such a value against ingrained habits and traditions and sees progress as irreducibly local, temporary, and finite. Dewey promotes what we might call compulsory liberation, whereas Santayana encourages a kind of liberated perception of constraint. Dewey inherits the tradition of infinite grasp, the sense that all things are possible if only we believe in them, while Santayana inherits the tradition of finite realization, the sense that only moderated desires are realized, and even those only precariously. Dewey envisages the use of scientific methods to establish a better social order; Santayana worries that such engineering will only introduce new forms of domination, all the more insidious for hiding behind a rhetoric of expanding freedoms. Dewey is an advocate of human intelligence as the only possible way to direct potentially aimless experience, whereas Santayana remains skeptical of this role of intelligence, adopting a more ironic attitude toward the inevitable human struggle with aimlessness.

The ground over which Dewey and Santayana disagree about spiritual, moral, and aesthetic values constitutes a significant divide within American pragmatic or naturalistic idealism. In Dewey, one sees the case made for the identification of material and ideal values. America — democratic, pluralistic, struggling to overcome its contradictions and imperfections — is the logical ground on which to work out, or to work toward, this identification. For Santayana, there are many possible spiritual ideals, most of which are unfortunately suppressed by the distinctly Protestant ideal promoted by James and Dewey. Santayana's unwillingness to adopt the label "pragmatist" is a reflection of his conviction that pragmatism is already an expression of distinctively American circumstances.

As these associations indicate, Santayana was an early and cogent critic of what he described as the coerciveness of American life, nowhere more so than in the essays collected in 1920 as *Character and Opinion in the United States:* "American life is a powerful solvent. As it stamps the immigrant, almost before he can speak English, with an unmistakable muscular tension, cheery

*The Poetics of Transition*

self-confidence and habitual challenge in the voice and eyes, so it seems to neutralise every intellectual element, however tough and alien it may be, and to fuse it in the native goodwill, complacency, thoughtlessness, and optimism" (CO 29). What seems to have rankled most for Santayana was the universal expectation of work and duty. However dedicated America might be to the many forms of freedom, no free act was considered worthy that did not dedicate itself to improvement and progress. As regards the content of belief, religious or secular, Americans were free to choose, but any who refused to dedicate their belief to the fulfillment of the American promise were sure to attract criticism: "In America there is but one way of being saved, though it is not peculiar to any of the official religions, which themselves must silently conform to the national orthodoxy, or else become impotent and merely ornamental. This national faith and morality are vague in idea, but inexorable in spirit; they are the gospel of work and the belief in progress. By them, in a country where all men are free, every man finds that what most matters has been settled for him beforehand" (CO 130–31). For all America's vaunted freedoms, freedom in America is universally conditioned by this quasi-moral purposefulness. Nowhere, Santayana suggests, do "people live under more overpowering compulsions" (CO 129). Writing of the atmosphere at Harvard around the turn of the century, Santayana describes the false sense of "academic freedom": "You might think what you liked, but you must consecrate your belief or your unbelief to the common task of encouraging everybody and helping everything on. You might almost be an atheist, if you were troubled enough about it. The atmosphere was not that of intelligence nor of science, it was that of duty" (CO 36–37). Freedom, for Santayana, must mean the freedom to pursue one's own ideals, so long at least as those ideals are not harmful to others. An atmosphere of duty discourages ideals that do not "fit in," in part by draining the sheer joy out of life.

This criticism is echoed in Santayana's descriptions of American life in his 1935 novel, *The Last Puritan*. Oliver Alden, the novel's protagonist, eventually recognizes the inadequacy of his Puritan worldview and so proceeds, in the best Puritan fashion, to rid himself of it. He is caught in a tight double bind: the harder he tries to release himself from his Puritan past, the more he reinscribes himself in it. In the words of another character, Oliver's puritanism "worked itself out to its logical end": "He convinced himself, on puritan grounds, that it was wrong to be a puritan" (WGS 4:14). Oliver is a tragic hero, marvelously capable of seeing his world's and his own limitations, their failure to live up to his ideal of the good, but incapable of delivering himself from the disabling grip of his conscience, largely because so pathetically trained in the arts of social being. At the heart of Santayana's critique is the individual moral

*The Politics of Transition*

will, the isolated conscience, for which the last imposed duty becomes a willed release from the fortress of the will. As Oliver tries to fit himself to the world through a conventional romantic pattern — marriage with one of two women both so idealized that he never has the least insight into their inner lives — it becomes clear that his admirable moral energy has made him unfit to live.

Oliver Alden has seen through the game but has none of the facilities that would allow him to experience his knowledge as a release. The only redeeming moments in *The Last Puritan* are moments of fugitive pleasure, either in the physical presence of Jim Darnley, the sailor who awakens Oliver's sensuality (in a passage with specifically homoerotic overtones), or in the company of nature, whose radical otherness Oliver always finds comforting, perhaps because it makes no demands on his moral will.[13] These are moments when Oliver's spiritual nature is not so much abandoned as brought into fleeting contact with overwhelming, sensually stimulating physical realities. But Oliver has internalized the sense of duty too completely to be anything other than a tragic hero. The narrator ("Santayana") captures this sense of tragedy in the prologue, addressing Oliver's cousin Mario Van de Weyer: "Human nature is engaged in an elaborate suicide. To be simple, sane and humble is to be a blackleg in the great tradesunion of strivers and busybodies who are sworn to make an artificial organism of everything. Now you, Vanny, dare to live, no matter on what level, as if living were the most natural thing in the world" (*WGS* 4:667).[14] The "strivers and busybodies" effectively impose their imaginative constraints on Oliver, whereas Mario (Vanny) and others like Jim Darnley simply embody their own ideal of living. Oliver Alden ultimately aspires to embody his own ideal of living too, but never manages to release himself from the grip of his moral imagination.

Oliver's state reflects the tragedy of the American temper as Santayana describes it in "The Genteel Tradition in American Philosophy," the talk Santayana delivered at Berkeley, California, in the summer of 1911, not long before he would permanently leave America. Calvinism, as Santayana notes in the talk, "is an expression of the agonized conscience" (*GT* 41). The Calvinist can only experience this world as a kind of beautiful tragedy. This, as Santayana suggests, is the ineluctable logic of its grounding ideals: "Calvinism, essentially, asserts three things: that sin exists, that sin is punished, and that it is beautiful that sin should exist to be punished" (*GT* 41). This leads the Calvinist to oscillate "between a profound abasement and a paradoxical elation of the spirit" (*GT* 41), abasement at the human condition, but elation to be the instrument of divine punishment. Hence the inability to experience joy in the simple pleasures of this world and the strenuous compulsion to overcome this scandalous world in heroic acts of conscience.[15]

*The Poetics of Transition*

*The Last Puritan* vividly re-creates the moral and intellectual atmosphere that drove Santayana, finally more like Vanny than like Oliver, to Europe. Santayana's criticism of America couldn't be clearer than in the 1911 Berkeley talk: "Serious poetry, profound religion (Calvinism, for instance) are the joys of an unhappiness that confesses itself; but when a genteel tradition forbids people to confess that they are unhappy, serious poetry and profound religion are closed to them" (*GT* 51). American faith in material progress, and the overwhelming sense that all Americans must optimistically participate in that progress, make serious thought suspect. Dewey's "naturalistic metaphysics" seemed to Santayana the last refinement of this hostility to the free expression of a variety of possible ideals. Indeed, variety would seem to constitute Santayana's highest ideal, as when he concludes "The Genteel Tradition in American Philosophy" by describing the potentially liberating influence of the western forests and Sierras on American intellectual life: "It is no transcendental logic that they teach; and they give no sign of any deliberate morality seated in the world. It is rather the vanity and superficiality of all logic, the needlessness of argument, the finitude of morals, the strength of time, the fertility of matter, the variety, the unspeakable variety, of possible life" (*GT* 62–63). This unspeakable variety is an end in itself. Santayana is perfectly uninterested in any possible progress beyond difference. Such progress could only diminish the unspeakable variety of possible life, a point made painfully clear in *Character and Opinion in the United States* when he describes the "luckless American" who is "born a conservative, or who is drawn to poetic subtlety, pious retreats, or gay passions" but "nevertheless has the categorical excellence of work, growth, enterprise, reform, and prosperity dinned into his ears: every door is open in this direction and shut in the other; so that he either folds up his heart and withers in a corner — in remote places you sometimes find such a solitary gaunt idealist — or else he flies to Oxford or Florence or Montmartre to save his soul — or perhaps not to save it" (*CO* 105). Santayana does not say who he is describing in this passage, but it is all but impossible not to recognize the autobiographical impulse at work here.[16]

Santayana is not, however, entirely critical of American social and political life. By the end of *Character and Opinion,* he contrasts English liberty, which is for Santayana perfected in the United States, with absolute liberty, which he associates with Germany (as well as with poets, madmen, criminals, and martyrs). English liberty, having evolved piecemeal, is based on the spirit of cooperation. The highest ideal is the functional one expressed in the will of a majority, working in good faith toward a government and a social environment that will minimize injustice and inequality and promote the general welfare. English liberty works in part because no single constituency insists on its absolute rights and prerogatives. The ideal of cooperation supersedes the absolute claims of individuals or individual groups. Absolute liberty, by contrast, supports a particular ideal as the best and only means of instituting the good life. Cooperation is rejected in favor of whatever means are necessary to establish what is definitely held to be best. Under a system of absolute liberty, a utopian reality is imagined which is then established as the only acceptable goal of social progress. Under the system of English liberty, by contrast, the radical imperfection of social institutions is acknowledged and compromises are accepted as the best means available to a shared, general progress.

Santayana clearly admires the spirit that animates any conception of absolute liberty. He repeatedly calls such a will "heroic." At the same time, though, he underscores the ultimate advantage of the system of English liberty: absolute liberty is "tragic and ridiculous" (*CO* 141). It is "too narrow," running up "against change, against science, against all the realities they had never reckoned with" (*CO* 142). Liberty loses "its massiveness, its plasticity, its power to survive change; it ceases to be tentative and human in order to become animal and absolute" (*CO* 143). Santayana allows that absolute freedom "would be more beautiful if we were birds or poets," but adds that "co-operation and a loving sacrifice of a part of ourselves — or even of the whole, save the love in us — are beautiful too, if we are men living together" (*CO* 144). There is a certain sadness in the tone of Santayana's recognition here. Writing at the close of World War I, Santayana allows that "mankind must make a painful and a brave choice" between absolute and English liberty. He almost seems to be offering to sacrifice passionately held human ideals: "The necessity of rejecting and destroying some things that are beautiful is the deepest curse of existence" (*CO* 144). Santayana is, nevertheless, willing to make this sacrifice, and more than willing to encourage his reader to make it with him: this is, as it happens, the concluding sentence of the book.

America appears here as the best possible soil for broad social and political progress, but its coercions exact a cost. Santayana is acutely aware of this cost, whereas James and Dewey are always optimistic about new prospects they associate with American democracy and pluralism. Writing in 1935 in *Liberalism and Social Action,* Dewey approaches "organized intelligence as the method for directing social change" (*LW* 11:61). His conception of everything mind does, from education to art and philosophy, reinforces this observation. Santayana is not so optimistic, either about the role of intelligence or the onward (which is also a pragmatically secularized way of saying upward) direction of social change. But this embrace of the finite limitation of this world and our experience of it also enables Santayana to appreciate the irreducible otherness of things, the dignity of life lived in the presence of such limits, the variety of possible forms of satisfaction still possible within those limits, and above all, the tragedy and comic irony of all human intelligence.

There are, then, two distinct faces of pragmatic naturalism apparent in the conflict between Dewey and Santayana: one that focuses on the duty to contribute to the ongoing progress, or in Dewey's phrase *reconstruction,* of social, intellectual, aesthetic, and moral conditions, and the other that focuses on the particular, often eccentric forms of social, intellectual, aesthetic, and moral beauty as they are shaped by ideals about, and responsive to, the world. Both perspectives emphasize the extent to which all ideals are contingently situated. For Dewey, however, this leads to an emphasis on the will to progress, whereas for Santayana it leads to a reverse emphasis on the distinctive value of the many diverse but limited ideals that are possible in this world. Dewey always insists on the importance of aesthetic experience and, almost interchangeably, the aesthetic structure of experience generally. His conception of pragmatism in fact hinges on his analysis of the ways in which individuals and cultures process experience through aesthetic mechanisms. In the absence of a stable moral authority, people keep their moral and intellectual bearings by grounding ideal values not in the material or ideal structure of being but in the "passage from disturbance into harmony" that constitutes the basic rhythm of art as experience. Dramatic and ritual forms thus provide the flexible mold from within which values and meanings can be adopted, shaped, and transformed. Ideals, whether moral or intellectual, are the product of dramatic, ritualized experience. They reflect the rhythm of experience as it is shaped, both individually and socially, into meaningful form.

Santayana would agree with Dewey's analyses of art as experience, though he would see these mechanisms less as means to other ends than as valuable experiences in their own right. As Santayana complained, Dewey's philosophy sets the transitive agency ahead of any value or ideal the transitive agency might possibly produce. Dewey calls this process "social progress" because, directed by intelligence, it serves to expand democratic practices and ideals. Santayana exactly reverses this formula: though such transitive agencies necessarily determine what realizations are possible, the realizations themselves constitute the ultimate prize in experience. If Dewey thinks of "organized intelligence" as a "method for directing social change," Santayana thinks of intelligence as a method for realizing possible ideals in a world that is not always terribly kind to ideals: "Intelligence consists in having read the heart and deciphered the promptings latent there, and then in reading the world and deciphering its law and constitution, to see how and where the heart's

*The Politics of Transition*

ideal may be embodied" (*RA* 222). Though human intelligence may well direct social change, the idea that this is its chief aim is, in Santayana's view, only a reflection of the characteristic temper of the New England mind.

Dewey and Santayana epitomize two strategies open to American post-liberal thought. Dewey's is the activist strategy, rejecting especially the individualism of liberalism in favor of an engaged historical agency that would reconstruct individualism in a socially responsible, responsive way. Santayana's is the reflective strategy, rejecting the coercive demands of responsible participation in a liberal culture of work and progress in favor of cultivating other ideals and satisfactions. If Dewey's more instrumentally inflected pragmatism has come to dominate our current conceptions of pragmatism, it is in part because these conceptions have evolved within the very social and political environment that Santayana so vigorously criticized. It has even proven difficult for critics to recognize and respond to the aesthetic and reflective content of Dewey's own project. Pragmatism has always been marked by these tensions. Though pragmatists have often emphasized engagement with immediate social circumstance, they have also cultivated reflective ideals, developing what might be called a reflective instrumentalism.

The American literary modernists I will discuss in the following chapters inherit precisely this tension within pragmatism. They sometimes exhibit Dewey's infinite grasp, and at other times cultivate Santayana's sense of finite limitation. They may display Dewey's optimism about the prospect of incessant change and growth or Santayana's skepticism toward the inherent progressiveness of that change and growth. Each of the writers I will discuss in the following chapters remains ambivalent on these crucial issues, which is only to say they are capable of feeling their way into both positions. None of the writers I will discuss, however, echoes Dewey's or Santayana's talk of "organized intelligence" and "rationality," each being more radically skeptical of imposed design, including their own. This is not to say that they believe that art must be irrational, but rather that the same imaginative energies that create art must also contribute to any intelligent design. If the pragmatists describe the permeability of real and ideal or subjective and objective realms, the literary modernists enact this permeability in the language and form of their writing. This shift does not reflect a retreat from the real-world contexts so important to Dewey and Santayana alike, but rather represents these writers' rigorous sense — sometimes joyful, sometimes skeptical and ironic — of the mutually determining interrelatedness of the world and the language and symbols by means of which we suffer and enjoy it.

*The Poetics of Transition*

# 5

## Henry James and the
## Drama of Transition

ACUITY OF PERCEPTION functions for Henry James to isolate and cultivate purely transitional agencies. James frequently depicts characters who are shocked, often quite brutally, into recognizing the inadequacy of long-held assumptions about their world or about the motivations of others in their world. He made an art of lingering over this process, tracing the slowly unfolding process of transition as characters' perceptions of their worlds evolve. But James's interest in transition also extends beyond his conception of character. James's prose, especially in his late phase, stages transition as the seemingly endless unfolding of perception. Even if this unfolding perception can be located in a character or narrative voice, it also enacts a perceptual and linguistic process that exceeds any definitive location. Transition, for James, figures the dynamic processes that subsume and exceed our always limited perception of those processes.

There are many ways of understanding James's claim to have "unconsciously pragmatised" all his life.[1] For one thing, Henry is as skeptical of abstractions as his brother William. Abstractions remove us from the dense particularity and temporal unfolding of experience. They enable certain efficiencies of thought and action, but they do so by turning attention away from the texture of actual experience. Both brothers are skeptical of intellectual habits that remove intelligence from the dynamic contexts of experience in this way. T. S. Eliot had something like this in mind when he called Henry James "the most intelligent man of his generation," praising him for having a mind so fine "that no idea could violate it."[2] An idea, in Eliot's sense, is the inflated currency of a dissociated sensibility, thought without feeling. It has none of the vital intelligence Eliot associates with Dante and the metaphysical poets. Both Henry and William James locate intelligence in a world of impinging realities. Intelligence is achieved not by detaching thought from these realities but rather by engaging them in all their teeming multiplicity and ambiguity. Both Henry and William project a self that is experimental, open to the perpetual emergence of novelty while still subject to the dislocations that necessarily accompany that emergence.

Whereas other critics have detailed this general pragmatic inheritance, I want to focus more specifically on Henry's distinctive poetics of transition. For William James, life is in the transitions as much as in the terms connected. Life is a dynamic, temporal unfolding, and to locate ourselves at the center of that unfolding is also to locate that unfolding at the center of ourselves. The "self" is merely another transitional agency, a progressive unfolding that is at the same time an ongoing reflection on that unfolding. Henry James's conception of character as well as his method of narration, especially in the late fiction, reflects the same dynamic model of self. His characters and his narrative voice do not simply develop or evolve through the course of a novel; rather, the process of development utterly overtakes the narrating and the narrated selves. Such passages are often marked by figures of violence or disruption, as, for example, in the famous scene late in *The Ambassadors* when Chad and Madame de Vionnet erupt through the surface of Strether's meticulously arranged scene.[3] James is frequently drawn to scenes which exceed either a character's or even the narrator's understanding of events, staging the literal disruption of surface that marks any transition.

This is apparent both at the broad level of character and plot development and at the more minute level of narrative description. For James, processes of thinking exceed their particular embodiment in specific thoughts. This is not because our thinking inadequately corresponds to a mysterious and inaccessible ideal reality but rather because thinking is a dynamic process linked to the dynamic processes that constitute the natural and social world. Just as William had insisted that a word stands for the thing it names and dimly a thousand other things, so Henry recognizes that the mind's thoughts are always advancing beyond themselves, always suggesting more than their reduced conceptual content. Some minds manage to content themselves with the available names and descriptions, learning to map the world in their image, while others follow words' indefinite threads of relationship, wherever they may lead. I have already noted in the introduction that James conceived the art of fiction as one of balancing the competing claims made by the need to name a thing and the need to acknowledge the dynamic web of relations that conditions its recognition as such. For James, fiction stages the complex, temporal interplay of definite impressions and the myriad related associations that accompany them, however dimly.

*The Poetics of Transition*

Almost as if to counter the elusiveness of this process, James emphasizes in his critical writing the importance of the novelist's formal control of materials. As he puts it in a letter to Hugh Walpole, "Form alone *takes,* and holds and preserves, substance—saves it from the welter of helpless verbiage that we swim in as a sea of tasteless tepid pudding."[4] The modernists admired James in part because he so insisted on the integrity of literary form and the artist's mastery of form against the background of impending chaos. The fact that he did so while choosing to live in exile from his native America further suggested, especially to Pound and Eliot, that the battle for integrity of form was one that provincial Americans were bound to misunderstand. But James's discussions of form can be misleading. The emphasis on economy and architecture, as well as on mastery of formal problems, suggests the kind of unified, autotelic work that became so central to the New Criticism. Indeed, James's own writing about form, as well as the writing of T. S. Eliot, which was to some extent influenced by James, constitutes one of the major sources of the New Criticism. But this trajectory of influence depends on a misreading of James's own fiction and criticism. James typically uses formal structure to stage the limits of such unity. His characteristic drama is one in which a coherent but partial view of the world finds itself in new circumstances that exert pressure on that view and ultimately force cracks and fissures to appear in it. So too the omniscient narrative voice of James's novels is perpetually reflecting on the limits of any singular understanding of the events that constitute a novel's or story's action. What the New Critical emphasis on form misses is the irreducible temporality of James's descriptions. As Dewey and Santayana also insisted, unity is an experience in time, always subject to the vicissitudes of time. James's late prose style cultivates a steady immersion in these vicissitudes.

Of course, James's style was one reason for his always modest success as a novelist. It is behind his brother William's dismissive impatience alluded to earlier; it is also behind what would become the classic parody of James, H. G. Wells's "Of Art, of Criticism, of Mr. Henry James," which appeared in Wells's 1915 *Boon* and led to the exchange of letters discussed later in this chapter. Others saw more deeply into the late style, saw it as a sharpening of James's verbal instrument: the vagueness and elusiveness is not the avoidance of statement, but rather the attempt to articulate ever more exact shades of meaning. James's verbal world is not less but more precise than other, more naturalistically rendered verbal worlds. James was never one to settle for a cheaply secured clarity of expression. His goal was always clarity, but a clarity so exact, so palpable even, that it bears no reduction into handy abstractions and generalizations. For James, an elusive formulation was only a better means of getting at the specificity and definiteness of all that is elusive in experience.

*Henry James and the Drama of Transition*

Pound describes this style in his 1918 essay on James: "In James the maximum sensibility compatible with efficient writing was present. Indeed, in reading these pages [*The Middle Years*] one can but despair over the inadequacy of one's own literary sensitization, one's so utterly inferior state of awareness." By comparison, Pound notes, "we may throw out the whole Wells-Bennett period, for what interest can we take in instruments which must by nature miss two-thirds of the vibrations in any conceivable situation?"[5]

James's mature prose works by indirection.[6] This is not an evasion of experience on James's part, but an attempt to incorporate as much experience and awareness into the fabric of his fiction as his writing can sustain: the "maximum sensibility compatible with efficient writing," as Pound had nicely put it. James notes in the preface to volume 18 of the New York Edition that even "the simplest truth about a human entity, a situation, a relation, an aspect of life, however small, on behalf of which the claim to charmed attention is made, strains ever, under one's hand, more intensely, *most* intensely, to justify that claim; strains ever, as it were, toward the uttermost end or aim of one's meaning or of its own numerous connexions; struggles at each step, and in defiance of one's raised admonitory finger, fully and completely to express itself" (*LC* 2:1278). This description recalls William James's claim that even the smallest pulse of experience includes "those indefinitely radiating subconscious possibilities of increase that we can only feel without conceiving, and can hardly begin to analyze" (*W* 2:761). As ever, perceptual or conceptual details cannot be isolated because they are always indicative of other details and patterns within the broader field of perception and understanding. For Henry James, every detail, no matter how minimally relevant to his characters and situations, strains for representation because every detail illuminates, in its own distinctive way, the broad web of relations that links his characters and their situations.

James proceeds to describe the art of fiction as "a controlled and guarded acceptance, in fact a perfect economic mastery, of that conflict: the general sense of the expansive, the explosive principle in one's material thoroughly noted, adroitly allowed to flush and colour and animate the disputed value, but with its other appetites and treacheries, its characteristic space-hunger and space-cunning, kept down" (*LC* 2:1278). James's suggestively animalistic metaphors here—"appetites and treacheries," "space-hunger and space-cunning"—indicate that "perfect economic mastery" is indeed a delicate affair. Something expansive, even explosive is being "kept down," on the model of the lion tamer keeping the lion's vicious savagery in line. James insists here, as he does throughout the prefaces, on his mastery of this "conflict," but his very insistence should draw our attention to the conflict and its frequent

*The Poetics of Transition*

eruption in his writing. Furthermore, when James refers to "the general sense of the expansive, the explosive principle," the striking transition from expansive to explosive is itself a minor eruption of this violence. Expansive is not necessarily the same as explosive, but James's collapsing of the two terms in this way suggests that in some sense they are the same. James's prose style indicates an eruption that it is attempting, in its very formulation, to contain. James recognizes that perception must be restrained if it is to issue in meaningful form. What he calls the "difficulty" of writing lies in balancing the claims of perception with those of meaningful form, an effect achieved by means of the device he labels here and elsewhere in the prefaces "foreshortening." Foreshortening allows him to write at the maximum pitch of suggestion while maintaining reasonable control of the potentially limitless details that crowd into his mind as he writes. Still, no reader of the late fiction has ever felt James to be lacking in detail. Indeed, the late style repeatedly stages the "expansive, the explosive principle" of James's transitional poetics.

Foreshortening is a formal, technical solution to a philosophical problem. This is the same problem faced by characters in James's fiction who struggle to perceive the subtle nuances of a scene or social situation. During one of Fanny Assingham's conversations with her husband in *The Golden Bowl*, Fanny objects to Colonel Assingham's summary reference to her "whole idea" regarding Maggie Verver: "It isn't my 'whole' idea. Nothing's my 'whole' idea — for I felt to-day, as I tell you, that there's so much in the air" (*GB* 302).[7] Indeed, one of the extraordinary features of this densely analytic novel is that clear and whole ideas are rarely formed by or about anyone; when they are formed, they are likely to prove inadequate, as when Amerigo and Charlotte independently reach mistaken conclusions about the Jewish shopkeeper who shows them the golden bowl. It is not possible to form a whole idea about any of the principal characters in this novel because they exist so elusively in their subtle gestures, their indirect habits of speech, their shifting relations to others around them. There is always too much "in the air" to allow for easy or even complex conclusions.[8] James appears to exult in this elusiveness. He would rather keep his characters incomplete in this way than lay them bare for all to see. Interesting people, in James's world, are never simply open to inspection. We see them, and often they see themselves, as mediated by the surface of their lives: their clothes, their drawing rooms, their houses and lawns, their tricks of speech, the objects they accumulate and sometimes lose, the friends they keep, the lovers they take or sacrifice. Even when he takes us into a character's thoughts, it is rarely for a view of what is deepest or most essential about that character. Instead, James will more likely focus on the trivial obsessions, the external details that crowd out or hold off the deeper thoughts, as if to suggest that such details are themselves the greater part of our psychological lives and even our self-conceptions.

William James, as well as both Dewey and Santayana after him, had insisted that nothing has its identity in itself. Everything is instead what its dynamic web of relations constitutes it as. So for Henry James any thing is indistinguishable from our sense (or our various senses) of that thing. Much as William could only define the core of self as the feeling of effort, so Henry conceives the recognizable core of self as an illusion, one often protected by clinging to a series of misconceptions and self-deceptions. Beneath these illusions, however, there is no singular truth about the self. There is, instead, only a far-reaching and temporally unfolding web of relations. By emphasizing psychological perspective in his fictional method, James does not seek to reinforce the classic subject/object division (though this is the usual effect of psychological readings of James). Instead, he attempts to break down that very division by acknowledging the mutual interdependence of what we call subjective and objective realms. The self is a transitional agency within the dynamic web of relations in which it appears. No element of that web has any meaning in isolation. Though many of James's most interesting characters are distinctively individual, his fictions invariably confront their individuality with the irreducible relationality of social experience.

This sense of the dynamic, relational dimension of people and things further explains James's fascination with inexact or indeterminate psychological states. Much like his brother, Henry embraces the vague fringe that suffuses even the most definite, exact experience. *The Turn of the Screw,* an important early work of James's late phase, can be read as an exercise in determining just how far James could take this indeterminate suffusing fringe. As James admits in his preface to the tale, everything in *The Turn of the Screw* is designed to suggest a dilemma that remains, and must necessarily remain, inexact: "The study is of a conceived 'tone,' the tone of suspected and felt trouble, of an inordinate and incalculable sort — the tone of tragic, yet of exquisite, mystification" (*LC* 2:1185). James explicitly conceives and designs a tone that will be evocative and indeterminate.

Nothing could be more beside the point of the tale than readers' attempts to determine the exact nature of Miles's words at school, of the ghosts' effect on the children, or of the narrator's psychological state. Even the attempt to separate the reality of the ghosts from the governess's psychological projection of them is singularly wrong-headed.[9] This is to ask the wrong kind of question of the story. In his preface (to volume 12 of the New York Edition), James calls the tale "a piece of ingenuity pure and simple, of cold artistic calculation, an *amusette* to catch those not easily caught (the 'fun' of the capture

*The Poetics of Transition*

of the merely witless being ever but small), the jaded, the disillusioned, the fastidious" (*LC* 2:1184–85). To hunt out the unspoken truth of the story is to fall into James's carefully laid trap: it is to attempt to read through the rich and endlessly suggestive surface of the tale and capture the definitive meaning hidden beneath that surface. But as James points out, the surface operates on the principle that there is nothing to hide beneath it. There is no depth, only the richly textured illusion of depth.[10]

The challenge James faced in writing *The Turn of the Screw* was to evoke a kind and degree of evil without having to specify it, since specification would undercut its purely suggestive horror:

> Thus arose on behalf of my idea the lively interest of a possible suggestion and process of *adumbration;* the question of how best to convey that sense of the depths of the sinister without which my fable would so woefully limp. Portentous evil—how was I to save that, as an intention on the part of my demon-spirits, from the drop, the comparative vulgarity, inevitably attending, throughout the whole range of possible brief illustration, the offered example, the imputed vice, the cited act, the limited deplorable presentable instance. (*LC* 2:1187)

Naming this evil would limit the dramatic impact of the story. In describing the sense he wanted to create in the story, James remains deliberately vague: "Of their being, the haunting pair, capable, as the phrase is, of everything— that is of exerting, in respect to the children, the very worst action small victims so conditioned might be conceived as subject to" (*LC* 2:1188). The evil, James decides, must be supplied by the reader's own imagination, there being "no eligible *absolute* of the wrong": "Only make the reader's general vision of evil intense enough, I said to myself—and that already is a charming job— and his own experience, his own imagination, his own sympathy (with the children) and horror (of their false friends) will supply him quite sufficiently with all the particulars. Make him *think* the evil, make him think it for himself, and you are released from weak specifications" (*LC* 2:1188). James proceeds to report his own surprise at his success, citing criticism of the story charging him with "indecently expatiating" despite the fact there is "not only from beginning to end of the matter not an inch of expatiation, but my values are positively all blanks save so far as an excited horror, a promoted pity, a created expertness—on which punctual effects of strong causes no writer can ever fail to plume himself—proceed to read into them more or less fantastic figures" (*LC* 2:1188). The joke is on the reader: the ghosts and their terrible depredations ("fantastic figures") are the product of the reader's own excited imagination.

*Henry James and the Drama of Transition*

I do not mean to suggest, as others have, that the ghosts are not real, by which readers usually mean that the narrator, under some psychosexual influence, makes them up. James is too playful with his ghosts to care much whether they are, or could be, real. He even apologizes in the preface for ignoring the general rules for apparitions, since to have followed the actual reports of apparitions would have left him with little to work with in the way of character and action. He slyly suggests that Peter Quint and Miss Jessel "are not 'ghosts' at all, as we now know the ghost, but goblins, elves, imps, demons as loosely constructed as those of the old trials for witchcraft; if not, more pleasingly, fairies of the legendary order, wooing their victims forth to see them dance under the moon" (*LC* 2:1187). James insists in the preface that the ghosts were useful to him in "having helped me to express my subject all directly and intensely" and proceeds to discuss the "villainy of motive in the evoked predatory creatures" (*LC* 2:1187). What matters is not whether or not they are in some sense real, but that they are intensely evoked. Their dimly horrible evocation is their full and sufficient reality.

James's preface makes clear (albeit retrospectively) that James is interested not in the nature of Miles's supposed evil, whether as passed on to him by Peter Quint or not, but rather in the way in which the reader supplies the evil that the story nowhere names. James was amused at critics who accused him of indelicacy of statement in the story, and he would likely also have been amused at efforts to understand what really happens in the tale. *The Turn of the Screw* in this sense provides an important clue to the puzzle of James's late fiction. James's psychological method is distinctly unpsychological—or at least, in the current phrase, it is anti-psychologistic. James conceives consciousness not as an inner property but rather as a set of evolving relations between human motives and the objects and events that shape and are in turn shaped by those motives. He never depicts a psychological state directly because a purely psychological state simply has no interest (or meaning) for him. What does interest James is a mind coming alive to its conditions, obstacles, and opportunities.[11]

William James was at the same time developing his idea that truth is not a "stagnant property inherent in" an idea, but rather "*happens* to an idea" (*W* 2:574). This is to say that our intellectual investigations, in philosophy as in science, do not discover true relations inherent in the nature of things but rather invent those relations, thus enabling human culture to harness things to human purposes. "True ideas," James notes, "lead us into useful verbal and conceptual quarters as well as directly up to useful sensible termini. They lead to consistency, stability and flowing human intercourse. They lead away from excentricity and isolation, from foiled and barren thinking" (*W* 2:580). This

*The Poetics of Transition*

is all very hopeful, in good William Jamesian fashion. One can readily trust in human intellectual capacities that are so well adapted to things, even if those capacities do not reveal anything of the inherent nature of those things. Henry James would surely agree with this understanding of truth, especially with the idea that truth happens to an idea as it is bandied about in conversation. When characters in James's fiction, especially his late fiction, speak together, it often appears that they are not discussing the same subject at all. These subjects are instead permeable, endlessly coming into, and again falling out of, focus.

In James's fiction, characters typically perform an intricate dance with language and ideas. There is shared ground in language and thought, but that ground is always permeable. The sense of a word will vary from character to character, will have a different inflection from one moment to the next because of some new development or revelation or will vary with changes of context or mood. What illuminates in one place bewilders in another. Passages of momentary clarification often give way to passages of deeper confusion. Then, too, James recognizes those moments of shared recognition, most often between a very small group of characters. *The Golden Bowl,* for example, provides in its conclusion an extraordinary understanding that is so limited in its range that the reader can never quite enter into it. All four of the novel's principal characters have reached some kind of mutual understanding, but that understanding is an astonishingly delicate affair. Adam Verver, for example, knows enough to move with his wife back to the United States, but it never becomes clear what he thinks is going on, even in his last reported conversation with his daughter. Adam remains opaque to the end. To some extent, this is true of all the characters in this novel. As deep as James takes us into their inner lives, we know them only through indirections.

William James would acknowledge that the consistency and meaning we read into things is always set against a background of uncertainty and confusion, but his cheerful positivism leads him to focus his intellectual energies on our ability to read consistency and meaning into things. Henry James focuses instead on the unstable process itself, the movement between uncertainty and tentatively posited meaning, between some definite element in the foreground and the shades of implication extending vaguely out on all sides. William's understanding of how we invent and use truths is illuminating, but Henry's understanding of these processes is designed to be at once illuminating and bewildering, allowing him to embrace dimensions of experience from which William shies away. Here again we can sense the affinity between the brothers and at the same time the gap that would make Henry's writing so inaccessible to William. William wanted to understand the psychological experience of bewilderment as well as the prospects for translating that be-wilderment into sufficient knowledge. For William, uncertainty exists to be overcome by understanding. "The Sentiment of Rationality" describes this process as the central dynamic of rational intelligence. Dewey would translate this into the social dynamic of organized intelligence: inadequate social forms are converted by applied intelligence into better, more expansive social forms. In the characteristic Deweyan rhythm of experience, disturbance always re-solves into harmony, however tentatively. For Henry James, by contrast, the dialectic of bewilderment and understanding does not necessarily move in the direction of progress and synthesis. Like Santayana, James does not see progress as the highest human value. The conflict between bewilderment and understanding is instead more genuinely indeterminate. One's only recourse is an unfaltering attentiveness, being bewildered to foster understanding and understanding enough to abide bewilderment.

Such unfaltering attentiveness constitutes the dramatic undercurrent in James's depiction of Lambert Strether in the early pages of *The Ambassadors*. Pausing in the street on the occasion of his first visit to Chad Newsome's Paris apartment, Strether becomes aware of the peculiar danger of pausing anywhere in Paris: "Poor Strether had at this very moment to recognise the truth that wherever one paused in Paris the imagination reacted before one could stop it. This perpetual reaction put a price, if one would, on pauses; but it piled up consequences till there was scarce room to pick one's steps among them" (*A* 69).[12] One senses here that Strether, or at least some part of him, still wants to stop his imagination from wandering and indulging itself, but finds himself unable to catch it before it has already gotten itself too far along. The "price" of pauses is the free-play of imagination, a respon-siveness to environment that always threatens to obscure Strether's reason for being in Paris: his effort, on behalf of Mrs. Newsome, to convince Chad to return to America to take charge of the family business. The world, or more specifically Europe and its charming culture, so overwhelms Strether that he hardly knows where to put his next foot forward. Indeed, Strether repeatedly pauses in this novel, and it is in such moments that he becomes sensible of the extraordinary imaginative appeal of his environment. At one point during Strether's first stroll with Maria Gostrey, the narrator comments parentheti-cally that they are "constantly pausing, in their stroll, for the sharper sense of what they saw" (*A* 25). The comment comes as a parenthetical aside, as if to underscore just how central peripheral awareness is to the steady unfolding of any richly conscious life.

Chad's balcony, to which Strether's lingering view from the street is in-evitably directed, is a privileged place in *The Ambassadors*. It is a marginal space, mediating between the interior apartment and the wide world of Paris. It presents its face to the world, but at the same time hides what transpires within. The balcony figures the possible transition between Strether's duties, represented in the repeated appeal to "Woollett," "Waymarsh," and "Mrs. Newsome," and his deepest, largely unacknowledged creative potential. It figures the movement from the abstract designs that have been imposed on Strether by Mrs. Newsome and the free responsiveness that calls out to him from every last seductive detail of the Parisian world. But perhaps most importantly, the balcony represents the ideal balance between public and private: it is the external face of a carefully cultivated interior world. It reaches out into the world, takes generous notice of that world, but at the same time nurtures and protects everything that goes on within. Strether is first depicted on the outside looking up, as "Little Bilham" eventually appears on the balcony, looking from the inside out. The movement of this most symmetrical of James's novels is to draw Strether into Little Bilham's position on the balcony. Here, at the outset of Strether's Parisian adventure, before he even knows who the young gentleman on the balcony is, Strether pauses, enjoying the admirable proportions of the building's facade, the fine look of its stone, even the quality of the young gentleman's "surrender to the balcony" and the "perched privacy" that appear to Strether as "the last of luxuries" (*A* 70). In short, Strether is smitten from the first. He takes his chances by entering, though not before he assuages his conscience by telling himself that he will later confess everything to Waymarsh.

The pause is one of James's favorite fictional devices. The famous fireside chapter in *The Portrait of a Lady* is an extended variation on the theme. But James pauses in more ways than one. In his scenic representation of action, characters are often caught mid-gesture, allowing James the opportunity to depict various aspects of the action in a kind of stopped time. By stopping narrative time, however, James is able to engage the temporal dynamic of his own unfolding prose. When Strether and Maria Gostrey meet for their first stroll through Liverpool, Strether observes Maria from a fixed position: "Before reaching her he stopped on the grass and went through the form of feeling for something, possibly forgotten, in the light overcoat he carried on his arm," though "the essence of the act was no more than the impulse to gain time" (*A* 20). James is also gaining time here, as he proceeds, in some 850 words of dense description, to trace Strether's state of mind, which includes his sense of his new friend, Maria Gostrey, and of his present predicament in Europe as he unaccountably delays his meeting with Waymarsh. Midway through the description, we are reminded that he is still feeling through his overcoat. As the passage begins to conclude, we are told that he "joined his guide in an instant" (*A* 22), as if the details outlined in the descriptive passage had registered for Strether in the space of a single glance.

The Jamesian pause is apparent on another level of James's prose as well. The late style is one of endless pauses: the Jamesian sentence begins like any other, but is always pausing to take in things along the way, as if the view at these points were always more interesting than the end in sight. Here is the narrator's report of Strether's own sense, at the outset of his little adventure (his walk!) with Maria Gostrey, of a new beginning that has somehow, already, been launched for him: "Nothing could have been odder than Strether's sense of himself as at that moment launched in something of which the sense would be quite disconnected from the sense of his past and which was literally beginning there and then. It had begun in fact already upstairs and before the dressing-glass that struck him as blocking further, so strangely, the dimness of the window of his dull bedroom; begun with a sharper survey of the elements of Appearance than he had for a long time been moved to make" (*A* 20). The passage continues in this vein. James keeps pushing back Strether's "beginning," qualifying the point of origins as he traces his character's realization further and further back. Strether's "launch" is first said to take place "there and then," apparently as he fumbles through his overcoat pocket before going on the walk with Maria Gostrey, but it is, "in fact," already begun, something that can be traced back to his survey of his appearance before his dressing room mirror. His attention focuses not just on the "dressing-glass," however, but on the way that it "struck him as blocking further, so strangely, the dimness of the window of his dull bedroom." Strether is making discriminations, surveying the elements of his scene more sharply, discovering further intimations of change as he inspects his surroundings. At the same time, James's prose, with its constant turns of qualification and modification, its movement from subordinate clause to subordinate clause and its subtly shifting tonal inflections, enacts that same process.

It is instructive to recall William James's comparison of thought to a bird's "alternation of flights and perchings." The transitional metaphor allows James to integrate dynamic process and relation into an otherwise static conception of thought. Henry effectively dramatizes this same transitional process, both as theme and as formal method. James pauses throughout his sentences, allowing himself an ever "sharper survey" of his own verbal scene. This enables him to indicate the dynamic, relational processes that suffuse all social and verbal experience. At one point, the narrator offers Strether's own sketch to himself of his impression of Maria Gostrey: " 'Well, she's more thoroughly civilised —!' If 'More thoroughly than *whom?*' would not have been for him a sequel to this remark, that was just by reason of his deep consciousness of

*The Poetics of Transition*

the bearing of his comparison" (*A* 21). The initial comment, offered as if it occurs word for word as such in Strether's own mind, breaks off abruptly, as indicated by the dash. For Strether, as for James, "more" grammatically implies "more than," an implication literally dashed by the dash, an indication of broken speech. The reference here is clearly to Mrs. Newsome, but James withholds this information, as well as any explanation of who she is in relation to Strether. Mrs. Newsome's symbolic presence is being delayed here, in order to give Strether sufficient leisure to pause. Strether does not name Mrs. Newsome to himself in relation with Maria Gostrey, and does not name her to himself because he is in some sense so deeply conscious of "the bearing of his [implicit] comparison" that he cannot, as yet, allow himself to be explicitly conscious of it. Strether is aware and at the same time not aware, and his broken speech is a perfect device by which to represent his real psychic state. The reader understands the importance of what Strether leaves unstated by the way James attends to its very unstatedness.

*The Ambassadors* records the process by which Strether awakens and responds to the world around him, a world that includes passionate love. It is this burgeoning responsiveness that enables him to advise Little Bilham, "Live all you can" (*A* 132). A fine responsiveness would be meaningless, even potentially destructive, if it did not cultivate a creative engagement with the material of experience. In his late correspondence with H. G. Wells occasioned by Wells's critical parody of James's fiction, James insists that his "poetic" and his "appeal to experience" rest upon his "measure of fulness — fulness of life and of the projection of it, which seems to you such an emptiness of both." For Wells, the fullness of life is conveyed with a minimum of aesthetic or formal fussiness. For James, the fullness of life is only realized in and through highly formalized aesthetic works: "I hold that interest may be, *must* be, exquisitely made and created, and that if we don't make it, we who undertake to, nobody and nothing will make it for us." Interest, in other words, is cultivated, not found. An art that takes its methods for granted will only diminish art's capacity to cultivate life's fullness and interest. In a second letter to Wells on the subject, James comments, "It is art that *makes* life, makes interest, makes importance, for our consideration and application of these things, and I know of no substitute whatever for the force and beauty of its process."[13] James does not advocate an art-for-art's-sake position here, but rather suggests that the sense of the fullness of life is itself cultivated by the peculiar force and beauty of art's processes. This is perfectly in keeping with the concluding address to the young novelist in "The Art of Fiction," which James had written over thirty years before: "All life belongs to you, and do not listen either to those who would shut you up into corners of it and tell you that it is only here and there that art inhabits, or to those who would persuade you that this heavenly messenger wings her way outside of life altogether, breathing a superfine air, and turning away her head from the truth of things. There is no impression of life, no manner of seeing it and feeling it, to which the plan of the novelist may not offer a place" (*LC* 1:64). A novelist is simply someone who is attentive and responsive to the dynamic web of relations that animates all things.

One of the comments in Walter Besant's talk to the Royal Institution that led James to compose "The Art of Fiction" is Besant's claim that "a young lady brought up in a quiet country village should avoid descriptions of garrison life." For Besant, a writer must write from experience, which means that "characters must be real and such as might be met with in actual life" (*LC* 1:51). James responds by redefining experience:

> What kind of experience is intended, and where does it begin and end? Experience is never limited, and it is never complete; it is an immense sensibility, a kind of huge spider-web of the finest silken threads suspended in the chamber of consciousness, and catching every air-borne particle in its tissue. It is the very atmosphere of the mind; and when the mind is imaginative—much more when it happens to be that of a man of genius—it takes to itself the faintest hints of life, it converts the very pulses of the air into revelations. The young lady living in a village has only to be a damsel upon whom nothing is lost to make it quite unfair (as it seems to me) to declare to her that she shall have nothing to say about the military. (*LC* 1:52)

Experience is not mere undergoing, but is rather a function of attentiveness and responsiveness. Like his brother William, though well before him, Henry refuses to separate the actual world from our imagination of it. Experience is itself constituted out of the incessant interplay of realms. The more imaginative the mind, the richer its experience.

Quality of mind, then, determines quality of experience. No amount of lived experience will lead a dull mind to perceptions that a lively mind may achieve at a glance. Colonel Assingham in *The Golden Bowl* is a case in point: "He knew everything that could be known about life, which he regarded as, for far the greater part, a matter of pecuniary arrangement. His wife accused him of a want alike of moral and of intellectual reaction, or rather indeed of a complete incapacity for either" (*GB* 86). Fanny is her husband's antithesis in this regard. As the colonel tries to bring their analysis of the Ververs' situation to a close, Fanny refuses to "have done with it," in her husband's phrase: "She was far, however, from having done with it; it was a situation with such different sides, as she said, and to none of which one could, in justice, be blind"

(*GB* 88–89). However dull a figure Fanny may cut on the social scene, she is a Jamesian analyst to the bone, full of imaginative responsiveness to the intricacies of the situation.[14]

In one of the prefaces to a collection of shorter works (volume 14 of the New York Edition), James suggests that no matter what the experience, what matters is *having* the experience:

> The thing of profit is to *have* your experience—to recognise and understand it, and for this almost any will do; there being surely no absolute ideal about it beyond getting from it all it has to give. The artist—for it is of this strange brood we speak—has but to have his honest sense of life to find it fed at every pore even as the birds of the air are fed; with more and more to give, in turn, as a consequence, and, quite by the same law that governs the responsive affection of a kindly-used animal, in proportion as more and more is confidently asked. (*LC* 2:1211)

Here is James's distinctive poetics of transition: to "have" an experience is to ask "more and more" from it and so, by extension, to cultivate more in it. As Dewey comments in *Art as Experience*, "We must summon energy and pitch it at a responsive key in order to *take* in" (*LW* 10:60). Nothing inherent in an experience constitutes or determines its meaning, short of one's will and ability to get from it "all it has to give." This is necessarily indeterminate, since what an experience has to give already depends on what is brought to it by the responsive sensibility playing over it. Two people in the same circumstance, undergoing the same events, will have different experiences. They will have "asked" differently in relation to those events, and so find themselves "fed" differently from them. Colonel and Mrs. Assingham will leave the same party having formed utterly different impressions of it. Artists are simply people who cultivate their experience more thoroughly, and by extension more subtly, than others.

James's meditation on the novel and the artist everywhere reflects his pragmatic understanding of how we form and use truths, what we do with them, how we revise them over time. This process, for James, is one that always takes place within this dynamic web of experience. The artist has no special vision of reality or of truth, but only a limited perspective formed in experience and always subject to the revision of further experience. The admonition to write from experience can be summarized in James's famous advice to aspiring novelists, "Try to be one of the people on whom nothing is lost!" (*LC* 1:53). The novelist's perceptive faculties are unusually sharp: "The power to guess the unseen from the seen, to trace the implication of things, to judge the whole piece by the pattern, the condition of feeling life in general so completely that you are well on your way to knowing any particular corner of it—this cluster of gifts may almost be said to constitute experience, and they occur in country and in town, and in the most differing stages of education" (*LC* 1:53). This power to guess, to trace, and to judge is a version of the Emersonian power of transition. By virtue of a heightened attentiveness and responsiveness, the artist or novelist sees beyond isolated or apparently trivial details into a more comprehensive reality. This flight of imagination in effect constitutes that reality.

In a letter to Henry Adams written in response to Adams's criticism of James's memoirs, James insists on the relationship between his accumulated experience and his art: "You see I still, in the presence of life (or of what you deny to be such,) have reactions—as many as possible—and the book I sent you is a proof of them. It's, I suppose, because I am that queer monster, the artist, an obstinate finality, an inexhaustible sensibility. Hence the reactions—appearances, memories, many things, go on playing upon it with consequences that I note and 'enjoy' (grim word!) noting. It all takes doing—and I *do*. I believe I shall do yet again—it is still an act of life." [15] As James had noted earlier in the letter, life is interesting "under *cultivation* of the interest." The exercise of imagination is "an act of life," and there simply is, for James, no more immediate or direct gesture of living that can serve the various interests of living more profoundly or effectively.

For James, who embraced the limitations of his own social milieu, the novel constituted the last great territory of freedom. James's perception of the overwhelming restrictions of the society he took as his subject reinforces his sense that freedom can only be cultivated as an aesthetic impulse. His is not, however, a blandly idealized freedom. It is instead an always difficult freedom, cultivated in response to impinging conditions. The quality of mind that James encourages in the novelist is one that acknowledges and indeed embraces its conditions, seeking to register their infinite detail while at the same time shaping that detail into coherent patterns. The novelist must, in good Emersonian fashion, passively "take in" the external world in order to impose shape on that world without simply distorting or idealizing it. When James emphasizes the fine perceptiveness of the novelist's mind, he is suggesting that the novelist is someone who has so thoroughly realized the external conditions of his or her world as to achieve significant freedom within those conditions. Thus, the Jamesian novel must serve no ulterior purpose but that of fine discriminating perception: "In proportion as that intelligence is fine will the novel, the picture, the statue partake of the substance of beauty and truth. To be constituted of such elements is, to my vision, to have purpose enough. No good novel will ever proceed from a superficial mind; that seems to me an axiom which, for the artist in fiction, will cover all needful moral ground" (*LC* 1:64).

A fine intelligence does not transcend its environment but is rather attentively responsive to that environment. Its freedom is not freedom from social conditions, but freedom within social conditions. The Jamesian novelist, like the intelligent hero or heroine of James's novels, displays an expansive attentiveness to the social environment, responding to the extraordinary drama constantly being played out in even the most ordinary circumstances. The introduction of a new character or setting, an unexpected admission or illumination by a familiar character, an uncertain, glimpsed perception: these constitute for James the basic material of the human drama. James places a surprising degree of emphasis on such scenes of incipient transition. In a sense, characters only become interesting to James as they learn to recognize how much more drama is going on around them than they realized. Characters who are stuck in pause, so to speak, could not possibly be interesting characters. They are not truly cultivating experience. James is endlessly fascinated by characters working their way through the early stages of transition, struggling to absorb some new fact about their world that literally changes everything for them. Such characters epitomize, for James, the human drama of transition.

One could multiply examples endlessly. I will focus, however, on two instances in James's fiction, one from the early reaches of the middle phase and one from the late phase. In each example, James represents a character coming alive to the implications and shades of implication of what has been going on around her. In the process, both characters begin to adjust their relationship to their environments. They become more significant actors in their own lives. The drama of unfolding sensibility is for both bound up with the exercise of individual agency.[16]

Isabel Archer's arrival at Gardencourt at the outset of *The Portrait of a Lady* immediately affects all three characters already on the scene: Mr. Touchett, Ralph Touchett, and Lord Warburton. It is as if they are stirred out of a deep sleep. From the start, *The Portrait of a Lady* is a novel of crossing thresholds. Isabel crosses the ocean, she crosses into the lives of her expatriate relatives, and she crosses Gilbert Osmond's threshold, transforming both their lives.

But Isabel also crosses many more subtle thresholds in this novel. A threshold, for James, can often be as simple as a passing glimpse. After she is already married to Osmond, Isabel, returning from a drive and a walk with Pansy, catches a fleeting glimpse of her husband in conversation with Madame Merle in the drawing room. The two apparently think themselves quite alone. It is here that Isabel gets her first sharp intimation of Osmond and Madame Merle's true relation. Isabel catches her view through the doorway:

> Just beyond the threshold of the drawing-room she stopped short, the reason for her doing so being that she had received an impression. The impression had, in strictness, nothing unprecedented; but she felt it as something new, and the soundlessness of her step gave her time to take in the scene before she interrupted it. Madame Merle sat there in her bonnet, and Gilbert Osmond was talking to her; for a minute they were unaware that she had come in. Isabel had often seen that before, certainly; but what she had not seen, or at least had not noticed—was that their dialogue had for the moment converted itself into a sort of familiar silence, from which she instantly perceived that her entrance would startle them. Madame Merle was standing on the rug, a little way from the fire; Osmond was in a deep chair, leaning back and looking at her. Her head was erect, as usual, but her eyes were bent upon his. What struck Isabel first was that he was sitting while Madame Merle stood; there was an anomaly in this that arrested her. Then she perceived that they had arrived at a desultory pause in their exchange of ideas, and were musing, face to face, with the freedom of old friends who sometimes exchange ideas without uttering them. There was nothing shocking in this; they were old friends in fact. But the thing made an image, lasting only a moment, like a sudden flicker of light. Their relative position, their absorbed mutual gaze, struck her as something detected. (*N* 611–12)[17]

James reiterates four times in these lines that there is to all appearances nothing unusual in this scene. The difference Isabel perceives is almost too subtle for words. For one thing, it is a quality of the silence that Osmond and Madame Merle are sharing which suggests something of the inexplicable intimacy of the meeting. For another, the difference in their positions—he sitting, she standing—marks an "anomaly" for Isabel. They are in the midst of a "desultory pause," as if some painful, irresolvable issue lay between them. Isabel has that strange but definite feeling of having come upon something she was not meant to see.

This marks the beginning of a new consciousness for Isabel, though it could hardly yet be classified as some new information about her husband and friend. Isabel is slowly beginning to recognize how thoroughly her bold act of self-determination was in fact a consequence of others' actions. It is not, however, as if the veil drops suddenly away. The winding syntax of the passage reinforces the impression of her unfolding discovery—one that in-

*The Poetics of Transition*

cludes uncertainty, half-formed intimations, baffling confusions. Phrases like "in strictness," "certainly," "as usual," and "in fact" casually reinforce what is most ordinary about the scene, as if to defuse what is at the same time dimly troubling about it. There are four "but" clauses in the passage, each one underscoring the interruption of something unusual against the background of what seems perfectly ordinary. As the passage shuffles between possibilities, James re-creates the uncertain play of Isabel's own mind, conservative in its speculation, struggling to maintain a sense of balance, but at every turn incapable of ignoring what is faintly disturbing in the scene.

Isabel returns to this image during her evening vigil in chapter 42. She is said to be "haunted with terrors which crowded to the foreground of thought as quickly as a place was made for them" (*N* 628). But she is not altogether sure why: "What had suddenly set them into livelier motion she hardly knew, unless it were the strange impression she had received in the afternoon of her husband and Madame Merle being in more direct communication than she suspected. This impression came back to her from time to time, and now she wondered it had never come before" (*N* 628). As Isabel proceeds to review her doubts and disappointments, this image hovers in the background. It is as if the glimpse releases the train of thought, though she can as yet not say exactly why. At the end of the chapter, as Isabel wonders why Pansy "shouldn't be married as you would put a letter in the post-office," the clock strikes four and Isabel prepares to go to bed: "But even then she stopped again in the middle of the room, and stood there gazing at a remembered vision — that of her husband and Madame Merle, grouped unconsciously and familiarly" (*N* 639). Again, the image haunts Isabel, but she can not yet put her finger on its exact significance. Isabel's awareness comes to her slowly and painstakingly. The transition is not instant, but requires a long and exhausting expense of energy.

Just before Madame Merle reveals the depth of her involvement by asking Isabel to use her influence to encourage Lord Warburton to marry Pansy, Isabel reverts once again to the glimpsed image:

> [Madame Merle] was nearer to her than Isabel had yet discovered, and her nearness was not the charming accident that she had so long thought. The sense of accident indeed had died within her that day when she happened to be struck with the manner in which Madame Merle and her own husband sat together in private. No definite suspicion had as yet taken its place; but it was enough to make her look at this lady with a different eye, to have been led to reflect that there was more intention in her past behaviour than she had allowed for at the time. (*N* 720)

*Henry James and the Drama of Transition*

Slowly and surely, Isabel's glimpse is transformed into the basis of action. Her first act is to release Lord Warburton, her second to return to England to be with her dying cousin, despite her husband's refusal of permission.

Readers have been divided about Isabel's return to Rome, both because she chooses to return to her husband and because she flees the one explicitly passionate act in the novel, Caspar Goodwood's kiss. Caspar's kiss is overwhelming to Isabel, who experiences the kiss (especially in the revised New York Edition text) as an aggressive "act of possession" on Caspar's part.[18] To give in to Caspar's passionate act would mean to abandon everything Isabel had chosen, everything she had cultivated in her experience, good and ill. In her escape from Caspar and from Gardencourt, Isabel pauses at the door, uncertain at first where she is going: "She looked all about her; she listened a little; then she put her hand on the latch. She had not known where to turn; but she knew now. There was a very straight path" (N 799). For all the considerable revision to which James submitted this paragraph, these lines remain the same in both editions. There is a quality of definiteness in Isabel's sense of "a very straight path." It is the path she has already been treading, and the one she must continue to tread. Isabel is still working through her transition, and recognizes that it is only in Rome that she can properly, and from a new position of power and knowledge, continue to do so.[19]

James allows the reader to see Isabel as she catches her first glimpse of something extraordinary in the relation between her husband and her ostensible best friend. He proceeds differently in *The Golden Bowl* when, in the opening of the second volume, he presents Maggie as having already begun to question the situation in which she finds herself. Maggie's suspicions begin vaguely, without her even being aware that she is suspicious. The situation has been all-too apparent to others, such as Fanny Assingham. As Maggie spends her time with her father (Adam Verver), her husband (Prince Amerigo) is thrown more and more on the company of Adam's young wife (Charlotte), who happens also, unbeknownst to Maggie, to be Amerigo's former intimate companion. Throughout the first half of the novel, the reader has no idea whether Maggie has even the slightest intimation of what is going on. She seems, on the surface at least, oblivious to the facts. From the first sentence of the second volume, which turns from Amerigo's to Maggie's point of view, the balance is tipped: "It wasn't till many days had passed that the Princess began to accept the idea of having done, a little, something she was not always doing, or indeed that of having listened to any inward voice that spoke in a new tone" (GB 327). Maggie becomes aware "many days" after the fact that she has already begun to have suspicions: strictly speaking, the suspicions begin without her even realizing they have begun. The delicate touch of this

*The Poetics of Transition*

sentence—Maggie has, after all, only begun to hear the new tone of her inward voice "a little"—underscores how uncertain Maggie's recognitions are and how reluctant she is even then to acknowledge them. Everything is left vague in this formulation and in those that will follow. Maggie will never name the deed, even as she brings it into ever sharper focus.

Maggie is, at this stage, becoming aware, but only dimly: "Yet these instinctive postponements of reflexion were the fruit, positively, of recognitions and perceptions already active; of the sense above all that she had made at a particular hour, made by the mere touch of her hand, a difference in the situation so long present to her as practically unattackable" (*GB* 327). Maggie's "recognitions and perceptions" are already active before they get translated into definite awareness. Her awareness, in other words, registers as a dynamic transitional process, unfolding even when she is least aware of it. This is similar to Isabel's initial recognition of her husband and Madame Merle's intimacy, except that in *The Portrait of a Lady* James depicts the scene directly and then allows Isabel's mind to play somewhat uncertainly over the scene over the course of many chapters. Here, at the outset of *The Golden Bowl*'s second volume, James summarizes the process of slow recognition through the extended metaphor of the "outlandish pagoda":

> This situation had been occupying for months and months the very centre of the garden of her life, but it had reared itself there like some strange tall tower of ivory, or perhaps rather some wonderful beautiful but outlandish pagoda, a structure plated with hard bright porcelain, coloured and figured and adorned at the overhanging eaves with silver bells that tinkled ever so charmingly when stirred by chance airs. She had walked round and round it—that was what she felt; she had carried on her existence in the space left her for circulation, a space that sometimes seemed ample and sometimes narrow: looking up all the while at the fair structure that spread itself so amply and rose so high, but never quite making out as yet where she might have entered had she wished. She hadn't wished till now—such was the odd case; and what was doubtless equally odd besides was that though her raised eyes seemed to distinguish places that must serve from within, and especially far aloft, as apertures and outlooks, no door appeared to give access from her convenient garden level. The great decorated surface had remained consistently impenetrable and inscrutable. (*GB* 327)

Maggie has been aware of something for some time. She has heard the ringing of the bells "stirred by chance airs," has circled round the structure, has wondered even how she might enter into the structure. James's sentences here have a marvelous roundabout quality, as if they too are circling something they cannot articulate any more directly. Maggie eventually begins to approach the structure more closely: "she had caught herself distinctly in the act of pausing, then in that of lingering, and finally in that of stepping unprecedentedly near" (*GB* 327–28). James's phrasing here separates the action from her awareness of the action. Maggie is doing something that she catches herself in the act of doing, her awareness lagging behind the action. Pausing gives way to lingering, which in turn gives way to "stepping unprecedentedly near." She is not there yet, and almost seems destined never quite to be there yet, but she is clearly approaching. The passage captures the slow drama of Maggie's dawning awareness by re-creating her deliberate, uncertain approach in the leisurely unfolding of its sentences. What it is that she is approaching remains as mysterious, for Maggie, as the outlandish pagoda itself.

Eventually, Maggie knocks on its surface: "She had knocked in short—though she could scarce have said whether for admission or for what; she had applied her hand to a cool smooth spot and had waited to see what would happen. Something *had* happened; it was as if a sound, at her touch, after a little, had come back to her from within; a sound sufficiently suggesting that her approach had been noted" (*GB* 328). This knock is the preliminary gesture in what will become, by the end, a confident and aggressive confrontation with the situation. This process is well under way by the time the shopkeeper returns to inform Maggie of the flaw in the golden bowl she has purchased, providing her with further information amounting to a glimpse of her husband and friend in an intimate setting even before Maggie had married the prince. Maggie's knock on the "wonderful beautiful but outlandish pagoda" is an initial gesture that will ultimately lead to the violence of Fanny Assingham's smashing of the bowl. The reader sees this dawning awareness before it takes shape as specific knowledge, and follows Maggie as it slowly unfolds. Maggie's consciousness of the situation is in a sense never complete, though it quickly embraces the essentials of the intimate relation between Amerigo and Charlotte. The narrator describes Maggie late in the novel thinking over the limited extent of the knowledge that she can share with Fanny Assingham: "This inability in her was indeed not remarkable, inasmuch as the Princess herself, as we have seen, was only now in a position to boast of touching bottom. Maggie inwardly lived in a consciousness that she could but partly open even to so good a friend and her own visitation of the fuller expanse of which was for that matter still going on" (*GB* 476–77). The boast of "touching bottom" was, it would seem, premature. There are always deeper, more recessed angles that open up to Maggie's vision, and the novel is finally resolved without ever fully exposing what there is to know. Just when the transitions seem to issue in a conclusive revelation or condition, it becomes apparent that the dynamic process is always "still going on."

The game of cards culminates this pattern of ever-deepening awareness for Maggie. The card game serves as a microcosm of the novel as a whole. The chapter centered upon it describes an expanding play of awareness that leads not so much to clarification of motive as to an almost brutal exercise of power. There are at this point only six people at Fawns: Adam and Charlotte, Amerigo and Maggie, and Colonel and Mrs. Assingham. The colonel excuses himself after dinner to write letters, his consciousness only serving as a foil to his wife's consciousness anyway. Maggie, meanwhile, takes the card game as an opportunity to settle in with her thoughts. Looking on, she imagines that each member of the foursome must be compensating for her conspicuous absence by an intense awareness of her: "Erect above all for her was the sharp-edged fact of the relation of the whole group, individually and collectively, to herself—herself so speciously eliminated for the hour, but presumably more present to the attention of each than the next card to be played" (*GB* 486). Maggie is shocked at the unruffled surface her friends maintain as they play cards and is even moved to entertain the monstrous possibility of speaking the "single sentence" that would "sound out their doom" (*GB* 487). The thought comes over her "as a beast might have leaped at her throat" (*GB* 488), but instead of speaking, she quietly moves out to the terrace.

From the terrace, her view of the card game is subtly transformed. Now that she is outside, the group strikes her as "almost consciously and gratefully safer" for her removal (*GB* 488). She imagines herself as a playwright, controlling the fates of the individual characters on stage: "the key to the mystery, the key that could wind and unwind it without a snap of the spring, was there in her pocket—or rather, no doubt, clasped at this crisis in her hand and pressed, as she walked back and forth, to her breast" (*GB* 488). Maggie recognizes that it is in her power to bring everything out into the open with a magnificent and violent flourish or to guide events in a more dignified fashion: "Spacious and splendid, like a stage again awaiting a drama, it was a scene she might people, by the press of her spring, either with serenities and dignities and decencies, or with terrors and shames and ruins, things as ugly as those formless fragments of her golden bowl she was trying so hard to pick up" (*GB* 488). Maggie realizes, even as her mind plays over the scene, that she has not availed herself of the usual outrage—"the straight vindictive view, the rights of resentment, the rages of jealousy, the protests of passion" (*GB* 489)—because she has meant, as much as possible, to preserve the unity of the group. She has been maneuvering all along to preserve her marriage as well as her father's. She has been walking an extraordinarily fine line from the start, as she only now begins to recognize.

Suddenly, however, she discovers that Charlotte has entered the empty smoking room, apparently in search of Maggie herself. There is a shift of emphasis in Maggie's mind, as if one of the characters in the drama she was imagining were threatening to assume control of her own role. She imagines Charlotte as having escaped from her cage: "The splendid shining supple creature was out of the cage, was at large; and the question now almost grotesquely rose of whether she mightn't by some art, just where she was and before she could go further, be hemmed in and secured" (*GB* 490). Charlotte may still have other ideas in mind, and so represents a threat to Maggie's vague (and only just articulated) plan. When Charlotte finally does face Maggie on the terrace, Maggie begins to crumble in fear. Their encounter is a veritable chess match of wills, and Maggie senses that Charlotte has taken the advantage. The shift in positions is indicated by the view they now share of the card game, in which Colonel Assingham has taken Charlotte's place:

> Side by side for three minutes they fixed this picture of quiet harmonies, the positive charm of it and, as might have been said, the full significance — which, as was now brought home to Maggie, could be no more after all than a matter of interpretation, differing always for a different interpreter. As she herself had hovered in sight of it a quarter of an hour before, it would have been a thing for her to show Charlotte — to show in righteous irony, in reproach too stern for anything but silence. But now it was she who was being shown it, and shown it by Charlotte, and she saw quickly enough that as Charlotte showed it so she must at present submissively seem to take it. (*GB* 493–94)

What Maggie now sees is Charlotte's potential control over her husband, the possibility that she will disrupt the visible harmony of the group. Maggie is uncertain of the power she can exercise over her father. She does not know what he knows, and so does not want to test that knowledge by breaking openly with Charlotte. Charlotte seems, to her, aware of this, and seems to want Maggie to act on the basis of that knowledge.

Charlotte proceeds to tell Maggie that she has sensed a change in Maggie's manner toward her and has wondered if she is in any way responsible for this change, claiming to be unaware of any cause she may have given (and so brazenly lying). After faltering briefly, Maggie herself lies: "'You *have* been mistaken'" (*GB* 497). The effect of her lie is instantaneous, giving her solid footing in the conversation: "Her companion's acceptance of her denial was like a general pledge not to keep things any worse for her than they essentially had to be; it positively helped her to build up her falsehood — to which accordingly she contributed another block" (*GB* 497). It is unlikely that Charlotte actually believes Maggie's lie. James's phrasing suggests rather that the two come to a mutual understanding to hold up the lie in the interest of the general unity. Maggie views her own lie as a companion to the false front her husband has been presenting to Charlotte since his view of the smashing of the bowl. It has the effect of making Maggie feel closer to Amerigo, at Charlotte's expense: "They were together thus, he and she, close, close together — whereas Charlotte, though rising there radiantly before her, was really off in some darkness of space that would steep her in solitude and harass her with care" (*GB* 498). This is Maggie's moment of triumph, as she foresees the arrangement by which her father and friend will return to America, while she and Amerigo get on with their lives together. The arrangement is sealed with a kiss, at Charlotte's insistence — a kiss which, by being overseen through the open doorway by the rest of the party, stages the reconciliation that will carry the day.

Though James conceived the novel as the last great territory of freedom, he never imagined such freedom as freedom from obligation or social relations. Neither *The Portrait of a Lady* nor *The Golden Bowl* envisions freedom in such absolute (or negative) terms. James's characters never wholly escape their socially constraining environments. At their best, they learn to negotiate their relationship to those environments from a position of heightened power. Their freedom is always a freedom within, not from, a restrictive social environment. James's characters remain relational through and through. Nothing is more revealing about a Jamesian character than the naive illusion that he or she can go it alone, standing apart from the corrupt social machinery in pursuit of his or her own values, ideals, and truths. Such visions of autonomous selfhood are always a recipe for disaster in James's fictional universe. James loves these characters because they are always superior to the worlds that destroy them, but they are almost always destroyed by their worlds.

Maggie Verver is a rare and wonderful exception to the rule. The intricate patchwork of lies, partial revelations, and half-truths that constitutes the resolution of *The Golden Bowl* is the consequence of Maggie's willingness to participate in the social game that has been going on around her all along. By not playing the card of righteous indignation — the one card that, in Maggie's imagination, might truly set her off from the others — she preserves a valuable degree of unity among all the players while at the same time gaining the advantage precisely where she most desires it — with her husband. Maggie realizes where she is and what the game is that is being played around her. She learns to become an active player in that game not by transcending those circumstances but rather by skillfully managing them. The simple, honest, naive, open, and easily manipulated woman of the novel's first volume becomes more of an actress, more of a player in its second volume: someone decidedly more like Charlotte. Nothing in *The Golden Bowl* redeems the petty manipulations and cruelties by which Maggie's friends betray her, and nothing suggests that this world could somehow be otherwise. In pragmatist terms, this social milieu constitutes the inescapable condition of Maggie's life. What Maggie learns to do is to recognize those conditions for what they are and to imagine new possibilities within them. Maggie steadily rises to the challenge of saving her marriage, while at the same time securing as much general agreement in the process as would allow her father the satisfaction of his own marriage as well.

Though James's characters, Maggie especially, do achieve a positive degree of understanding through the course of the novel, they also learn, as importantly, to cultivate abiding obscurities. Maggie has to settle for a series of dense obscurities before she is allowed to embrace her husband at the end of *The Golden Bowl*. In parting with her father, Maggie insists on Charlotte's being "great." Their agreement on this point becomes something she and her father "could close upon": "it was firm under their feet" (*GB* 577). As if to confirm this judgment, Adam comments, "I know her better," to which Maggie returns, "You know her best." Adam then responds, "Oh but naturally!" (*GB* 577). Every phrase here resonates as if dense with meaning, but the reader would be hard put to say just what that meaning is.

This exchange leads the narrator to comment on this gap between agreement and obscurity: "On which, as the warranted truth of it hung in the air—the truth warranted, as who should say, exactly by the present opportunity to pronounce, this opportunity created and accepted—she found herself lost, though with a finer thrill than she had perhaps yet known, in the vision of all he might mean" (*GB* 577). The "warranted truth" is itself a product of an opportunity "created and accepted." Father and daughter have tacitly conspired to settle things between them in the best possible light. The problem is that they both mean so much in their praise of Charlotte, but each understands so little of what the other means. When Adam comments, "She's beautiful, beautiful," Maggie hears something of "the shade of a new note" and determines that her father is speaking of Charlotte's social value (*GB* 577). As much as she is alive with the "finer thrill" of his potentially infinite and unfathomable meaning, Maggie needs something solid to hold on to: "If Maggie had desired at so late an hour some last conclusive comfortable category to place him in for dismissal, she might have found it here in its all coming back to his ability to rest upon high values" (*GB* 577–78). Her father could always appreciate Charlotte's material, social value: "Great for the world that was before her — *that* he proposed she should be: she wasn't to be wasted in the application of his plan" (*GB* 578). As James's description indicates, this line of thought works to comfort Maggie: "Maggie held to this then — that [Charlotte] wasn't to be wasted" (*GB* 578). Like Maggie's and Charlotte's earlier willingness to share their lie, Maggie and her father conspire to part on mutually supportive terms.

Something similar happens in the novel's last scene, as Maggie and Amerigo find themselves alone, facing their future together for the first time. Maggie worries, as Amerigo approaches her, that her own appearance may make him fear that she expects some kind of confession from him. She acts quickly to alleviate this fear: "All she now knew accordingly was that she should be ashamed to listen to the uttered word; all, that is, but that she might dispose of it on the spot for ever" (*GB* 579). Having already played this scene with her father, she knows how to accomplish that: " 'Isn't she too splendid?' she simply said, offering it to explain and to finish." Amerigo responds, "Oh splendid!" and then moves toward Maggie (*GB* 579). Nothing more needs to be said. Like Maggie's earlier term "great" and her father's term "beautiful," Maggie's exclamation can, and in an important sense does, mean just about everything. The term settles things nicely because it is so hard to pin down.

There is, however, a final play on "truth" in the novel's last lines. Maggie says in response to Amerigo, "That's our help, you see," as if to drive home the point that their agreeing to classify her in this way gives them firm ground on which to stand. The novel's last paragraph then begins: "It kept him before her therefore, taking in — or trying to — what she so wonderfully gave" (*GB* 580). Amerigo could not possibly fathom what Maggie means, so he takes in what he can. James's "trying to" could stand as an emblem for the many partial understandings that filter through the book. It appears here in a spirit of generosity. Maggie is "wonderfully" giving, and Amerigo is trying to take from her as much as he can. As he embraces her (but James's prose is stronger: "close to her, her face kept before him, his hands holding her shoulders, his whole act enclosing her"), he echoes her, " 'See'? I see nothing but *you*" (*GB* 580). It is as if the dense web of discourse simply collapses around the couple embracing. Maggie is the only reality that matters to him now: "And the truth of it had with this force after a moment so strangely lighted his eyes that as for pity and dread of them she buried her own in his breast" (*GB* 580). Amerigo's physical presence, figured here by the strange light in his eyes, speaks a truth so vivid and overwhelming that Maggie must avert her own eyes. This too is a little obscure. Their communication is still proceeding by verbal indirections. But the indirections have at least brought them together and made them secure in each other's presence. Why, James almost seems to ask, would anyone demand more definitive "truth" than that?

What is striking about this conclusion is that even after having removed his heroine's obstacles from the scene and brought her into intimate contact with her husband, James draws his readers' attention to the gaps in their communication, to everything that they haven't said to one another and that, in this last gesture by which Maggie buries her eyes in her husband's breast, they agree to leave unspoken. Isolated at last from the larger social milieu, Maggie and Amerigo still carry the scars from that environment, and so still approach each other with a certain caution. This is not to say that James compromises their happiness. Indeed, what is remarkable is that he still allows them such prospects of happiness. But their happiness has been earned in the difficult arena of their social world, and James's last point is that both have learned to appreciate what that means. If much is left unspoken in this conclusion, it is because both have learned to value something more than dragging the truth out into the open. Maggie and Amerigo conspire to leave some things unspoken and so seal the shared perspective from which their love can at last prosper.

It is the unspokenness in this conclusion that reaffirms James's distinctive drama of transition. By not attempting to spell out the novel's resolution James reinscribes this concluding embrace in the unfolding and open-ended dynamic processes that have all along constituted Maggie's and Adam's experience of each other. The departure of Adam and Charlotte will put these processes on a new footing, but just how Maggie and Amerigo will grow from here is precisely what James refuses to say. The moral lesson of *The Golden Bowl*, very much like that of *The Portrait of a Lady*, is that dynamic processes include our creative responsiveness to them. We summon energy and pitch it, as Dewey would say, in order to take in. For James, this happens not only in the larger dramatic events of life but even in the simplest response to the most minute details of experience. By keeping so much unstated — by actively striving to sustain this quality of unstatedness — James allows for the dynamic play of seemingly endless implication. The remarkable elusiveness of James's late fiction, which so discouraged William as a reader of his brother's fiction, encourages readers to summon energy and pitch it, enacting their own attentive responsiveness to the unfolding dynamic web of relations, both of fiction and of life.

# 6

## Gertrude Stein and the
## Movement of Words

IN "COMPOSITION AS Explanation," Gertrude Stein describes the lag between "entering the modern composition" and becoming "classical," by which she appears simply to mean widely acknowledged: "Those who are creating the modern composition authentically are naturally only of importance when they are dead because by that time the modern composition having become past is classified and the description of it is classical" (*GSW* 1:521). Stein's phrasing suggests a correlation between classification and the classical. Once a working vocabulary has been developed, an audience can assimilate works which had previously seemed ugly or offensive, meaningless or inconsequential. Stein's own writing had been subject to this lag, as the sheer volume of her unpublished (as well as her self-published) work testifies.

Even as modernism was gaining steam, however, Stein's writing continued to resist assimilation.[1] Edmund Wilson set the tone as early as 1931 in his influential *Axel's Castle,* damning Stein with faint, if memorable, praise:

Most of us balk at her soporific rigmaroles, her echolaliac incantations, her half-witted-sounding catalogues of numbers; most of us read her less and less. Yet, remembering especially her early work, we are still always aware of her presence in the background of contemporary literature—and we picture her as the great pyramidal Buddha of Jo Davidson's statue of her, eternally and placidly ruminating the gradual developments of the processes of being, registering the vibrations of a psychological country like some august human seismograph whose charts we haven't the training to read. And whenever we pick up her writings, however unintelligible we may find them, we are aware of a literary personality of unmistakable originality and distinction.[2]

Thus Wilson grants Stein's status as a significant figure of modernism without in the least impelling us to read her work. She is for Wilson, as she continued to be for most readers over the next several decades, both a literary personality and an enigma.

Stein is taken more seriously now, as the steady stream of reprintings and even first printings that have appeared over the past decade suggests.[3] Feminist critics and revisionary scholars of modernism alike have turned to Stein to uncover a largely neglected dimension of modernism, while avant-garde poets have turned to her writing as an exemplary and prescient example of postmodern techniques and concerns.[4] Classification, it is safe to say, is doing its work in transforming Stein from a forbidding enigma into a leading example of what might be called modernist anti-modernism: a proto-postmodern sensibility struggling against modernist aestheticism and pointing the way beyond modernist impasses. Thus Marianne DeKoven describes the "abolition of the censoring authorial ego" that accompanies the "vision of extreme fragmentation, abstraction, non-selectiveness, open-endedness, randomness, flux" that Stein's later writing shares with more recent postmodern texts.[5] This is an apt description of Stein's writing, but these attitudes also have a distinct history in American writing, not only in pragmatism's general embrace of open-ended experience but even more specifically in Emerson's conception of self-reliance as a form of abandonment and William James's fascination with all forms of ecstatic abandonment, the more marginal the better. Selection had always been a key problem in this tradition, one that was frequently resolved by resorting to images and metaphors indicating the immersion of an individuated self into a suffusing dynamic process.

To some extent, this tradition was mediated for Stein by Henry James. It is easy to imagine Stein reading a novel like *The Golden Bowl* and delighting in its reported conversations:

"Well *now*," he smoked, "we see."
"We see."
"I know her better."
"You know her best."
"Oh but naturally!" (*GB* 577)

James's effort to locate the drama of his fiction in the surface of his language, both in reported speech and in narration, struck Stein as a remarkable advance in literary representation.

Indeed, Stein takes the reader closer to the heart of James's accomplishment than any other modernist, even though her reading of James is dense and quirky. Pound, Eliot, and Ford Madox Ford recognized James's relationship to the French prose tradition that was so influential for their own methods, but Stein responded to something different in James: the beginning of an abstract method which would foreground the nonrepresentational dimensions of language. In "What Is English Literature," the first of her 1934–35 *Lectures in America,* she presents James as her own immediate precursor. In her broadly sketched history of English literature, Stein first groups James with Browning, Swinburne, and Meredith, but then distinguishes him from this group by suggesting that "although they did in a way the same thing, his had a future feeling and theirs an ending." "It is very interesting," she elliptically adds (*GSW* 2:221). The native British writers come at the end of a tradition, but can only close it out. Theirs is the tradition Stein describes as "daily island life." The English "had poetry, because everything was shut in there with them and these things birds beasts woods flowers, roses, violets and fishes were all there and as they were all there just telling that they were all there made poetry for any one" (*GSW* 2:219–20). In America, by contrast, the "daily everything was not the daily living and generally speaking there is not a daily everything. They do not live every day. And as they do not live every day they do not have the daily living and so they do not have this as something that they are telling" (*GSW* 2:220). Perhaps this is to say that in America, there is no shared conception of "American life": Americans are too various, and the American continent too vast, to be reduced to anything so blandly homogeneous as "daily living." England's established institutions and traditions provide the stability from within which poets can describe and otherwise invoke England's essential lyrical nature ("flowers, roses, violets," and so on).

In America, by contrast, things are not so thoroughly "connected." American life thrives on its productive engagement with what Stein calls "separation" and "disconnection." American literature, by contrast with British literature, "tells something because that anything is not connected with what would be daily living if they had it" (*GSW* 2:220). These passages recall Stein's description in *The Autobiography of Alice B. Toklas* of her discussion with Bertrand Russell on the relation between "Greek island culture" and English and American culture:

At any rate greek was essentially an island culture, while America needed essentially the culture of a continent which was of necessity latin. This argument fussed Mr. Russell, he became very eloquent. Gertrude Stein then became very earnest and gave a long discourse on the value of greek to the english, aside from its being an island, and the lack of value of greek culture for the americans based upon the psychology of americans as different from the psychology of the english. She grew very eloquent

*Gertrude Stein and the Movement of Words*

on the disembodied abstract quality of the american character and cited examples, mingling automobiles with Emerson, and all proving that they did not need greek, in a way that fussed Russell more and more and kept everybody occupied until everybody went to bed. (*GSW* 1:810–11)

As Russell comments in his *History of Western Philosophy,* Roman culture was marked by a "loss of vigour through the breach with tradition" and by "a more individual and less social ethic." Where the Greeks conceived "virtue" as a relation to the state, the Stoics thought of it as Christians also would, as a relation of the individual soul to God. Once political power passed from the Greeks to the Macedonians and later to the Romans, people "no longer asked: how can men create a good State? They asked instead: how can men be virtuous in a wicked world, or happy in a world of suffering."[6] For Russell, this is a fundamentally apolitical and dispiriting reduction. The Romans would perfect the administration of the state while utterly losing sight of the fundamental meaning of life within that state.

Stein and Russell were obviously talking at cross purposes, though one imagines, at least from Stein's description, that she enjoyed the resulting dissonance rather more than the ever-fussing Russell. The "disembodied abstract quality of Americans" that she describes is the same quality she would soon associate with Henry James's prose. In America, everything is always moving, or perhaps more accurately, everything is always moving everywhere, but in America, that movement becomes a basic principle of life. The "disembodied abstract quality of Americans" is an effect of being subject to this constant movement. One is not known by one's high passions, on the model of Greek character, but rather by one's ability to master the movements of the day, whether in technology (automobiles) or the arts (Emerson). The whole question of "virtue" would have struck Stein as itself too fundamentally Greek and, by extension, British. Stein's interest was in something much more abstract, something that preceded the formulation of virtuous intentions.

As British literature comes to its end, American literature discovers its own motive: "In the meantime Henry James went on." As Stein suggests in "What Is English Literature," James also, like the British, "needed the whole paragraph," but, "and that is the thing to notice, his whole paragraph was detached what it said from what it did, what it was from what it held, and over it all something floated not floated away but just floated, floated up there" (*GSW* 2:222). James's "disembodied abstract quality" is not, Stein insists against his critics, a failure of feeling (the same point on which Pound, Eliot, and Ford had insisted in their own appreciations of James): "Some say that it is repression but no it is not repression it is a lack of connection, of there being no connection with living and daily living because there is none, that makes American writing what it always has been and what it will continue to become" (*GSW* 2:222).[7] America is an open circuit for Stein, a space, as she says in another of her 1934–35 lectures, that is "filled with moving." The effort to convey and extend this moving, to see it as movement and not just as an array of objects that happen to be moving, calls for the methods of disconnection and abstraction Stein associates with James. After James, in this history of English literature, comes Gertrude Stein: "And now, the paragraph having been completely become, it was a moment when I came and I had to do more with the paragraph than ever had been done. So I thought I did. And then I went on to what was the American thing the disconnection and I kept breaking the paragraph down, and everything down to commence again with not connecting with the daily anything and yet to really choose something" (*GSW* 2:222).

As Gertrude Stein read through the New York Edition of James's work in the years of her own most far-reaching experiments in language and form, she recognized in James's peculiar obscurity, and especially in his habit of endlessly delaying and qualifying his subject through the course of a paragraph, a form of abstraction that detached and broke down the continuities of social and cultural life. Of course, Stein drew inspiration from many sources. Critics have documented the influence of the new methods of painting in particular. Cézanne, Picasso, and Matisse probably gave her as many ideas about how she could transform the "composition" of a literary portrait as any other source.[8] Stein was, however, uniquely prepared to absorb the work of these painters. Unlike James, who tried very hard to raise American literature to the level of its British and Continental models, Stein seems always to have thought of herself as bringing America to Europe in order to act as the catalyst to the modernization of literature. In fact, the catalysis works in both directions for each writer, but Stein surely came to Europe uniquely prepared to absorb its atmosphere of artistic and literary experiment.

In "The Gradual Making of *The Making of Americans*," another of the *Lectures in America* she delivered in 1934–35, Stein would insist on the connection between her American background and what she described as the continuous movement of her writing: "I am always trying to tell this thing that a space of time is a natural thing for an American to always have inside them as something in which they are continuously moving. Think of anything, of cowboys, of movies, of detective stories, of anybody who goes anywhere or stays at home and is an American and you will realize that it is something strictly American to conceive a space that is filled with moving, a space of time that is filled always filled with moving" (*GSW* 2:286). Stein's cowboys, movies, and detective stories constitute a virtual iconography of perpetually circulating

American energy. In a similar vein, William Carlos Williams would compare Stein's words to "a crowd at Coney Island, let us say, seen from an airplane." Williams goes on to describe "the modern imperative" of writing as "an alertness not to let go of a possibility of movement in our fearful bedazzlement with some concrete and fixed present. The goal is to keep a beleaguered line of understanding which has movement from breaking down and becoming a hole into which we sink decoratively to rest."[9] Williams not only shares Stein's sense that words should keep on the move, but that theirs is a distinctly American preoccupation. Stein repeatedly resorts to this imagery of movement, as in the passage cited above: "a space that is filled with moving, a space of time that is filled always filled with moving." The oblique repetition here brings us to the crux of Stein's enigma: Stein wants less to clarify a point or drive home a specific idea than to keep the movement — of words, of ideas, of self-awareness — on the go.

In his 1908 book *Abstraction and Empathy,* Wilhelm Worringer linked abstraction in the modern arts to the primitive response to an external world experienced as "an incomprehensible chaos, a meaningless or terrifying confusion of occurrences and sensations." According to Worringer, naturalists could imitate the external world because of the felt "equilibrium between man and the cosmos." The abstractionist, on the other hand, seeks "stability," "harmony," and "a sense of order" by reducing the incomprehensible and unpredictable "appearances of the natural world to a liner-geometric form."[10] Joseph Frank would later draw on Worringer's account as an explanation of spatial form in modern literature. Because "the history of modern culture since the last quarter of the nineteenth century" is dominated by "insecurity, instability, the feeling of loss of control over the meaning and purpose of life amidst the continuing triumphs of science and technics," modern culture was (and presumably remained as Frank wrote in 1945) ripe for nonorganic art.[11]

But Stein would have recognized an impetus toward formal abstraction in Henry James's fictional method as well his brother William's discussions of psychological experience. Stein was an admiring (and admired) student of William James when she attended Harvard Annex from 1893 to 1897 (during which time it was renamed Radcliffe). She had read James's *Principles of Psychology* as a freshman in Hugo Münsterberg's course in psychology. As a junior, she managed to gain admission to James's advanced seminar on psychology, a course in "Consciousness, Knowledge, the Ego, the Relation of Mind and Body, etc."[12] It was in this course that she first teamed with Leon Solomons to conduct the research on habits of attention that led to two papers which appeared in the *Harvard Psychological Review*.[13] As a number of critics have noted, Stein would have first discovered the relation between

*The Poetics of Transition*

perception and abstraction as a student of William James, and without the added burden of modernist despair so central to Worringer's formulations.[14] James's comments on perception in *The Principles of Psychology*, which Stein had read even before she studied with James, carefully expose the artifice of naturalistic vision. James's point is made near the beginning of his chapter on the perception of things: "Infants must go through a long education of the eye and ear before they can perceive the realities which adults perceive. *Every perception is an acquired perception*" (*PP* 2:724). What we see depends on our training in how to see. We learn to recognize what are in effect distortions and to see them as natural representations. One of James's key points in this chapter is that pure sensations cannot be separated from the contextual current that gives them form. He offers the French phrase *Pas de lieu Rhône que nous* in order to point out that one could read the phrase over repeatedly (the reader might want to do so before finishing this sentence) without realizing that its sounds are identical to those in the English sentence, "Paddle your own canoe." "As we seize the English meaning," James comments, "the sound itself appears to change" (*PP* 2:726).[15] The "associative irradiations" of the sounds are temporarily inhibited, but once that inhibition is relaxed, the interpretation "suddenly occurs," an experience often accompanied by "a change in the very *feel* of the word." Words will acquire very different meanings as the contexts in which they are viewed or heard shift.

James proceeds to recommend a word experiment which it is hard to imagine Gertrude Stein having been able to resist:

> This is probably the reason why, if we look at an isolated printed word and repeat it long enough, it ends by assuming an entirely unnatural aspect. Let the reader try this with any word on this page. He will soon begin to wonder if it can possibly be the word he has been using all his life with that meaning. It stares at him from the paper like a glass eye, with no speculation in it. Its body is indeed there, but its soul is fled. It is reduced, by this new way of attending to it, to its sensational nudity. We never before attended to it in this way, but habitually got it clad with its meaning the moment we caught sight of it, and rapidly passed from it to the other words of the phrase. We apprehended it, in short, with a cloud of associates, and thus perceiving it, we felt it quite otherwise than as we feel it now divested and alone. (*PP* 2:726–27)

What James describes here could be thought of as an analytic exercise in the abstraction of language. By isolating a word on an otherwise blank sheet of paper and repeating it for a minute or two, the word is emptied of all secondary association. It is reduced to a bare sensation. In James's phrase, it has lost

*Gertrude Stein and the Movement of Words*

its "speculation," a term that plays both on the figure of the glass eye (Latin *speculari*, to spy out, examine) and on the assumption that words mirror the world (Latin *specularis*, of a mirror). One can imagine Stein arranging words and phrases on separate sheets, then beginning to shape them into repeating forms. In other words, one can imagine Stein beginning to develop her distinctive style under the impetus of such abstract word experiments.

Such fascinations further suggest why Stein was the ideal reader of Henry James's fiction. One can see even from this description that, for William, the word experiment is something that takes place in a vacuum. It is an interesting experiment, but James's larger point is that an engaged mind does not operate in a vacuum. As James summarizes the point, "*whilst part of what we perceive comes through our senses from the object before us, another part* (and it may be the larger part) *always comes* (in Lazarus's phrase) *out of our own head*" (PP 2:747). That is to say, it is one thing to experiment with the bare sensation caused by the visual or acoustic impression of a word and quite another actually to *use* language. The engaged mind always provides a context. Hence William's impatience with Henry's prose style, with its lingering appreciation of words and phrases that so often seem to be abstracted from their contextual streams. And hence Stein's instinctive understanding of Henry's prose. But where Henry James continued to rely on naturalistic techniques which he would deform from within, Stein would attempt to compose her representations without recourse to those techniques. Stein is always insistent that she is writing "portraits," describing "objects," or composing "landscapes," but she refuses to rely on ordinary conventions of portraiture or description. She follows William James in recognizing that words acquire meaning from the mind's stock of associations, but she refuses to allow habitual patterns of association to obscure the multiple associative contexts of words.

Stein's writing, especially those aspects of it which have seemed so enigmatic, is designed to resist the repose that would put an end to the continuous movement of perception and understanding. Her style develops, and endlessly changes over time, from the conviction that perception and conception are essentially dynamic processes that we renew and transform in every new moment of language use. The continuous present which she seeks to represent is the dynamic moment of this renewal and transformation. Stein's words are always in transition, foregrounding the processes that make and remake meanings. In his chapter "The Perception of 'Things'" in *The Principles of Psychology*, William James describes the "everlasting struggle in every mind between the tendency to keep unchanged, and the tendency to renovate, its ideas" (PP 2:753). Echoing Emerson, he comments, "Our education is a ceaseless compromise between the conservative and the progressive factors" (*PP* 2:753). Stein must have been energized by James's insistence that "most of us grow more and more enslaved to the stock conceptions with which we have once become familiar, and less and less capable of assimilating impressions in any but the old ways" (*PP* 2:754). Genius, James comments, "means little more than the faculty of perceiving in an unhabitual way" (*PP* 2:754). Thus James describes a painting viewed upside down: "We lose much of its meaning, but, to compensate for the loss, we feel more freshly the value of the mere tints and shadings, and become aware of any lack of purely sensible harmony or balance which they may show" (*PP* 2:727). Stein's own literary genius would cultivate these unhabitual shocks of perception, seeking to renovate meaning by multiplying and relocating it.

Stein probably found another stimulus to her abstract literary practice in "The Perception of Time," the chapter of *The Principles* in which James analyzes the role of repetition in the perception of "the sensible present" or what he also calls "specious duration." "In short," James comments, "empty our minds as we may, some form of *changing process* remains for us to feel, and cannot be expelled" (*PP* 1:584). The changing process is experienced as the rhythmic repetition of our "heart-beats, our breathing, the pulses of our attention, fragments of words or sentences that pass through our imagination" (*PP* 1:584). There is no purely present time that is not constituted from our awareness of these changing processes. Even "empty time" is an experience of repetition: "We say 'now! now! now!' or we count 'more! more! more!' as we feel it bud" (*PP* 1:585). To hear a steady sound, we "*take it in* in discrete pulses of recognition, calling it successively 'the same! the same! the same!'" (*PP* 1:585–86). Interestingly, for James, the sense of duration is "specious" since it is only an effect of such repetitions. James distinguishes specious duration from symbolic time, which includes clock and calendar time. Symbolic time is not experienced as duration. While the feeling of immediate duration is real, it is a synthetic product of these rhythmic repetitions. Indeed, James recognizes repetition and substitution as the basic mechanism of our awareness of time, space, and other conceptual categories. We could not be aware of our thoughts if we were not aware of them as repetitions or substitutions of previous thoughts: "As a rule we are fully aware that we have thought before of the thing we think of now. The continuity and permanency of the topic is of the essence of our intellection. We recognize the old problems, and the old solutions; and we go on to alter and improve and substitute one predicate for another without ever letting the subject change" (*PP* 1:454). All thought and awareness are the result of these transitional processes of repetition and substitution.

*Gertrude Stein and the Movement of Words*

Lisa Ruddick has demonstrated the ways in which Stein incorporates William James's theory of "habits of attention" or conscious selectivity in her representation in "Melanctha" of characters who are "fluid" and "solid": characters who remain fluidly receptive to the multitudinous and random stimuli that come to us from the world and others who block off such experience by filtering everything through the categories and available terms that organize and weed out the excess of stimuli.[16] As Ruddick points out, language is, in this regard, viewed by James as a positive obstruction to experience that is "fresh and alive to fact." To recall the previous discussion of James's metaphorics of transition, language "works against our perception of the truth" that meaning is always relational and that our ideas serve not as ends-in-themselves but rather as transitions to other ideas. Language, James writes, "almost refuses to lend itself to any other use" than "recognizing the existence of the substantive parts alone" (*PP* 1:234, 1:238). James's "almost" suggests that language can compensate for its habit of encouraging us to conceptualize our thought as a static series of nouns. He would counter this propensity of language by emphasizing those aspects of language that exceed conceptual meaning: conjunctions and prepositions, adverbial phrases, inflections of voice indicating finely nuanced shades of meaning.

Stein was influenced not only by James's general conception of the stream of thought and habits of attention, but also by his conception of the sensible present and the role of repetition and substitution in our perception of changing processes. By recognizing repetition and substitution within patterns of language, we perceive the flow of time. The "constant recurring and beginning" to which Stein refers in "Composition as Explanation" marks Stein's first attempt to foreground the movement of words within patterns of repetition in her writing. To recall the passage cited at the outset of this chapter, Stein uses repetition and substitution to make movement visible or audible without the relatively stable block against which that movement is classically perceived. It is in this sense that "Melanctha" constituted, in Stein's words, "the first definite step away from the nineteenth century and into the twentieth century in literature" (*GSW* 1:714).

"Melanctha" also dramatizes the conflict between static and dynamic conceptions of language use as one between two psychological types, characters with different conceptions of love, understanding, and communication. Critics have often noted Stein's early interest, dating from her years at Radcliffe, in psychological types. It is obvious that characters like "The Good Anna" and "The Gentle Lena" were conceived as such types. Stein described *The Making of Americans* as an effort to "really describe every kind of human being that ever was or is or would be living" (*GSW* 2:274). Eventually, she even "began to make charts of all the people I had ever known or seen, or met or remembered" (*GSW* 2:273), a sign of a certain scientific pretension in Stein's conception of her writing that has been often noted.

Richard Bridgman reaches the logical conclusion when he writes in the context of "Melanctha" that Stein's sentences seek "to stabilize a chaotic world by progressively elevating particular cases of isolation and estrangement to more general categories. Stated at a sufficiently high level of abstraction, individual problems appear to become universal dicta." [17] The opposition here between a chaotic world and a stabilizing art is, of course, familiar. The conflict in "Melanctha" between Jefferson Campbell and Melanctha Herbert is, in this analysis, a version of the universal conflict between the analytical and the spontaneous, between reason and passion, mind and body. The narrator repeatedly informs us that Jeff favors "living regular" and opposes the "excitements" that his people—inner-city African Americans around the turn of the century—appear to favor: "Dr. Campbell said he wanted to work so that he could understand what troubled people, and not to just have excitements, and he believed you ought to love your father and your mother and to be regular in all your life, and not to be always wanting new things and excitements, and to always know where you were, and what you wanted, and to always tell everything just as you meant it" (*GSW* 1:148). "New things" and "excitements" represent experience that overflows the borders not only of certain normative ethical standards but of established conceptual and linguistic patterns as well. "Living regular," for Jeff, means fulfilling preestablished expectations for his own and other Black Americans' fate.[18] Melanctha, whose most significant characteristic in the early part of the story is what Stein calls her "wandering," would appear to be one of those against whom Jeff defines himself. She is drawn to spontaneous and often suggestively sexual excitements and finds it hard to achieve the more measured pleasures of responsible behavior that she claims to desire: "Melanctha Herbert was always seeking peace and quiet, and she could always only find new ways to get excited" (*GSW* 1:129). Or, as Stein subtly shifts the emphasis a page later, "and all her life for herself poor Melanctha could only find new ways to be in trouble" (*GSW* 1:130).[19]

Jeff's and Melanctha's mutual definitions of love further reflect these styles of being. In one definition, Jeff embeds his love for Melanctha in a larger narrative that serves to ground his love in his social commitment: "Why sure no, yes I do Miss Melanctha," he begins in reply to Melanctha's claim that he does not believe "it's right to love anybody": "I certainly do believe strong in loving, and in being good to everybody, and trying to understand what they all need, to help them" (GSW 1:152). This effort to understand and help others is reflected in Jeff's repeatedly staged desire to help people overcome what he sees as their laziness and recklessness, his effort to advance the position of Black Americans in society. When he comes to define love more specifically, his definition emphasizes not passion but, again, what makes love socially useful and good: "One kind of loving seems to me, is like one has a good quiet feeling in a family when one does his work, and is always living good and being regular, and then the other way of loving is just like having it like any animal that's low in the streets together, and that don't seem to me very good Miss Melanctha" (GSW 1:153). Jeff's conception of proper love here places little emphasis on the person who is loved. Rather, it focuses on how love is good — socially acceptable and useful — for the person in love. His example of a negative kind of love underscores his discomfort with any passion not being directed to higher, more socially useful ideals.

Melanctha's conception of love is altogether different. In response to Jeff's claim to believe in loving, in being good to everybody, and in trying to understand and help people, Melanctha comments, "Oh I know all about that way of doing Dr. Campbell, but that certainly ain't the kind of love I mean when I am talking. I mean real, strong, hot love Dr. Campbell, that makes you do anything for somebody that loves you" (GSW 1:152). Melanctha is less interested in what good her love might do for her people than in how it makes her and the person she loves feel. This is not love in the service of higher principles or social utility. Indeed, doing "anything for somebody that loves you" implies a distinctly antisocial disregard for conventional moralities or practices.

Yet as the passages I have quoted indicate, Stein's language always does a great deal more than establish the patterns by which we come to recognize these types. Even as Stein constructs a variety of psychological types and sends them spinning through a naturalist downward spiral that ends in Melanctha's inevitable death, the telling of the story constantly interferes with the sense one would make of it. Her description in "The Gradual Making of *The Making of Americans*" of her writing during this period reveals this conflict between the set patterns characteristic of psychological types and the dynamic movement of her characters' thoughts and words:

> I then began again to think about the bottom nature in people, I began to get enormously interested in hearing how everybody said the same thing over and over again with infinite variations but over and over again until finally if you listened with great intensity you could hear it rise and fall and tell all that that there was inside them, not so much by the actual

words they said or the thoughts they had but the movement of their thoughts and words endlessly the same and endlessly different. (*GSW* 2:272)

Like James, Stein is more interested here in the movement of people's thoughts and words than in the isolated thoughts and words themselves. Her assumption that the rhythm of rising and falling words reveals a "bottom nature" reflects her early conception of character. In *Everybody's Autobiography*, Stein suggests that this conception of character came to her as she was involved in the psychological research she conducted with Leon Solomons in Cambridge. She describes herself as being interested at that time in the way their subjects "had their nature in them" and the way their "bottom nature" was "mixed up with the other natures in them."[20] One's "bottom nature," then, is in some way qualified or modified by the "other natures" that also go into the constitution of the self. In "Melanctha," important transformations of self are frequently registered, placing the emphasis on the shifting rhythms of selfhood that are reflected in the shifting rhythms of the language of the story.

It is significant that Stein describes these linguistic effects as a result of "hearing how everybody said the same thing over and over again," of hearing their rhythms rise and fall. Spatial understanding abstracts a visually conceived paradigm, like a chart, from the flow of experience; temporal attentiveness registers the subtle shadings and nuances that can be associated with vocal intonation and emphasis. Stein had worked with charts in writing *The Making of Americans,* trying, as she put it, to "describe every individual man and woman who ever was or is or will be living."[21] Though Stein clearly has a spatial conception of what might be called the possibilities of character, her representation of any particular character is decidedly temporal. In a story like "Melanctha," the reader is invited to overhear the unfolding rhythms of character. Indeed, character is a function of these unfolding rhythms, dense repetitions and subtle variations that occur in time. Stein effectively magnifies the process James had described in his chapters on the perception of time and space and on conception, emphasizing the way in which meaning turns on repetitions and substitutions of terms and ideas as they unfold in time.

Stein's use of repetition in "Melanctha" underscores this dynamic quality in the experience of language. Stein extends the meaning of James's claim in the "Conception" chapter of *The Principles of Psychology* that "nothing can be conceived twice over without being conceived in entirely different states of mind" (*PP* 1:453). It is as if she refuses ever to take for granted what has already been said in the story, as if no important details or character traits can possibly be established which could then, without further mention, contribute to the coherent sense the reader might form of an action being presently described. Nothing is ever said just once because consciousness never registers anything in isolation. It works by slow and steady accretion, by perpetual reference and by the constant transformation of other moments. In Stein's writing, patterns of meaning never quite coalesce. Meanings can only be established by constant repetition and transition. Every moment in Stein's writing is a new beginning, a continuation and transformation of the last moment, a movement forward into the next moment. By foregrounding this continuous present, Stein breaks the spell of naturalistic illusion, restaging the repetitions and transitions obscured by such illusion.

Stein's description of the breakdown of Melanctha's relationship with Jane Harden is an example of this "constant recurring and beginning" as it occurs locally, within a short passage: "Then slowly, between them, it began to be all different. Slowly now between them, it was Melanctha Herbert, who was stronger. Slowly now they began to drift apart from one another" (*GSW* 1:140). The repetitions of "slowly," "between them," and "began" reinforce the sense of an event unfolding in time. Stein offers three separate beginnings here, three moments in the slow unfolding time of the event of Jane and Melanctha's breakup. The repetition draws out the constant new beginning that *is* every new moment of experience. The words here continue to signify meanings, but their repetition suggests something more than just what the words mean: the temporal, rhythmic unfolding of conscious experience.

The statement that "it was Melanctha Herbert, who was stronger" also enacts another, more extended repetition which looks back to the duration of Melanctha's relationship with Jane Harden. "Strength" had been one of Jane's defining traits, one that Melanctha finally learns from her. Jane "had power and she liked to use it" (*GSW* 1:139); Melanctha could feel Jane's "strength and the power of her affection" (*GSW* 1:139). And importantly, "In the first year, between Jane Harden and Melanctha Herbert, Jane had been much the stronger" (*GSW* 1:139–40). Sometimes, the lesson Jane taught "came almost too strong for Melanctha" (*GSW* 1:140). Still, significantly, "somehow she always managed to endure it and so slowly, but always with increasing strength and feeling, Melanctha began to really understand" (*GSW* 1:140). Then comes the crucial reversal that falls in the passage cited above: "Slowly now between them, it was Melanctha Herbert, who was stronger." The terms continue to be repeated even after this turn, though with the now reversed associations. The meaning of *strength* throughout the story, and of *power* (which is further nuanced by recalling the important association of *power*, earlier in the story, with Melanctha's father), is largely a function of its relation to its many appearances elsewhere in the story. The constant repetition of such terms denaturalizes them, underscoring the way in which their meaning is a function of an abstract design.

What makes "Melanctha" such an astonishing book to read is the way in which Stein's concern to draw out these dynamic, nonreferential qualities of language is integrated into the central dramatic conflict of the story. The struggle between Melanctha and Jeff is not only one between spontaneity and reason, but also between antithetical conceptions of language and communication. Jeff is frequently disturbed by his sense that he and Melanctha are failing to communicate. He says to Melanctha at one point, "I certainly do wonder, if we know very right, you and me, what each other is really thinking. I certainly do wonder, Miss Melanctha, if we know at all really what each other means by what we are always saying" (*GSW* 1:157). The repetitions here function much like those described above. It is the painful, unfolding experience of doubting, not the static fact of his doubt, that Stein thus conveys to her reader, something inseparable from his shifting vocal inflections and tones. Jeff's uncertainty about what each of them means by what each says soon resurfaces as an uncertainty about what Melanctha really is: "He did not know very well just what Melanctha meant by what she was always saying to him. He did not know very well how much he really knew about Melanctha Herbert" (*GSW* 1:157–58). Jeff suffers from a variety of epistemological anxiety: he does not know how or how much he knows, and the condition troubles him. This leads to the wavering he experiences in the relationship, the constant return of his feeling that perhaps, as he puts it, Melanctha is "really just a bad one" (*GSW* 1:180), that he has simply forgotten "about what was the right way for me, to live regular and all the colored people" (*GSW* 1:180). "The right way," "to live regular," and "all the colored people" all refer back to Jeff's characteristic thought and speech before he met Melanctha. Jeff repeatedly reverts in this way to familiar word-motifs in order to cope with his anxiety. He even doubts that he has ever *known* Melanctha: "He did not know the least bit about Melanctha. He did not know what it was right that he should do about it. He wondered if it was just a little play that they were doing. If it was a play he did not want to go on playing, but if it was really that he was not very understanding, and that with Melanctha Herbert he could learn to really understand, then he was very certain he did not want to be a coward" (*GSW* 1:158). Jeff distinguishes a false from a real kind of love— "playing" from "really understanding"—and, like any good skeptic, questions whether he can distinguish one from the other. When he determines that Melanctha's love must be "playing" (a determination which does not last for long), he decides he "certainly will stop fooling, and begin to go on with my thinking about my work and what's the matter with people like 'Mis'

Herbert [Melanctha's ailing mother]." Taking a book out from his pocket, he begins "with some hard scientific reading" (*GSW* 1:158–59). Thus epistemological skepticism paves the way for empirical science, the facts that defend against latent and encroaching doubts. Jeff proposes to eliminate his anxiety about what Melanctha "is," about whether or not their love is "real" and they are "understanding" one another, by returning to his scientific studies and his social program for good living.

Melanctha is quick to criticize Jeff's need for certain knowledge: "I certainly never did see no man like you, Jeff. You always wanting to have it all clear out in words always, what everybody is always feeling. I certainly don't see a reason, why I should always be explaining to you what I mean by what I am just saying" (*GSW* 1:190). Whereas Jeff is constantly troubled by the gap between words and meanings and seeks to repair it by repeating familiar language, Melanctha refuses to be held to any model of correspondence. Feeling cannot necessarily be summed up in words, and she does not consider explaining the meaning of what is said conducive to understanding. Melanctha immediately recognizes that for all his talk about knowledge and understanding, Jeff "really was never knowing about anybody and certainly not being really very understanding" (*GSW* 1:154). She explains this by pointing to his reliance on a familiar word-motif and his fear of losing its security: "It certainly is all Dr. Campbell because you is so afraid you will be losing being good so easy, and it certainly do seem to me Dr. Campbell that it certainly don't amount to very much that kind of goodness" (*GSW* 1:154). To Melanctha, Jeff's speeches about "being good," his efforts to define the good conceptually and to hold himself to his definition, end by constraining experience. Melanctha recognizes the way in which fear of the unknown — and here it is quite distinctly the unknown that resides at the center of their love — forces Jeff to retreat into a readily available rhetoric of moral and intellectual commitment that effectively limits the range of his possible experience in the name of an abstract good. In short, Jeff's reliance on familiar ways of using words determines his world and his self in advance of further experience, whereas Melanctha's resistance to available language keeps her open to fresh discoveries of world and self.

Jeff's understanding, always abstractly intellectual, is related to his sense of the good as something that one arrives at by reason, whereas for Melanctha understanding always has a physical dimension, a result of intense interpersonal, even sexual knowledge. For Melanctha, the good remains tied to what is immediately, rather than abstractly, useful. The ambiguity of the term *understanding* is crucial to the story. "Understanding," "real understanding," "to really understand," "being really very understanding": these few examples, taken just from passages already cited, demonstrate how words get mobilized, with constantly changing inflections, as they recur throughout the story. The same is true of such terms as *strength* and *power*. The deceptively simple words and phrases that characterize Stein's style are made to bear the intense emotion and even intellectual weight that is largely the product of *how* they are used. Words and phrases are differently inflected as they fall into different patterns of speech, into different clusters of terms and streams of feeling. They convey the vague but powerfully felt rhythms of feeling that the story is "about." To represent the "continuous present" is to be always registering the constant variations of these rhythms.

These rhythmic disjunctions are perhaps most potently reflected in the debate on how Melanctha and Jeff each "remembers." Each suggests that a distinct style of remembering in the other is related to a flawed mode of loving. Thus Jeff describes Melanctha:

> You certainly Melanctha, you ain't got down deep loyal feeling, true inside you, and when you ain't just that moment quick with feeling, then you certainly ain't ever got anything more there to keep you. You see Melanctha, it certainly is this way with you, it is, that you ain't ever got any way to remember right what you been doing, or anybody else that has been feeling with you. You certainly Melanctha, never can remember right, when it comes what you have done and what you think happens to you. (*GSW* 1:197)

To which Melanctha replies:

> It certainly is all easy for you Jeff Campbell to be talking. You remember right, because you don't remember nothing till you get home with your thinking everything all over, but I certainly don't think much ever of that kind of way of remembering right, Jeff Campbell. I certainly do call it remembering right Jeff Campbell, to remember right just when it happens to you, so you have a right kind of feeling not to act the way you always been doing to me, and then you go home Jeff Campbell, and you begin with your thinking, and then it certainly is very easy for you to be good and forgiving with it. . . . No, Jeff Campbell, its real feeling every moment when its needed, that certainly does seem to me like real remembering. (*GSW* 1:197–98)

Are Melanctha and Jeff "communicating" here? Many of their words are the same: "certainly," "feeling," "right," "remembering," "remembering right." There is enough overlap between these speeches to indicate some shared ground of discourse. But surely these passages suggest more emphatically a slippage of meanings. Remembering right, for Jeff, is a process of recalling precisely what has happened, a process he considers rational and objective. Because she demands moments "quick with feeling," Melanctha is impatient with the intellectual reflectiveness necessary to bring about such objectivity. Accordingly, Melanctha counters by wrenching Jeff's phrase from its rationalist context: remembering right is "to remember right just when it happens to you," which Melanctha believes Jeff incapable of doing. This seems to be something other than memory altogether. Melanctha's "remembering" is geared to the dynamic moment of mental activity, not to some distant moment recalled by it.

Not only do Jeff and Melanctha take and inflect "remembering" differently, but even Jeff's qualifying adjective—"to remember *right*"—is differently inflected in Melanctha's response, where "right" ceases to signify an objectively correct memory and suggests as well, perhaps even instead, the precise instant when experience occurs: "right just when it happens to you." While the two versions of "remembering right" can be taken to suggest two personality types in conflict, Stein is clearly as interested in the way in which the same patently vague phrase is drawn into antithetical streams of discourse and consciousness. The real thrill of these passages, and the source of the disturbing gap between Melanctha and Jeff, is in this interplay of varying inflections.

A dialectic of thrill and disturbance is conveyed every time Melanctha and Jeff—or Melanctha and Jane Harden, Melanctha and Rose Johnson, Melanctha and Jem Richards—come together for a time and then break away from one another in rising and falling cycles that constitute the action of the story until Melanctha dies. During a long walk, Melanctha and Jeff achieve an apex of harmony which Stein underscores by repeating and varying earlier word-motifs like "understanding," "feeling," "strength," and "thinking things out in words":

> More and more every day now they seemed to know more really, what it was each other one was always feeling. More and more now every day Jeff found in himself, he felt more trusting. More and more every day now, he did not think anything in words about what he was always doing. Every day now more and more Melanctha would let out to Jeff her real, strong feeling.
>
> One day there had been much joy between them, more than they ever yet had had with their new feeling. All the day they had lost themselves in warm wandering. Now they were lying there and resting, with a green, bright, light-flecked world around them. (*GSW* 1:177)

*The Poetics of Transition*

Such is the ecstasy to which Melanctha and Jeff are sometimes allowed access. Stein builds the ecstasy up slowly by shifting around phrases like "more and more," "every day now," "always feeling," "always doing," and releases it in the climactic paragraph that abruptly begins, "One day . . ." The image of the two of them having "lost themselves in warm wandering" obliquely captures the sense of discovering their connection with each other and with their world in a moment of mutual and vaguely sexual abandonment.

Yet this state of grace is no sooner established than it is undermined:

> What was it that now really happened to them? What was it that Melanctha did, that made everything get all ugly for them? What was it that Melanctha felt then, that made Jeff remember all the feeling he had had in him when Jane Harden told him how Melanctha had learned to be so very understanding? Jeff did not know how it was that it had happened to him. It was all green, and warm, and very lovely to him, and now Melanctha somehow had made it all so ugly for him. What was it Melanctha was now doing with him? What was it he used to be thinking was the right way for him and all the colored people to be always trying to make it right, the way they should be always living? Why was Melanctha Herbert now all so ugly for him? (*GSW* 1:177–78)

The repetitive questions—"What was it?" "What was it?" "What was it?", followed by two declarative sentences, then "What was it," "What was it?" "Why?"—pointedly deflate the unexpected ecstasy of the previous passage. The transition is overwhelming and sharp, focused mid-paragraph on a bare comma and coordinating conjunction that interrupt a lush, bouncing rhythm: "It was all green, and warm, and very lovely to him, and now Melanctha somehow had made it all so ugly for him." Here is Stein's life in the transitions, the emphatic, even shocking movement from a past to a new state. The suddenness of the turn is underscored again at the end of the following paragraph when Stein writes, "He sort of turned away then, and threw Melanctha from him" (*GSW* 1:178). "Melanctha" is, in all the interpersonal relations it represents, a story of such turnings, of the rise and fall of abruptly alternating moments of connection and separation, ecstasy and loss. The rhythms point to nothing universal short of constant change: the inevitable transformation of every connection into a fissure and every fissure into the impulse to achieve some new connection.

In "Melanctha," people flow together and then flow apart, just as the words used to describe them flow in given patterns of association only to be crossed into different streams of association, forming new, always varying patterns.

*Gertrude Stein and the Movement of Words*

Stein is responsive to the moment like other modernists, but her sense of the moment is unlike anyone else's. Every moment, for Stein, is the site of a new transition; every word, every time it is spoken, is the agent of that transition. To some extent, Stein utilizes naturalistic techniques in "Melanctha," even offering something like psychological realism in her juxtaposition of Melanctha with other characters like Jeff Campbell and Jane Harden. At the same time, however, she undoes such naturalistic illusions of plot and character by repeating and subtly varying words and patterns of words. Stein's characters in "Melanctha" are as much abstract groupings of words as they are personalities.

Henry James was among the first to draw this abstract dimension of language to the foreground of his fiction. Many readers concluded that he was simply a cold writer, when in fact nothing interested him more than the ways in which felt emotion became entangled with abstract designs of words, in literature as in life. At the same time, William James had analyzed the mechanism by which mind makes sense out of its immediate flux, even pointing the way to word experiments that would foreground the irreducibly senseless component of that process. Stein inherited these concerns and took them to a new extreme. Though her style would constantly develop in new directions, it is marked throughout by an effort to create a composition of words abstract in design and resistant to the illusions and clichés of narrative and lyric conventions. Like Henry James, Stein always seeks to achieve a balance between the emotional appeal of her language and the abstract form in which it is composed. Having mastered the method in "Melanctha," she returned to *The Making of Americans* and attempted to fulfill her dream of recording every possible type of person. The emphasis, however, on a universal system of types is countered by the effort to capture different rhythms of feeling as they are embodied in constantly varying verbal arrangements.

In her portraits of the early 1910s, Stein would break even more thoroughly with naturalistic representational techniques, offering only the most reduced and oblique references to personality and action and relying even more thoroughly on the careful repetition and variation of words and phrases. These portraits, however abstract, convey depths of character without relying on conventional methods of representing a character's innermost thoughts or psychological conflicts. Not long after writing the portraits, Stein would also begin to represent objects and what she still later called "landscapes," seeking to render verbal arrangements that would evoke the object or landscape without relying on habitual patterns of perception or description. It is hard to imagine a more complete rejection of the standard repertoire of representational strategies. Stein's prose still refers to objects and feelings in the world, but even as one looks "through" her words to their referents, one is forced to look "at" them, teasing out acoustic echoes, playful ambiguities, and dimly evoked associations.

One way to think of these verbal arrangements is as found phrases, something like the found objects that artists like Marcel Duchamp made famous. In reading an apparently nonsensical description in *A Long Gay Book* or *Tender Buttons,* one recognizes and even comprehends snippets, though it is often hard to piece the snippets together into a coherent whole. Consider even a brief passage from *A Long Gay Book:* "Carpet sweeping is so timely and a comb would be useful if there was poverty." [22] Phrases like "is so timely," "would be useful," and "if there was" are the common currency of linguistic expression. What is unusual here is simply the way in which the phrases are strung together. The juxtaposition of "carpet sweeping" and "comb," both instruments of cleaning or grooming traditionally associated with women, may be significant, though the sentence hardly imposes that association or any particular meaning arising from it. Stein's sentence teases the reader with possibilities of sense, while at the same time it challenges our habits of sense-making. We are meant to see (or hear) the unusual combinations and juxtapositions, not just to see through them to some obvious coherent meaning. Reading this sentence, however, one is faced not with sheer nonsense, as if Stein were emptying language of any potential meaning, but rather with a proliferation of possible meanings. By drawing attention to the seams within the sentence, Stein's language stages the transitional movements of words that constitute the endless activity of meaning-making.

Perhaps another clue to Stein's method in a passage like this can be found in James's description in *The Principles of Psychology* of his increasing awareness of fugitive thoughts: "Many years ago, after reading Maury's book, *Le Sommeil et les rêves,* I began for the first time to observe those ideas which faintly flit through the mind at all times, words, visions, etc., disconnected with the main stream of thought, but discernible to an attention on the watch for them" (*PP* 2:729). These fleeting glimpses "can often be explained by subtle links of association, often not at all" (*PP* 2:729). Here again, James's model of the stream of thought foregrounds those aspects of thought that exceed or even challenge the "main stream of thought." The difference in the example from Stein's experimental prose is that there is no longer any discernible main stream of thought. The actual model here remains James's single word, abstracted from all context and repeated ad nauseam. The word is voided of its context. It is, in James's phrase, reduced to its "sensational nudity." So too Stein's words here are reduced (almost) to their sensational nudity. Stein exposes naturalistic illusion in order to intensify the reader's awareness of the

*Gertrude Stein and the Movement of Words*

multiple implications and connotations of words. By attending to the resonant fringe of language in this way, she foregrounds the role of association, repetition, and substitution in even the most rational and normative thought processes.

It is hard to imagine a more rigorous or inventive refusal of naturalistic illusion. Indeed, one is tempted to say that it is, by now, classic: now that we can begin to classify it, we can see and hear it for the first time, and in ways that are relatively cogent. But to understand this writing too well would be to miss its meaning, or perhaps more accurately, to miss the way in which it stages the production of meaning. There is much in Stein's writing that, to echo Melanctha, will not come "clear out in words always." The challenge of reading Stein's poetry and prose is in attending to the movements of words as they enact the transitional processes that make meanings.

# 7

## Wallace Stevens and the Pragmatist Imagination

THE EMPHASIS ON process and relationality within the unfolding instant of perception forms a background to American literary modernists' efforts to represent the moment of transition between an available stock of familiar meanings and an emerging novelty that can potentially transform that stock of meanings. To recall William James's definition of genius in *The Principles of Psychology*, the literary modernists set out to cultivate habits of perceiving in unhabitual ways. While for Henry James this meant an interest in characters of heightened perceptiveness and a method of narration that integrated an excess of perception into the texture of even the most mundane observation or description, for Stein it meant increasingly detaching these processes from characters as well as from any authoritative narrational sensibility in order to cultivate transition as an abstract linguistic process.

For Wallace Stevens, poetry serves to refine and extend powers of perception. It is not, however, conceived in opposition to mere prose or to more explicitly practical or engaged forms of communication. Poetry is rather a means of cultivating possible forms of engaged experience as well as a more richly and diversely enlightened understanding of that experience. Poetry's vital integration of imagination and reality leads Stevens to embrace fiction, or poetic distortion, as an aspect of true understanding. This essential feature of Stevens's pragmatist imagination is reflected in his defense of metaphor, as in these lines from "Someone Puts a Pineapple Together":

> He had not to be told

> Of the incredible subjects of poetry.
> He was willing they should remain incredible,
> Because the incredible, also, has its truth,

Its tuft of emerald that is real, for all
Its invitation to false metaphor.
The incredible gave him a purpose to believe.
(*CPP* 695)

Stevens's willingness that the "incredible subjects of poetry" should "remain incredible" reflects his conviction that even in a modern, skeptical age we depend on habits of knowledge and belief that exceed rational intelligence. He acknowledges that the "tuft of emerald"—a characteristic Stevensian figure for some irresistibly attractive object or belief—invites "false metaphor," or a distorted understanding of things. Yet he remains willing to engage that metaphor for the sake of the incredible and the "purpose to believe" it establishes.

Like William James, who in "The Will to Believe" defended the right to adopt beliefs that may in the end prove false, Stevens considers this "purpose to believe" every bit as important to our cognitive life as the methods of rational investigation that aim at eliminating demonstrably false beliefs. What is unusual in Stevens's formulation is his refusal to separate rational and pre-rational processes. The incredible, which "also, has its truth," works together with the credible, even determining the latter's possibility. The incredible does not contradict belief or the will to believe, but instead generates a viable "purpose to believe." Stevens offers a gloss on these lines in his "Adagia," the epigrams he collected in a notebook: "The relation of art to life is of the first importance especially in a skeptical age since, in the absence of a belief in God, the mind turns to its own creations and examines them, not alone from the aesthetic point of view, but for what they reveal, for what they validate and invalidate, for the support they give" (*OP* 186). The "tuft of emerald" is real not because it corresponds to anything in the world, which in a narrow sense it does not, but because of what it reveals and makes possible in this broader sense.

This mingling of the credible and the incredible is also the source of Stevens's resistance, in his 1948 essay "Imagination as Value," to what he calls the "deliberate exploits of the abnormal" in Rimbaud and Kafka: "It is natural for us to identify the imagination with those that extend its abnormality. It is like identifying liberty with those that abuse it" (*CPP* 738). Stevens's real target here is not the literature of Rimbaud and Kafka—he objects, but as only an insider can—so much as the conception of the "normal" their most exaggerated effects imply: "A literature overfull of abnormality and, certainly, present-day European literature, as one knows it, seems to be a literature full of abnormality, gives the reason an appearance of normality to which it is not, solely, entitled" (*CPP* 738). Reason, in other words, already includes imagina-

*The Poetics of Transition*

tion. The "incredible" should be recognized as a component of the world we "normally" inhabit. A fantastic literature only reinforces the artificial division between reason and unreason, and it is precisely this division that Stevens, in his poems, seeks to unhinge.

Stevens's defense of the incredible reflects his pragmatist belief that our ordinary conceptions are in fact a subtle and constantly evolving fusion of rational and imaginative elements. His poetry typically sets out to reveal the extraordinary dimension of the ordinary. More like Santayana than like Dewey, Stevens rarely seeks to apply rational intelligence to the problems of men, but rather explores the imaginative dimensions of that rational intelligence. This insistence on *imagination* has led some critics to classify Stevens as more essentially late Romantic than modernist.[1] In one sense, this view is indisputable: Stevens was deeply influenced by the Romantic poets and often appropriated their vocabularies. But the affinities and borrowings often lead readers to underestimate his distinctive modernity, especially as it is conveyed through the dense obscurity of his language. Like Henry James and Gertrude Stein, Stevens makes elusiveness a positive virtue in his poems.[2] This elusiveness marks a style of attentiveness to things that recognizes their dynamic relationship to unfolding, imaginative processes. If anything, Stevens's poetry makes it increasingly difficult to rest content with such classifications as "Romantic," "modern," and "avant-garde." Stevens roams freely between such conceptions and, by doing so, complicates our understanding of the relations between literature, imagination, and the real, historical world.[3]

One reason for the confusion about Stevens's modernist credentials is that critics have rarely understood his distinctive metaphorics of transition. As I have already suggested in my previous discussion of the aesthetics of pragmatism, Stevens is interested in the exchange between imagination and reality, an exchange so complete and fundamental that the terms themselves, in isolation, have no proper meaning. There is no imagination without reality, just as there is no reality without imagination. In "Imagination as Value," Stevens hesitates to aggrandize human imagination: "The romantic belittles [the imagination]. The imagination is the liberty of the mind. The romantic is a failure to make use of that liberty" (*CPP* 727–28). To "make use" of the liberty of the mind would be to set it to work within concrete, material conditions.

Like the pragmatists, Stevens was skeptical of any effort to posit hidden or ideal realities somewhere behind the actual appearances and processes of the material, social world. From his religious skepticism in "Sunday Morning" to his recognition in "Esthétique du Mal" that "the greatest poverty is not to live / In a physical world" (*CP* 325), Stevens felt that whatever the imagina-

*Stevens and the Pragmatist Imagination*

tion could accomplish, it could only accomplish it through its engagement with the actualities and particularities of this world. Like James and Stein, Stevens believed that literature was not "about" life, but that in an important sense, it *made* life. He copied into his commonplace book James's comment in a letter to H. G. Wells that "art *makes* life, makes interest, makes importance," later citing the passage in his 1951 talk "The Relations between Poetry and Painting." He also copied a passage from James's notebook that he found in a review of F. O. Matthiessen's *Henry James: The Major Phase:* "To live *in* the world of creation—to get into it and stay in it—to frequent it and haunt it—to *think* intensely and fruitfully—to woo combinations and inspirations into being by a depth and continuity of attention and meditation—that is the only thing."[4] These passages underscore James's characteristic effort to link the experience of writing with the world of experience.

In his poetry, Stevens dramatizes the same interrelation between the world and its ongoing realization in poetry. This interrelation is the subject of the famous anthology piece, "Anecdote of the Jar."

> I placed a jar in Tennessee,
> And round it was, upon a hill.
> It made the slovenly wilderness
> Surround that hill.
>
> The wilderness rose up to it,
> And sprawled around, no longer wild.
> The jar was round upon the ground
> And tall and of a port in air.
>
> It took dominion everywhere.
> The jar was gray and bare.
> It did not give of bird or bush,
> Like nothing else in Tennessee.
> (CP 76)

Dimly echoing Keats's urn, the jar is a static *objet d'art,* a bit ridiculous in its rural simplicity but nonetheless distinct as art from its surrounding environment. Indeed, wilderness and jar are set against each other here. The jar takes dominion by imposing its order on the scene. By actively placing the jar in the Tennessee wilderness, the speaker transforms that wilderness. The last lines of the poem bluntly state the gap that still remains between jar and environment: the jar, "gray and bare," did not "give of bird or bush, / Like nothing else in Tennessee."

Frank Lentricchia, drawing on a reference to the poem in Michael Herr's book on the war in Vietnam, *Dispatches,* writes of the jar's dominion as a kind of imperialistic aggression. Jars "seem to have designs upon power. They take dominion, they can even make something as unmanageable as a wilderness shape up, imitate their structural roundedness. A jar can make a wilderness surround itself; a jar can make the very ground into its mirror. Jars are humorless narcissists who think they are ungrounded." Lentricchia further suggests that whereas Wordsworth and Keats could comfortably differentiate between an imposing sociopolitical/aesthetic order and their own poetry ("they might have said: 'The jar is them'"), Stevens could not. Unsentimental about democratic America, he concludes, and forces us to conclude, "'The jar is us.'" [5]

Incisive as this reading is, it also somewhat overdetermines the poem, especially since Stevens seems so delighted by its scenario. "Anecdote of the Jar" is positively charming in its representation of the gulf between world and poem. This is an effect of rhyme, rhythm, diction, and tone, in short, of poetic form. "Anecdote of the Jar" is a masterful performance, a lot like the jar in its mastery. For the space of twelve charming lines, the poem effectively transforms the source of Stevens's most profound and recurrent anxiety—how valid are his meager poems, mere jars in the wilderness?—into a delightful display of confidence and wit.[6] Stevens recognized that if his poems were, like the jar, arrogantly false and dominating representations of the world, the process of writing them effected something altogether different. To write a poem is to exercise energies that are both entirely natural (like bird or bush, perfectly organic) and inventive of genuine differences (like nothing else in Tennessee). If the poem as a representation is a violent domination, the process of writing still cultivates fundamental and indispensable creative energies.

The argument of this poem turns on a set of animating paradoxes that together constitute the dynamic tension of Stevens's best poetry. I will reduce these paradoxes to two, one concerning the nature of the real, the other concerning language. Consider two contiguous "Adagia": "The ultimate value is reality," "Realism is a corruption of reality" (*OP* 192). Broadly speaking, realism in art and literature seeks to isolate and represent what is most authentically real about the world, by which novelists and critics have generally meant the social, economic, or even sexual conditions of experience. But Stevens's aphorisms suggest that the effort to purify reality of all imagination is itself a delusion. The paradox about reality, for Stevens, is that to isolate and approach it, one has to recognize that it is always and inevitably intermixed with what we pejoratively call "illusion." Reality, Stevens's explicit ultimate value, is never simply the opposite of fiction or illusion: as he puts it in "Notes toward a Supreme Fiction," "A fictive covering / Weaves always glistening from the heart and mind" (*CP* 396).

And just as, in the final analysis, reality depends, as Stevens will elsewhere say, on the unreal, so the impulse to purify language is met by an impulse to multiply words. "Anecdote of the Jar" suggests the limitations of language, and would almost seem to be a prelude to the rejection of language as a mechanism of domination, but for the poem's charming playfulness. In fact, even as he criticizes the limitations of language, Stevens exults in his powers of language. Naming is a dangerous business, full of risk and potential violence, but it is at the same time a wonderful game and a great chance, altogether sensuous, especially as an affair of sound. This is the second paradox, never quite resolved in Stevens: language functions as both an obstruction and a link to reality.

Stevens does not want his reader to decide between the real Tennessee wilderness and the jar's "gray and bare" Tennessee. These are false opposites that constitute a set of deeply intellectualist expectations about the world, that the "real" will be distinct from what is "illusory," "metaphorical," or "fictive." Stevens engages this language because the language has engaged him already—he is, in other words, never entirely beyond such false binaries— but the point of the poem is not to choose one side or the other but rather to recognize how the two sets of terms mutually determine one another. This is the poem's subject, but it is also its effect. As readers, we can resist the temptation to decide for or against the jar. And it is this sort of elusiveness that confuses readers who come to Stevens's poems with expectations about definitive structures of meaning. "Anecdote of the Jar" stages a double-movement toward imposed orders that focus meanings and away from those orders toward details that are never fully assimilated into the poem's structure. The poem offers a view of the wilderness and at the same time reminds us of the constructedness of that view. It demonstrates the capacity of words to effect transitions from one view to another, without staging any given view as absolute or definitive.

A similar double movement is apparent in "The Idea of Order at Key West." The poem hardly conveys anything like a sense of an order that is a permanent, stable dimension of Key West, but rather explores a momentary sense of such order, and is as much about the precariousness of that sense as it is about the comfort or pleasure that derives from it.

> Whose spirit is this? we said, because we knew
> It was the spirit that we sought and knew
> That we should ask this often as she sang. (*CP* 129)

The woman's song is powerful enough to create a sense that some spirit is at play, whether it is the spirit of the sea, her self, or some other source. The point of these lines, however, is not to identify or define that spirit but rather to suggest that the song raises the unanswered, and perhaps unanswerable, question of the origins of that spirit, a question that "we should ask often . . . as she sang." The next stanza begins in Stevens's characteristic conditional voice — "If it was only the dark voice of the sea / That rose . . ." — and, after proceeding through a number of options, ends with an accumulating sense that the spirit in question is "more" than anything the speaker has been able to figure:

> But it was more than that,
> More even than her voice, and ours, among
> The meaningless plungings of water and the wind,
> Theatrical distances, bronze shadows heaped
> On high horizons, mountainous atmospheres
> Of sky and sea.
> (*CP* 129)

"Meaningless plungings" states the case rather frankly, that without the woman's song the sea has no cosmic significance beyond its perfectly mundane activity. But "theatrical distances" and the dramatic language that follows — "bronze shadows heaped / On high horizons, mountainous atmospheres / Of sky and sea" — suggest that some kind of meaning is in fact being staged here. "It was her voice that made / The sky acutest at its vanishing": the intensities described in the woman's song (and by extension, in the poem itself) are generated by this theatrical, singing voice.

"The Idea of Order at Key West" is about the "idea of order," not about order per se. The difference marks what is most distinctive about Stevens's pragmatist imagination. The idea of order does not correspond to something in Key West or to some ideal type or form indicated by Key West. It may not even outlast the song that is overheard or the poem that describes it. The poem's conclusion underscores this distinction between an inherent, unchanging order and the idea of order as poetry:

> Ramon Fernandez, tell me, if you know,
> Why, when the singing ended and we turned
> Toward the town, tell why the glassy lights,
> The lights in the fishing boats at anchor there,
> As the night descended, tilting in the air,
> Mastered the night and portioned out the sea,

Fixing emblazoned zones and fiery poles,
Arranging, deepening, enchanting night.

Oh! Blessed rage for order, pale Ramon,
The maker's rage to order words of the sea,
Words of the fragrant portals, dimly-starred,
And of ourselves and of our origins,
In ghostlier demarcations, keener sounds.
(*CP* 130)

The effect here is much like the effect described in "Anecdote of the Jar." The lights of the boats, suffused as they are by the experience of the song, organize the scene, almost as constellations map the night sky. The last stanza moves from the starlike lights of the fishing boats to words themselves, which are also "dimly-starred" and which, like the fishing lights, reflect two distinct axes, one recognizable and mundane, almost realistic ("of ourselves and of our origins") and the other strange and haunting, almost fantastic or phantasmatic ("ghostlier demarcations, keener sounds"). The effect of these lines is to make it difficult to separate these axes from one another.

The trope of mastery on which the poem's conclusion turns marks the poem's most difficult movement. Stevens's singer appears to be imposing authoritative form over heterogeneous materials. One is reminded of Stevens's later admonition in "Notes toward a Supreme Fiction": "But to impose is not / To discover" (*CP* 403). But this reading simplifies a more complicated, more modulated response to the woman's song and to the view of the boats that the poem is also recording. Stevens himself frequently complains that all the old efforts to master the world are inadequate ("the solar chariot is junk," as he puts it in one poem), yet it is apparent that, under certain circumstances, nothing is more extraordinary than to have mastered, even if only tentatively, what had been pure chaos. Stevens would not have us choose between an enchanted cosmos and a disenchanted one, religious and secular worldviews, or authoritarian mastery and liberated free-play, as if all enchantments were equal and all authority equally despicable. We inherit these oppositions as part of our reasoning about the world, but they are themselves profoundly inadequate to that world and our experience of it. The deeper, more elusive problem for Stevens is how to inhabit the world responsively without losing the world because of our response to it. Even as we familiarize the world in linguistic patterns, the poet recognizes the power of words to disrupt and reshape those patterns. Words constitute the familiarizing patterns as well as the transitional power to recast those patterns.

Stevens began developing a theory of poetry in his first major talk, his 1936 Harvard address, "The Irrational Element in Poetry." After staking poetry's claim to the territory of "the irrational," however, he rigorously avoided the term thereafter. Indeed, this would be the only major talk to be excluded from the 1951 collection of prose essays, *The Necessary Angel.* Stevens seems to have recognized the disservice the association of poetry and the irrational would do to his poetics. He wanted to make the rational and irrational permeable, but by highlighting the irrational in this way, he made it seem to be something separable from the rational. This is the basis of his criticism of the surrealists, and it likely accounts for his decision to exclude the essay from *The Necessary Angel.* After this first early talk, Stevens's descriptions of imagination and reality would turn on various tropes suggesting interdependence. The composition the following year of *The Man with the Blue Guitar* constitutes Stevens's major breakthrough in this regard: "things as they are," in the vocabulary of the poem, are constantly transposed on the poet's "blue guitar." The sequence cycles between two extremes: "The earth is not earth but a stone" (*CP* 173) and "The world washed in his imagination" (*CP* 179). The thirty-three sections of the poem develop variations on the theme of the mutual inherence of imagination and reality. The balance tips in each direction through the course of the sequence, but the larger drift of the sequence is to suggest that no single description of the relation between imagination and world can be definitive. *The Man with the Blue Guitar* is the first of Stevens's many successful sequence poems composed in two- or three-line stanzas, a form he would pass on to such poets as A. R. Ammons, William Bronk, and Mark Strand.

"Two things of opposite natures seem to depend," the fourth poem of the second section of another of Stevens's major sequences, "Notes toward a Supreme Fiction," describes this interdependence.

Two things of opposite natures seem to depend
On one another, as a man depends
On a woman, day on night, the imagined

On the real. This is the origin of change.
Winter and spring, cold copulars, embrace
And forth the particulars of rapture come.

Music falls on the silence like a sense,
A passion that we feel, not understand.
Morning and afternoon are clasped together

And North and South are an intrinsic couple
And sun and rain a plural, like two lovers
That walk away as one in the greenest body.

In solitude the trumpets of solitude
Are not of another solitude resounding;
A little string speaks for a crowd of voices.

The partaker partakes of that which changes him.
The child that touches takes character from the thing,
The body, it touches. The captain and his men

Are one and the sailor and the sea are one.
Follow after, O my companion, my fellow, my self,
Sister and solace, brother and delight.
(*CP* 392)

Two things "of opposite natures" should logically be separable, yet Stevens figures their qualities here as mutually dependent. Somehow, "the particulars of rapture" hinge on this mutual inherence of opposite natures or terms. The metaphors here are even explicitly sexual, playing on the apparent opposition of man and woman and on the mutuality implicit in their embrace. The experience Stevens describes is not logical so much as prelogical: "Music falls on the silence like a sense, / A passion that we feel, not understand." Nothing can explain a responsive rapture, but it is not any less rapturous because it cannot be explained. By the end of the poem, boundaries are being blurred everywhere, so that identity becomes a function not of autonomous selfhood, but rather of the contexts that mediate and shape the formation of any self: "The partaker partakes of that which changes him." Stevens insists on the subtle effect of physical touch, suggesting that the child who touches objects in her environment takes her own character from "the thing, / The body, it touches." This is one of Stevens's most perfectly Whitmanesque passages, from the moment of the child's touch to the end of the poem: "Follow after, O my companion, my fellow, my self, / Sister and solace, brother and delight." The address to the reader, like Whitman's address in "Crossing Brooklyn Ferry," is an acknowledgment that the poem itself, in this case Stevens's "Notes," has become a part of the reader's living context. What seemed opposite, a writer and a reader, is recognized here as strangely but altogether concretely interrelated.

For Stevens, poetry is a means to realize identity as a series of open-ended, unfolding relations. Such poetry represents things as they are irreducibly suffused by processes of imagining. Nor is there any one definitive or ideal imagination of things in Stevens's poetry. Everything is in transition because imagination is an implicitly unfinished process. Hence what in "An Ordinary Evening in New Haven" Stevens calls "this endlessly elaborating poem." But this perpetual multiplication of meanings is also the source of a peculiar irony, for Stevens has set himself the unenviable task of creating a vocabulary for something that, in his own words from the first section of "Notes," "never could be named." This is a point to which Stevens returns, one way or other, repeatedly in his talks. In "The Noble Rider and the Sound of Words," for example, he comments on the elusiveness of the figure of nobility: "Nothing could be more evasive and inaccessible. Nothing distorts itself and seeks disguise more quickly. There is a shame of disclosing it and in its definite presentations a horror of it. But there it is." This leads Stevens to comment that he is "evading a definition": "If it is defined, it will be fixed and it must not be fixed. As in the case of an external thing, nobility resolves itself into an enormous number of vibrations, movements, changes. To fix it is to put an end to it. Let me show it to you unfixed" (*CPP* 664). To evade a definition is to leave an element of possibility active in that which is not being defined. But what can it mean to "show it to you unfixed"? What is a figure of nobility if it can only be represented as "an enormous number of vibrations, movements, changes"? Certainly the structure of the essays, with their restless movement from source to source, their progress not by logical argumentation but by pulses of thought, represents one strategy for keeping the subject unfixed.

Still, Stevens's ambivalence about his prose—where he seems to have felt acutely the burden of description—is often apparent, nowhere more so than in the short introduction he wrote for *The Necessary Angel*. "Obviously," the second paragraph of the introduction begins, "they are not the carefully organized notes of systematic study" (*CPP* 639). Stevens must have been anxious to make this clear from the start, since he had to know that his effort to articulate a theory of imagination had run up against the problem of having to organize or systematize a mode of perception that, by virtue of its double allegiance to the realistic and the imaginative, resisted systematic organization. Stevens comments further on in the introduction, after describing his ambition to write a theory of poetry, "The few pages that follow are, now, alas! the only realization possible to me of those excited ambitions" (*CPP* 639).

These ambivalences reflect something quite central to Stevens's poetic imagination, the gap between the ambition of poetry and the reality of poems. To some extent, this is a product of Stevens's Emersonian ambition. It was Emerson, after all, who commented in "Fate" that "every spirit makes its house; but afterwards the house confines the spirit" (*EL* 946). The rather obvious problem with imagination is that its projections may impose themselves, like the jar in Tennessee, all too successfully. In his "Essays on Reality and the Imagination," the subtitle of *The Necessary Angel*, Stevens is everywhere anxious to balance the claims of both realms as a safeguard against this effect of confinement. And so he proposes definitions that will ideally be self-consuming. Here is how Stevens finally describes the essays in the introduction: "To their extent they are a realization; and it is because that is true, that is to say, because they seem to me to communicate to the reader the portent of the subject, if nothing more, that they are presented here" (*CPP* 639). Stevens's prose here is fraught with nervous qualifiers: "to their extent," "seem to me," "if nothing more." Somewhere between the ideal of anticipation and the disappointment of actualization falls the "portent of the subject," not quite the subject itself, it would seem, but a fair enough approach to it, enough, at least, to indicate what it *would be* if it *could be* named.

Stevens's ongoing defense of imagination should be understood in light of these ambivalences. Stevens almost never invokes imagination in his prose without first qualifying it, indicating that any imagination not grounded in reality and answerable to it is not worth having: "The real is only the base. But it is the base," as one of the "Adagia" has it (*OP* 187). "The interest of life," he writes in another "Adagia," "is experienced by participating and by being part, not by observing nor by thinking" (*OP* 200). Or: "Poetry is a response to the daily necessity of getting the world right" (*OP* 201). Poetry belongs to life in its most ordinary contexts, and anything that detaches it from that life and those contexts drains it of its vitality. These comments indicate one important aspect of Stevens's poetics, his sense that imagination for its own sake, or for the sake of establishing a poetic universe outside the universe of ordinary experience or of actual fact, is an empty ideal.

But for all this apparent realism, to engage the real is also for Stevens to engage the ideas that we invariably form of the real. William James comments provocatively in "The Will to Believe" on the absurdity of our single-minded devotion to truth: "Biologically considered, our minds are as ready to grind out falsehood as veracity, and he who says 'Better go without belief forever than believe a lie!' merely shows his own preponderant private horror of becoming a dupe" (*W* 1:469). James concludes: "Our errors are surely not such awfully solemn things. In a world where we are so certain to incur them in spite of all our caution, a certain lightness of heart seems healthier than this excessive nervousness on their behalf" (*W* 1:470). Nietzsche would say much the same thing, right down to the necessary "lightness of heart," though he would say it in thunder, as if only he were strong enough to stand the truth about truth. What James and Nietzsche share is the sense that there is a tyranny of truth that is itself more deeply and dangerously "false" than the beliefs people tentatively adopt that may, in the end, need to be revised.[7] Stevens's poet may also grind out falsehood, but that falsehood is, at least, always attuned to the need to remain open to further revision, much as intelligence, for Dewey, requires what in *Reconstruction in Philosophy* he called "constant alertness in observing consequences, an open-minded will to learn and courage in re-adjustment" (*MW* 12:135).

Stevens's pragmatist imagination takes this constant alertness to a new level. By "consequences," Dewey means changes in physical or social properties. The "will to learn" and "courage in re-adjustment" refer to one's ability to assume the risks and uncertainties associated with the processes of intellectual and social transformation. For Stevens, consequences cannot be located so definitely in the external world. This is because an attentive eye will see transition and its unfolding consequences everywhere. Dewey deconstructs the opposition between internal (conscious) and external (physical and social) realms in order to locate the conscious self in the world of impinging realities. Stevens also deconstructs this opposition, but with more of an eye to complicating our sense of what is internal and what is external. Where Dewey folds mind back into the world, Stevens weaves his way in and around and across the always permeable, impossible boundary between mind and world.

Stevens's prose can be disappointing, in part because he is always bumping his head against the limitations of his key terms, reality and imagination. However savvy he may be in his use of these terms, the terms never take him very far. His poetry, though, is another matter altogether. "A Lot of People Bathing in a Stream," first collected in the 1947 *Transport to Summer,* is a delightfully strange poem that incorporates these tensions, weaving and unweaving the fabric of a world with astonishing confidence and ease. The poem describes an outing to a local stream, where the activity of swimming is mixed indiscriminately with the poet's perception of light, color, and shape playing around and apparently on the stream.

It was like passing a boundary to dive
Into the sun-filled water, brightly leafed
And limbed and lighted out from bank to bank.

That's how the stars shine during the day. There, then,
The yellow that was yesterday, refreshed,
Became to-day, among our children and

Ourselves, in the clearest green — well, call it green.
We bathed in yellow green and yellow blue
And in these comic colors dangled down,

*Stevens and the Pragmatist Imagination*

Like their particular characters, addicts
To blotches, angular anonymids
Gulping for shape among the reeds. No doubt,

We were the appropriate conceptions, less
Than creatures, of the sky between the banks,
The water flowing in the flow of space.

It was passing a boundary, floating without a head
And naked, or almost so, into the grotesque
Of being naked, or almost so, in a world

Of nakedness, in the company of the sun,
Good-fortuner of the grotesque, patroon,
A funny foreigner of meek address.

How good it was at home again at night
To prepare for bed, in the frame of the house, and move
Round the rooms, which do not ever seem to change . . .
(*CP* 371–72)

The guiding trope of this poem is the initial figure of "passing a boundary."
There is a literal boundary, constituted by the water's actual surface, but the
poem also describes a figurative boundary, on the other side of which all that
is solid melts. Stevens begins immediately to confuse the different physical
spaces of the poem. The surface of the water in particular functions not as
a strict boundary, but as a surface at once transparent and opaque, allowing
simultaneous perception of what is in the water, on its surface, both in and
out (like the swimmers themselves), and, by reflection, above and around it.
The water is "sun-filled," even though the sun is supposedly outside the water,
and is "brightly leafed / And limbed" despite its apparent separation from the
surrounding banks.

The oddest passage in the poem is the one in which the speaker and his
companions are reduced to aspects of the physical geography, of the play of
light and color on and in the river. These are strangely depersonalized people,
"appropriate conceptions" of a physical geography that is itself reduced to
a shapeless play of light, color, reflection, and motion. No wonder Stevens
calls them "angular anonymids / Gulping for shape among the reeds," underscoring the erasure of identity which they undergo in the poem/stream. To
adopt such form, or to escape in such ways from form, is to become the "appropriate conception" of place so formless that it will hardly stand still to
be described: "the sky between the banks, / The water flowing in the flow

of space." It is as though the speaker imagines himself in a modern painting and attributes to the others and to himself as much "humanity" as a figure in such a painting would have, which is to say none at all. The image of "floating without a head" probably refers to an actual appearance, a reflection on the surface, say, or bodies partly submerged, but it also suggests the temporary relaxation of reason on which the poem depends. One must suspend the tyrannous forms of knowledge in order to comprehend everything that such knowledge obscures—here, a fluidity of identity that opens the speaker to the radical otherness of his world. The "grotesque / Of being naked, or almost so" captures the strangeness of what is in fact seen on the other side of such knowledge. Stevens sometimes uses the term "comic" in this sense, as in "these comic colors dangling down," suggesting the uninhibited delight of color, shape, and motion as they precede organization into recognizable and meaningful form.

Interestingly, Stevens returns, in the poem's last stanza, to such an organized space. The "frame of the house" suggests a kind of intellectual and even moral framing. While movement in the stream promotes a sense of the finality of change, movement in the house provides the illusion of permanence. Everything turns on the tone of "seem," which quietly underscores the speaker's recognition that the frame provided by the house is as illusory and finally irrelevant as human identity had seemed in the stream. The ellipses, an infrequent typographical ploy with Stevens, underscores this sense, as if announcing the change still to come. But there is also warmth and recognition in this stanza. It is good to return home after such disjunctive visions, and good to feel some confidence, however qualified, in the relative stability of a home.

Like other poems by Stevens, "A Lot of People Bathing in a Stream" is an effort to get into words certain perceptions that exceed the organizing and rationalizing tendency of words. Only a proliferation of language can counter the reductive effect of language and form: more language, and more rhetorical play, to suggest the "more" of all identity. Rather than seek to minimize language, or to purify it, as a means of resisting its distortions, as if some simple reality or identity really did abide beneath the encrustations of language, Stevens writes to multiply linguistic effects. Hence, not, for Stevens, an ideal of simple nakedness, but rather a "grotesque / Of being naked, or almost so." Language does not aim at accuracy of representation but rather stages the perpetual play of form and formal rupture. The poem foregrounds our irreducible relation to these transitional processes.

Stevens everywhere reminds his reader that fictions about the world cannot simply be erased or avoided. Indeed, fictions only seem avoided when one fiction has been successfully naturalized. This is when people speak with the greatest assurance about what is real, natural, or true. When any received fiction dominates, it does so by attaining the status of truth. The alternative is not a truth that rigorously eschews the mechanisms of fiction, but rather proliferating fictions that resist being taken as final truths. For Stevens, there is an intricate complication at the heart of all of these categories—the real, the natural, the true—a complication that stems from the mixed condition of fact and fiction. Consider another "Adagia": "To live in the world but outside of existing conceptions of it" (OP 190). To live by "existing conceptions" of the world would not be to live in the world, but there is no way simply to step apart from those existing conceptions into the world pure and simple. Hence, in Stevens's most significant reversal, to live in the world is also to live in poems, and in ways that make the dichotomy increasingly hard to uphold.

Poetry, for Stevens, is an extended inquiry into new possibilities of transition. Stevens's poetry attempts to think beyond the received imperatives of thinking. It is not clear that he ever succeeds, or that it is even possible wholly to succeed, but the effort led him to compose an extraordinarily challenging body of poetry. Writing in canto 22 of "An Ordinary Evening in New Haven," Stevens suggests that an imaginative reduction can serve as the basis for a further imaginative investment:

> To re-create, to use
>
> The cold and earliness and bright origin
> Is to search.
> (CP 481)

Stevens's "cold," "earliness," and "bright origin" are all tropes for the will to clear away false or tired imaginative ideals, while his verbs—"To re-create, to use," "to search"—remind the reader that this return is not designed to achieve a state of settled repose but rather to initiate or extend an already unfolding process. In this spirit, Stevens appropriates the "evening star," a figure sedimented with conventional associations, as the material for still further discovery:

> Likewise to say of the evening star,
> The most ancient light in the most ancient sky,
>
> That it is wholly an inner light, that it shines
> From the sleepy bosom of the real, re-creates,
> Searches a possible for its possibleness.
> (CP 481)

*The Poetics of Transition*

Stevens muddies the classic distinction between origins and ends, as well as between internal (subjective) and external (objective) realms. The "evening star" is "wholly an inner light," but it shines "From the sleepy bosom of the real." The figure of the star is intended to complicate our usual sense that these are separable realms. More importantly, once we realize their mutual inherence, the figure of the evening star "re-creates, / Searches a possible for its possibleness."

Stevens's pragmatist imagination reaches a fever pitch in its vigilance to search "a possible for its possibleness." He is never more opaque and bewildering than when he is seeking to tease out or intensify his perception of the mutual inherence of imagination and reality. It is a process of continuous re-creation because the received imaginings of things — whether ancient mythologies, conventional poetic associations, or long-dominant metaphors — ultimately obstruct one's relation to the world. The old imaginings limit the play of imagination over things. For Stevens, poetry is the realization of the latent possibility in things, so long as that realization does not fix that possibility. To search "a possible for its possibleness" is to replace settled identifications, definitions, intentions, and designs with the open-ended unfolding of possibility as realized in the indeterminate, transitional play of verbal implication, association, suggestion, tone, or acoustic and imagistic juxtaposition.

Stevens repeatedly stages the destruction of some old form of imagination and the new beginning that the imagination undertakes in its place. I have already cited in my introduction the first poem of "Notes toward a Supreme Fiction," in which Stevens writes,

> You must become an ignorant man again
> And see the sun again with an ignorant eye
> And see it clearly in the idea of it.
> (*CP* 380)

The sun is seen clearly only in "the idea of it," which is the idea formed of it once all the false and distorted ideas of it have been washed away. It is an imagined sun, but a sun imagined without the mediation of its old imaginings: "Phoebus is dead, ephebe. But Phoebus was / A name for something that never could be named" (*CP* 381). What makes this new idea of the sun different is that it is not so much *imagined,* as it is *being imagined.* The process of imagining is going on in, or as, the poem itself.

In canto 24 of "An Ordinary Evening in New Haven," Stevens describes the destruction of a statue of Jove. Instead of describing the god or theological tradition that replaces Jove, however, he describes what emerges as an unresolved state of being suspended between gods and traditions:

It took all day to quieten the sky
And then to refill its emptiness again,

So that at the edge of afternoon, not over,
Before the thought of evening had occurred
Or the sound of Incomincia had been set,

There was a clearing, a readiness for first bells,
An opening for outpouring, the hand was raised:
There was a willingness not yet composed,

A knowing that something certain had been proposed,
Which, without the statue, would be new,
An escape from repetition, a happening

In space and the self, that touched them both at once
And alike, a point of the sky or of the earth
Or of a town poised at the horizon's dip.
(CP 482–83)

Between afternoon and evening ("at the edge of afternoon, not over"), Stevens posits a condition of pure preparedness: after the old forms have been turned away, before the new ones have yet taken shape. Something "certain" has already been proposed and will assuredly replace the old certainty. Stevens focuses, however, not on that new certainty but rather on the condition of excited readiness that extends between old and new, the "opening for outpouring." No descriptive word or phrase could possibly capture this condition, which is finally conveyed most suggestively by the suspended syntax of the passage, with its repetitions (of "there was" especially) and parallel construction ("a clearing," "a readiness," "an opening," and so on). It is here, suspended not only between certainties but also between available descriptions, that the self glimpses possibility as "an escape from repetition." Something "new" is being proposed, without, as yet, any propositions about the "new" being formulated. In this uncertain state, sky and earth are indistinguishable, as New Haven momentarily becomes one with the distant horizon: "poised at the horizon's dip."

Stevens delights in achieving such poise in suspended states of verbal irresolution: "still speech / As it touches the point of reverberation," as he describes it elsewhere in "An Ordinary Evening" (CP 475). The juxtaposition between the stillness of speech and the reverberation of the language of that speech suggests a subtle mediation of the antithetical forces of resolution and irresolution. "Touch" is the crucial term here, as it was also in the passage from "Notes" discussed above. "Touch" is also suggested in the statue of Jove passage, where the "happening // In space and the self" is said to have "touched them both at once / And alike" (*CP* 483). This figure of touch lends an aura of materiality, even physical intimacy to an otherwise elusive and abstract conception. It is as if the visible and invisible worlds, the one hard matter, the other ideal, have themselves mysteriously "touched," a meeting collapsed into the paradoxical space—physical and verbal—of "the horizon's dip," another "point of reverberation" figured as the meeting of earth and sky, sky dipping into earth.

The reference to the "still speech / As it touches the point of reverberation" occurs in canto 14, the canto in which Professor Eucalyptus, one of Stevens's many cartoonlike personages, first appears:

> The dry eucalyptus seeks god in the rainy cloud.
> Professor Eucalyptus of New Haven seeks him
> In New Haven with an eye that does not look
>
> Beyond the object.
> (*CP* 475)

Where the eucalyptus tree's "natural supernaturalism" points up, figuring its god not as the inhabitant of the cloudy heavens but as the actual clouds, Professor Eucalyptus's philosophical project resists this vertical projection. In place of rainy clouds, he sits "close to the ramshackle spout in which / The rain falls with a ramshackle sound." Stevens knows that this is not to "possess" the object, the rain; it is only to "seek" it (always searching a possible for its possibleness) along a horizontal axis, in its actual, earth-bound sounds. "Ramshackle" is evocative because of its jangling sound, an acoustic effect Stevens could rarely resist. Professor Eucalyptus "seeks // God in the object itself, without much choice," but this minimum of choice—like all of Stevens's reductions—is also of immeasurable import:

> It is a choice of the commodious adjective
> For what he sees, it comes in the end to that:
>
> The description that makes it divinity, still speech
> As it touches the point of reverberation.
> (*CP* 475)

Thus language momentarily, precariously, "touches" the movingness of things, the unspeakable, ungraspable quality that renders our representations of objects inadequate. There is an enormous burden on the figure of touch here, mediating as it does between palpable and impalpable dimensions of being.

The figure of touch reappears in the next canto as well, where it again functions to establish a continuity between the "instinct for heaven" and the "instinct for earth." Insubstantial, shadowy projections—like the divinity of "Sunday Morning" that can come "Only in silent shadows and in dreams" (*CP* 67)—are returned to earth where we can touch them and be emotionally touched by them:

> The hibernal dark that hung
> In primavera, the shadow of bare rock,
>
> Becomes the rock of autumn, glittering,
> Ponderable source of each imponderable,
> The weight we lift with the finger of a dream,
>
> The heaviness we lighten by light will,
> By the hand of desire, faint, sensitive, the soft
> Touch and trouble of the touch of the actual hand.
> (*CP* 476)

"Glittering," a conspicuously commodious adjective for the "rock of autumn," suggests that the insubstantial, or imponderable, qualities of objects have a substantial, ponderable basis. "Ponderable" indicates something subject to, or perhaps the subject of, meditation, but the term also suggests something "ponderous," or weighty, a gross physical object. The word reminds us that all that glitters is something, whether or not that something happens to be gold. Weight and weightlessness, object and dream, are strangely intermingled in these lines. The object is a "weight we lift," but lift with "the finger of a dream"; it is a "heaviness," but a heaviness "we lighten by light will." And the hand that touches is a "hand of desire, faint, sensitive": a physical hand, but one whose "soft / Touch" is conspicuously "touching," or moving. All of these verbal maneuverings suggest a realm in which distinctions between physical and spiritual, object and desire collapse. Indeed, such distinctions distort both object and desire by relegating them to separate and distinct spheres, when in fact they abide only in "still speech / As it touches the point of reverberation."

For Stevens, the "point of vision and desire are the same." The world we see is also the world we desire. Stevens's "point of reverberation" reverberates *with* desire. So in the third canto of "An Ordinary Evening" he describes the way in which desire instills a certain irreducible movement in all perception:

Say next to holiness is the will thereto,
And next to love is the desire for love,
The desire for its celestial ease in the heart,

Which nothing can frustrate, that most secure,
Unlike love in possession of that which was
To be possessed and is. But this cannot

Possess. It is desire, set deep in the eye,
Behind all actual seeing, in the actual scene,
In the street, in a room, on a carpet or a wall,

Always in emptiness that would be filled. . . .
(*CP* 467)

Stevens appropriates the religious phrase "celestial" and attaches it to specifically human passion. The "celestial ease in the heart" recalls James's
"strong feeling of ease, peace, rest" in "The Sentiment of Rationality," though
here Stevens even more vehemently distinguishes this ease in the heart from
the desire for it. This love never reaches a final, permanent stage of settled
affection, and so is never fully realized in fact. Desire attaches itself to that
which is not in possession, circulating around what hovers just out of our
possessive reach: what we touch, but cannot hold.

In all of these examples, Stevens describes a world that is situated so exactly
at the point where imagination and reality meet that we can neither possess
nor, paradoxically enough, even describe that world. Stevens writes from the
leading edge of unfolding transitions, the edge where novelty emerges and
reconstructs habitual patterns of perception and understanding. Stevens's
poetry begins in what might be called a dis-imagination of things that is indistinguishable from their re-imagination.[8] Most importantly, Stevens never
offers a definitive imagination of things. In this regard, canto 32 of *The Man
with the Blue Guitar* stands as one of the central poems in Stevens's canon:

Throw away the lights, the definitions,
And say of what you see in the dark

That it is this or that it is that,
But do not use the rotted names.

How should you walk in that space and know
Nothing of the madness of space,

Nothing of its jocular procreations?
Throw the lights away. Nothing must stand

*Stevens and the Pragmatist Imagination*

Between you and the shapes you take
When the crust of shape has been destroyed.

You as you are? You are yourself.
The blue guitar surprises you.
(*CP* 183)

This is one of Stevens's earliest invitations to the reader to become an "igno-
rant man" by suspending the vocabularies and conceptual paradigms that
mediate between us and our world. As ever, once these mediations are rejected, imagination is still present on the scene: "The blue guitar surprises
you." Phrasings like "the madness of space" and "its jocular procreations"
hardly suggest the bareness of an unimagined, plain, or natural world. As
Stevens peels away the encrusted layers of past imaginings, he finds not the
naked world, but the mad and jocular play of imaginative energies.

Stevens's poems become occasions for writer and reader alike to experience the peculiar pleasure and enlightenment generated by these unresolved,
unresolvable tensions. In "Landscape with Boat," the "anti-master-man, flori-
bund ascetic," who seeks to rid his world of all its falsifying magnifications,
allows Stevens to reaffirm the pervasiveness of these magnifications. While
the "anti-master-man" may allude to Nietzsche's master being, as David
Bromwich has suggested, it is important not to lose sight of the epithet's
more obvious reference to "the masters" of painting. The poem is, after all,
explicitly about painting a "Landscape with Boat."[9] Painting was, for Stevens,
a recurrent metaphor for creative activity. Here, the "anti-master-man" for-
goes traditions of painting which have obscured their subjects by failing to
separate simple seeing from layers of feeling. The speaker demands a sight
more pure than that which is "indifferent to the eye": "He wanted to see. He
wanted the eye to see / And not be touched by blue" (*CP* 241). This true and
untouched seeing is associated with true knowing:

He wanted to know,
A naked man who regarded himself in the glass
Of air, who looked for the world beneath the blue,
Without blue, without any turquoise tint or phase,
Any azure under-side or after-color.
(*CP* 241)

The "naked man" evokes the mythical ideal of the denuded American self,
divested of all the cultural (and emotional) baggage that interposes between
the cultivated self and its world. "Turquoise tint or phase" and "azure under-

side or after-color" suggest minor variations on the sky's transcendent blue, last, lingering hints of the sky's mythic suggestiveness.

Yet the anti-master-man insists that even these must be rejected, "brushed away" as a painter might conceive it:

> He brushed away the thunder, then the clouds,
> Then the colossal illusion of heaven. Yet still
> The sky was blue.
> (*CP* 241)

This persistent blue, which the anti-master-man also wants to dispose of ("He wanted imperceptible air"), recalls the "dividing and indifferent blue" of "Sunday Morning" (*CP* 68) and the "spaciousness and light / In which the body walks and is deceived" in "Anatomy of Monotony" (*CP* 108).[10] The anti-master-man epitomizes Stevens's intense desire not to be deceived by comforting illusions. Yet Stevens also recognizes that the skeptical impulse can go too far:

>         He never supposed
> That he might be truth, himself, or part of it,
> That the things that he rejected might be part
> And the irregular turquoise, part, the perceptible blue
> Grown denser, part, the eye so touched, so played
> Upon by clouds, the ear so magnified
> By thunder, parts, and all these things together,
> Parts, and more things, parts.
> (*CP* 242)

The anti-master-man's pursuit of pure truth leads him to reject magnifications and intensifications that are in fact a significant and vital, even necessary part of his world.

But transcendent magnification is always, in Stevens, held in abeyance by the gestures of style that embody his desire to achieve such experience without sacrificing the integrity of the world in which it is had. If the speaker in "Landscape with Boat" is allowed to acknowledge magnification by thunder as itself part of the world, it is because he does so in response to someone who would reduce the world to "imperceptible air." Moreover, the speaker of "Landscape with Boat" repeatedly insists that these magnifications are "parts" of truth, echoing the title of the volume in which the poem appeared, *Parts of a World.* These "parts" not only resist becoming monolithically imposed meanings that would account for the whole, but, because of their sheer multiplicity, they also function to unsettle the very possibility of such an all-encompassing, impartial meaning.

In "Description without Place," Stevens captures these paradoxes in an almost oxymoronic formulation: "the actual seemings that we see, / Hear, feel and know. We feel and know them so" (*CP* 340). Without these "actual seemings," the world would lack dimension: "In flat appearance we should be and be, / Except for delicate clinkings not explained" (*CP* 340). These "delicate clinkings," which by definition cannot be defined (there is always something "not explained" about them), are precisely what keep us attached to the world, convinced that it has dimension, depth, color, brilliance. As Santayana points out, we never experience such qualities directly, but rather assume them in a spirit of animal faith. They are "actual seemings," at once real and imaginary, true and fictive. Thus Stevens defines "description" not as mimetic reproduction but rather as the constant making-visible of the "seemings" of things:

Description is revelation. It is not
The thing described, nor false facsimile.

It is an artificial thing that exists,
In its own seeming, plainly visible,
Yet not too closely the double of our lives,
Intenser than any actual life could be. . . .
(*CP* 344)

Such intensification is an entirely legitimate, even essential element in any human experience. Description neither mirrors nor falsifies the "object" described, but rather posits the seemings that shape human interest in relation to the world of things.

Emerson makes a similar point in a discussion of human motivation in the short essay "Nature." Having claimed that "exaggeration is in the course of things," that "a little violence of direction in its proper path, a shove to put it on its way . . . a slight generosity, a drop too much" functions to keep the self actively engaged with its world, Emerson proceeds to describe a form of deception that works to human advantage: "This glitter, this opaline lustre plays round the top of every toy to [the child's] eye, to ensure his fidelity, and he is deceived to his good. We are made alive and kept alive by the same arts. Let the stoics say what they please, we do not eat for the good of living, but because the meat is savory and the appetite is keen. . . . All things betray the same calculated profusion" (*EL* 550). The "good of living" is an abstraction. As an ideal, we might readily give it our thoughtful assent, but it would still have little power to affect our lives. We eat, as Emerson comments, not to satisfy an ideal but for pure bodily satisfaction — to alleviate the pain of appetite, to enjoy the pleasure of taste. Such is the model, for Emerson, of all human behavior: "No man is quite sane; each has a vein of folly in his composition, a slight determination of blood to the head, to make sure of holding him hard to some one point which nature had taken to heart" (*EL* 550). Not the plain truth of our intentions and designs, but the folly of our attachment to them, constitutes the working principle of the universe, its "calculated profusion."

So too Stevens's magnifications and intensifications are positive components both of his world and of his poetic style. Like Emerson's exaggeration, Stevens's intensifications reflect the fundamentally dramatic quality of all reality. We do not just occupy the world, but we act out our lives in it, play out our affections and attachments. This explains why Stevens's ascetic impulse, the drive to a simplified, purified reality, is almost always overcome by his expansive impulse. For the reality includes the dramatic intensification, the stylistic excesses that the ascetic, like the "anti-master-man" in "Landscape with Boat," rejects and denies.

Stevens repeatedly stages the transformation of ascetic denial into passionate affirmation. Thus he concludes the eighth section of "Esthétique du Mal":

How cold the vacancy
When the phantoms are gone and the shaken realist
First sees reality. The mortal no
Has its emptiness and tragic expirations.
The tragedy, however, may have begun,
Again, in the imagination's new beginning,
In the yes of the realist spoken because he must
Say yes, spoken because under every no
Lay a passion for yes that had never been broken.
(*CP* 320)

The cold vacancy, with its emptiness and tragic expirations, reflects the snow-man's vision of a world divested of accumulated meanings and values, a world from which to behold (in the language of "The Snow Man") "Nothing that is not there and the nothing that is" (*CP* 10).[11] And yet it is also the occasion of "the imagination's new beginning." The unbroken "passion for yes" derives from the same regions of the self's experience of things as Emerson's "over-faith of each man" and James's "will to believe." The cold vacancy does not represent a final and absolute denudation, but is rather one term in a rhythm that moves just as surely through a new beginning as it does through a tragic expiration. Hence the cycles of affirmation and denial, the interplay of realism and romance, that constitute the rhythms of Stevens's poetry.

*Stevens and the Pragmatist Imagination*

This rhythm is the basis of Stevens's emphasis on creative renewal, his orientation, as in the opening lines from "The Well Dressed Man with a Beard," toward the future world: "After the final no there comes a yes / And on that yes the future world depends" (*CP* 247). This orientation is also prominent in "Description without Place":

> The future is description without place,
> The categorical predicate, the arc.
> It is a wizened starlight growing young,
> In which old stars are planets of morning, fresh
>
> In the brilliantest descriptions of new day,
> Before it comes, the just anticipation
>
> Of the appropriate creatures, jubilant,
> The forms that are attentive in thin air.
> (*CP* 344)

The "brilliantest descriptions of new day" are produced "before it comes, the just anticipation" of that new day. The future is not "defined," as from without, but is rather anticipated and projected in description, as part of that future's unfolding. The "forms that are attentive in thin air" represent those changes, renewals of the world, that are literally *becoming* in the process of their description. The anticipation is "just" not because it is in any sense accurate or justified — it is still "a little different from reality" — but because it renews and refreshes the world and our experience of the world. Its "justice" is in what James called the "feeling of tendency." "Reality is the great *fond*," Stevens comments in a letter of June 20, 1945, to José Rodríguez Feo, "and it is because it is that the purely literary amounts to so little. Moreover, in the world of actuality, in spite of all I have just said, one is always living a little out of it" (*LWS* 505–6). Description, especially as it bears toward the future, is also always "a little out of it," "attentive in thin air" as if to find its "place" materializing there.

Description mediates for Stevens between imagination and reality, underscoring the interrelations of words and things:

> Thus the theory of description matters most.
> It is the theory of the word for those
>
> For whom the word is the making of the world,
> The buzzing world and lisping firmament.

It is a world of words to the end of it,
In which nothing solid is its solid self.
(*CP* 345)

There is an idealist cast to these lines that may make them difficult to comprehend. The last line especially seems to deny the physical world, or at least to lose touch with it through the dense mediation of words. But Stevens's "world of words" also refers to creative activity, the speaking of the world into being, an act of poetic language that incorporates tendency, direction, movement, into description. "Nothing solid is its solid self" because everything solid remains subject to the magnifications and intensifications that suffuse its substantive value and significance. Released from the solid world of given, finished realities, the self enters a "place" characterized by what Stevens aptly describes in the late poem "Reality Is an Activity of the Most August Imagination" as "an insolid billowing of the solid" (*CPP* 472). This antithetical "place" is the site not of direct access to some simple, solid reality, but of constant, tentative, and precarious creative renewal.

So Stevens writes of description itself in the final lines of "Description without Place":

It matters, because everything we say
Of the past is description without place, a cast

Of the imagination, made in sound;
And because what we say of the future must portend,

Be alive with its own seemings, seeming to be
Like rubies reddened by rubies reddening.
(*CP* 345–46)

Because these "seemings" correspond to nothing solid, they cannot simply be described. Bringing them to life, or rather bringing a description "alive with its own seemings," must be a delicate and complicated procedure. A "cast //  Of the imagination" suggests both a mold, as if having frozen imagination in a single shape, and an active casting, a throwing forward, or projection. This anticipates the "portend[ing]" of "what we say of the future," its incorporation, in the "delicate clinkings" of its language, of what is not yet fully manifest in the world. There is a life, Stevens insists, in portending language, "alive with its own seemings." Thus rubies are not simply red, but are figured here as "reddened by rubies reddening." They are constituted actively, by this very forward projection implicit in our impassioned response to them.

Stevens's pragmatist imagination never simply embraces a world of things that is figured as preceding the imagination. Stevens instead locates imaginative activity in the realm of things. All things have already been imagined, and the world we inhabit is necessarily a world dense in prior imaginings. Dewey suggests in *The Quest for Certainty* that "nature as it exists at any particular time is a challenge, rather than a completion; it provides possible starting points and opportunities rather than final ends" (*LW* 4:81). Nature is always coming-into-being, and it is the poet, in Stevens's view, who perceives and extends that process. To ignore the role of the poem in the constitution of the real is to assume that we could have some conception of the real without the intervention of human imagination. In fact, without imagination we would be incapable of distinguishing any one thing from any other, probably even incapable of formulating a conception of any "thing."

But these negative formulations are themselves inadequate. For Stevens, the pragmatist imagination establishes its authority by virtue of its positive acts of imagining. One of Stevens's last poems, "The Planet on the Table," will serve to exemplify this point, as well as to underscore the animating paradoxes implicit in Stevens's attitudes to poetry and language:

Ariel was glad he had written his poems.
They were of a remembered time
Or of something seen that he liked.

Other makings of the sun
Were waste and welter
And the ripe shrub writhed.

His self and the sun were one
And his poems, although makings of his self,
Were no less makings of the sun.

It was not important that they survive.
What mattered was that they should bear
Some lineament or character,

Some affluence, if only half-perceived,
In the poverty of their words,
Of the planet of which they were part.
(*CP* 532–33)

The "planet on the table" probably refers to the manuscript of Stevens's *Collected Poems*. Holly Stevens dates the composition of the poem to 1953, probably around the time Stevens began to gather his poems for the collected edition. In the poem, the speaker is pleased to recognize that his poems are the product of both "his self" and "the sun." In the last two stanzas, he expresses his willingness to entertain the destruction of his poems, in which case they would only be following the sun's "other makings." Everything is "waste and welter" in this world. Still, for all their impermanence, the poems might bear some vital trace of the life they responded to and intensified. The words themselves will always display a certain "poverty," a bareness that sets them off from life itself, but they may, at the same time, convey some "lineament or character, // Some affluence, if only half-perceived" that belongs as much to the planet as to the poet, reflecting and extending the creative processes that encompass and subsume poets and their collected poems.

Affluence and poverty: these conflicting terms mark Stevens's sense of the abiding, animating paradox of the pragmatist imagination. There is no transcendence that finally overcomes our human poverty, but also no purely reductive condition that utterly defeats the irresistible play of imagination. There is an affluence that abides even in the poet's most reductive words and that coexists with their essential poverty. Better that this affluence remain only half-perceived, since to perceive it whole might be to neglect the poverty of words, to mistake their occasional and uncertain glimmering for complete illumination. Stevens's poetics of transition is a poetics of such half-perceptions: the transitions are still in the making, partial and tentative, but always actively unfolding. Such words do not create final satisfactions, but they can orient us toward the endless satisfaction of creative activity. "Alpha continues to begin," as Stevens puts it in "An Ordinary Evening in New Haven," "Omega is refreshed at every end" (*CP* 469).

There is something tantalizingly oxymoronic in the phrase "pragmatist imagination." To the extent that our conception of imagination is shaped by late-eighteenth- and early-nineteenth-century poetics and critical theory, it is difficult to wrest the term away from its fringe (to echo James) of idealist affinities. Pragmatism was conceived as a rejoinder to the deeply ingrained idealist habits of mind that have characterized a good deal of Western philosophy since Plato. I have been suggesting throughout, however, that even in its high-instrumentalist phase, pragmatism was always also a last refinement on idealism: conceived in reaction to idealism, especially in its neo-Hegelian forms, and mediated by its strong (if also qualified) affinity with the philosophical style of British empiricism, pragmatism was not so much a step beyond idealism and metaphysical systems, though pragmatists would sometimes describe their work in such terms, as an attempt to reimagine them. Rejecting the supernaturalism implicit in traditional metaphysics, pragmatists

*Stevens and the Pragmatist Imagination*

sought to reincorporate imaginative, creative processes on a more naturalistic basis.

The pragmatist imagination is the site where this reincorporation is endlessly negotiated. For the pragmatist, imagination is exercised in full awareness of its limitations. Pragmatists posit the ultimate value of imaginative activity even as they underscore the inadequacy of any metaphor or narrative that activity might produce. The pragmatist imagination thus seeks to balance visionary and skeptical impulses. It attempts to keep its visionary flights tethered to the material and social facts of the world, but never to allow the cumulative weight of those facts to obscure its creative imperative. Because it identifies itself with the rhythm of fact and creative vision, the pragmatist imagination faces the inevitable conflict between what is and what might be with equanimity. Its voice is sometimes tragic, to the extent that its creative vision is invariably thwarted, and sometimes comic, so far as its creative impulses are continuously renewed and revived.

I want to offer, in lieu of definitive conclusion, one last example of this pragmatist imagination in action. It is a poem by William Bronk, written in the early 1970s. "The Mind's Limitations Are Its Freedom" is a poem of remarkable poise, situated at the margin between a reality perfectly inaccessible to mind and an imagination nevertheless exercised in defiance of that strict limitation. I quote the poem in full:

> The mind has a power which is unusable
> and this is its real power. What else but the mind
> senses the final uselessness of the mind?
>
> How foolish we were, how smaller than what we are,
> were we to believe what the mind makes of what
> it meets. Whatever the mind makes is not.
>
> You know there are always messages we find
> — in bed, on the street or anywhere, and the mind
> invents a translation almost plausible;
> but it hasn't any knowledge of the language at all.
>
> Sometimes the translations are cryptic in themselves.
> I read them in wonderment. It is a wonderment
> not usable. What could it all mean?
> The mind does this. I stand in awe of the mind.[12]

This is a poem that both recognizes and embraces its imaginative limits. The mind has a "power," but that power is perfectly "unusable." It is not a power that can readily be harnessed to human designs, however well intentioned those designs may be. Bronk suggests that we are mistaken if we suppose that the mind's imagined values, whether its concepts or ideals, in any way correspond to the world. Of the messages sent our way by the world, the mind "hasn't any knowledge of the language at all."

But Bronk draws his reader, on the basis of this very recognition, into the realm of "wonderment." The mind may not grasp its reality, but it produces cryptic "translations" which compel our assent despite their inevitable distortion. Examples of such translation would include scientific models, philosophical systems, and even an individual's working sense of self. To "believe in" any of the mind's constructions is to willingly adopt a fiction, usually because it is somehow useful to adopt that fiction. Like Stevens, Bronk balances faith in the mind's processes with a profound skepticism of the particular fictions that these processes have generated. His skepticism, like Santayana's, is more a reflection of intellectual modesty than of rational arrogance. Bronk simply does not believe that any thought will be adequate to the diverse and multiple reality of things. Skepticism and faith are mutually reinforcing here, both together keeping the mind on an even keel, capable of acknowledging its limits and of recognizing its real power, or the real power to which it has access, within those limits.

For any pragmatist, there is no definitive ideal or belief that puts us in closer contact with the inherent nature of things or the absolute moral grounds or ethical imperatives of being. What poets like Bronk and Stevens and other literary pragmatists offer is a strong sense of the inadequacy of all received ideals, coupled with a powerful creative impulse to imagine new and different ideals. One of the hazards of neopragmatism (as well as postmodern theory more generally) is that implicitly antifoundational attitudes and intellectual practices may be reduced to a set of true ideas which are then promoted as the only viable replacement for the false foundational ideas that were once the province of philosophy. The literary pragmatists do not make this mistake because their skepticism is so thoroughly integrated with their faith in the processes of imaginative transition. These writers use literary language and specifically aesthetic dynamics to foreground the creative activity that precedes and outlasts any search for adequate foundations or any supposed discovery or formal realization of them.

Bronk's claim that "Whatever the mind makes is not" echoes Stevens's snow man, who "nothing himself, beholds / Nothing that is not there and the nothing that is" (*CP* 10). For both Stevens and Bronk, the negative assertion, rather than generating despair at the collapse of traditional values or beliefs, makes possible an affirmation that is at once detached and sympathetic, cautious but ever hopeful. Their emphatic rejection of inadequate ideals opens the space for fresh creative activity, an activity that does not issue in final ideals in which we can repose but rather initiates new transitional processes. Our wonderment serves to cultivate this creative power, but it remains a wonderment "not usable," which is the basis of its "real power." This is the most distinctive and difficult aspect of the pragmatist legacy: the mind's power is indistinguishable from its abiding powerlessness. "Life, transition, the energizing spirit": these Emersonian terms mark a power that suffuses and exceeds the pragmatist imagination and all its works. Literature and other imaginative arts are valuable, despite their essential poverty, for the "affluence" they bear of this transitional dynamic. "The mind does this. I stand in awe of the mind."

# Notes

## PREFACE

1 Stanley Fish, *Doing What Comes Naturally: Change, Rhetoric, and the Practice of Theory in Literary and Legal Studies* (Durham: Duke UP, 1989) 321, 323.

2 Cornel West, *The American Evasion of Philosophy: A Genealogy of Pragmatism* (Madison: U of Wisconsin P, 1989) 5, 237.

## INTRODUCTION

1 For a discussion of "actualist hope" in American writing, see Robert Weisbuch, *Atlantic Double-Cross: American Literature and British Influence in the Age of Emerson* (1986; Chicago: U of Chicago P, 1989). Weisbuch defines American actualism as "the attempt to make literary vision literally available to everyday living." Actualism is "mimeticism in reverse, life imitating art, and in a manner having nothing to do with *fin de siècle* aestheticism and everything to do with the sense of the possible in dawn-driven America" (207). Weisbuch balances his presentation of American actualism with a discussion of a related intellectual and literary phenomenon he traces to an "ontological insecurity" and associates especially with Melville. For such writers, Americans' release from received forms and traditions generates a profound anxiety: possibility overwhelms as optimism shades into a dark moodiness and even despair. My own discussion of Emerson, pragmatism, and American literary modernism owes much to Weisbuch's formulations.

2 Many neopragmatists have foregrounded what they take to be the implicit politics of pragmatism. As social constructionists, they assume that pragmatism opens the way to a politicized intervention in the processes of social formation. In fact, the only political advantage of pragmatism (or of any social-constructionist position) is in providing a hedge against the hegemonic authority of any given construction. See especially Richard Rorty's incisive comments in *Consequences of Pragmatism* on the absence of any narrative of moral assurance even in the face of totalitarian disaster (xlii–xliv). There is nothing in pragmatism to ground a progressive (or a conservative) politics. Pragmatism may help us to question authoritarian accounts of the world, but our own accounts will always be subject to the same questioning. See Rorty, *Consequences of Pragmatism: Essays, 1972–1980* (Minneapolis: U of Minnesota P, 1982).

3 In an autobiographical essay, Rorty has described himself as having "gotten more and more raucously secularist" over time (41), linking this secularism to his steady disillusionment with the dream of a coherent, rational, and unifying philosophical perspective. See Rorty, "Trotsky and the Wild Orchids," in *Wild Orchids and Trotsky: Messages from American Universities,* ed. Mark Edmundson (New York: Penguin, 1993) 31–50.

4 John Patrick Diggins, *The Promise of Pragmatism: Modernism and the Crisis of Knowledge and Authority* (Chicago: U of Chicago P, 1994) 17.

5 Qtd. in Richard Hocks, *Henry James and Pragmatistic Thought* (Chapel Hill: U of North Carolina P, 1974) 52.

6 See especially Ross Posnock, *The Trial of Curiosity: Henry James, William James, and the Challenge of Modernity* (Cambridge: Harvard UP, 1991).

## 1 DIVINE OVERFLOWINGS: EMERSON'S PRAGMATIC IDEALISM

1 On pragmatism and nineteenth-century neo-Hegelianism, see especially the first three essays collected in William James's 1909 *A Pluralistic Universe*: "The Types of Philosophic Thinking," "Monistic Idealism," and "Hegel and His Method" (*W* 2:631–89). Richard Rorty grapples with the problem of Dewey's latent Hegelianism in his essay "Dewey's Metaphysics," in *Consequences of Pragmatism* 72–89. For a reading that links Emerson's idealism with his "incipient pragmatism," see Russel B. Goodman, *American Philosophy and the Romantic Tradition* (Cambridge: Cambridge UP, 1990). In *Emerson's Pragmatic Vision: The Dance of the Eye* (University Park: Pennsylvania State UP, 1993), David Jacobson also demonstrates that "Emerson altered the meaning of transcendence . . . mainly by indicating that it is a matter of action, not contemplation, by inverting the traditional priority of theory over practice and rendering universality finite" (60). Jacobson further suggests that Emersonian Transcendentalism "inheres in what is presented by the clearing of the eye, the space opened up within the horizon of the eye," making his a "humanist and phenomenological transcendence, not a rationalist one" (60). For a contrasting view of Emerson's visual metaphors suggesting that "inherent in his resistance to rationalization is the detached contemplative stance of reified consciousness" (201), see Carolyn Porter, "Reification and American Literature," in *Ideology and Classic American Literature*, ed. Sacvan Bercovitch and Myra Jehlen (Cambridge: Cambridge UP, 1986) 188–217, as well as the larger work from which this essay is taken, Porter, *Seeing and Being: The Plight of the Participant Observer in Emerson, James, Adams, and Faulkner* (Middletown: Wesleyan UP, 1981).

2 Stephen Whicher, *Freedom and Fate: An Inner Life of Ralph Waldo Emerson* (Philadelphia: U of Pennsylvania P, 1953) 58.

3 Robert D. Richardson Jr. briefly summarizes Emerson's reading outside Western religious traditions in *Emerson: The Mind on Fire* (Berkeley: U of California P, 1995) 392–93. The standard work on Emerson's Eastern influences remains Frederic Ives Carpenter, *Emerson and Asia* (1930; New York: Haskell House, 1968). See also Arthur Christy, *The Orient in American Transcendentalism* (1932; New York: Octagon, 1969); Elamanamadathil V. Francis, *Emerson and Hindu Scriptures* (Cochin, India: Academic Publications, 1972); and Daniel J. Thottackara, *Emerson the Advaitin: A Study of the Parallels between Emerson and Samkara's Advaita Vedanta* (Cochin, India: L. F. I. Press, 1986).

4 In "Emerson's Constitutional Amending: Reading 'Fate,'" Stanley Cavell refers to the "power of what Emerson calls patience, which he seeks as the most active of intellectual conditions" (38). Patience is vital to what Cavell calls "Emersonian perfectionism" because of the recalcitrant imperfection of the world we inhabit. Through patience, we train our capacity for response; this responsiveness, for Cavell, is the basis of all human responsibility. For another, related view of the relationship between response, responsiveness, and responsibility, see Emmanuel Levinas, especially the essays on Martin Buber in *Outside the Subject*, trans. Michael B. Smith (Stanford: Stanford UP, 1994) and "Substitution," rpt. in *The Levinas Reader*, ed. Seán Hand (Oxford: Blackwell, 1989). Cavell often links Emerson with Heidegger, but his insistent emphasis on ethics should also bring Levinas to mind.

*Notes to Chapter One*

See Cavell, "Emerson's Constitutional Amending," in *Philosophical Passages: Wittgenstein, Emerson, Austin, Derrida* (Oxford: Blackwell, 1995) 12–41.

5   Many scholars have noted the apparent collapse of moral standards in Emerson's anti-nomian celebration of "whim" in "Self-Reliance." In "The Standard Oil Trust as Emersonian Hero," Howard Horwitz comments that Emerson provides no means "for distinguishing degraded from virtuous practice, for distinguishing, that is, merely private interest from inspiration, investment in a higher plane" (106). Horwitz links the logic of Emersonian self-reliance with the rise of the Standard Oil Trust, suggesting that both are designed to exercise power without having to answer to anyone for any of its potentially destructive effects. Horwitz, like many of Emerson's critics, views Emersonian perfectionism as something between a ruse and a naive political ideal. See Horwitz, "The Standard Oil Trust," *Raritan* 6.4 (1987): 97–119.

6   Emerson's bitter denunciations of the market are amply documented in Sacvan Bercovitch, *The Rites of Assent: Transformations in the Symbolic Construction of America* (New York: Routledge, 1993) 307–52. Bercovitch locates a shift in Emerson's attitudes around 1842, after which his championing of individuality against the forces of the market (a position Bercovitch links to the socialist rhetoric of the day) slides into what Bercovitch describes as a more complacent individualism that views the laissez-faire market as the best, indeed the only hope for progress. Bercovitch does not address the way in which Emerson's attitudes toward slavery evolve after his apparent "complacency" has set in. For another, related view of "Self-Reliance, Politics, and Society," see George Kateb, *Emerson and Self-Reliance* (Thousand Oaks, Calif.: Sage, 1995) 173–96.

7   The racism appears in what is very nearly Emerson's opening gambit in the talk, as if to "allow" what his audience would already take for granted: "I think it cannot be maintained by any candid person that the African race have ever occupied or do promise ever to occupy any very high place in the human family. Their present condition is the strongest proof that they cannot. The Irish cannot; the American Indian cannot; the Chinese cannot. Before the energy of the Caucasian race all other races have quailed and done obeisance" (*JMN* 12:152). Emerson's sense of the limits of what Northern whites can and should attempt on behalf of the slaves appears late in the essay: "But when we have settled the right & wrong of this question I think we have done all we can. A man can only extend his active attention to a certain finite amount of claims. We have much nearer duties than to the poor black slaves of Carolina and the effect of the present excitement is to exaggerate that" (*JMN* 12:154). For three distinct views of Emerson on the problems of race and slavery, see Cornel West, *The American Evasion of Philosophy* 9–41; Len Gougeon, *Virtue's Hero: Emerson, Antislavery, and Reform* (Athens: U of Georgia P, 1990); and John Carlos Rowe, *At Emerson's Tomb: The Politics of Classic American Literature* (New York: Columbia UP, 1997) 17–41.

8   Qtd. in Robert D. Richardson Jr., *Emerson: The Mind on Fire* 278, 275–76.

9   See also Emerson's comment on the effect of speaking with éclat in "Self-Reliance" (*EL* 261) and Richard Poirier's astute observations on this passage in *The Renewal of Literature: Emersonian Reflections* (New York: Random House, 1987) 48–49.

10  This view forms the basis of the classic criticism of Emerson's individualism. For a recent restatement of this view, see Cary Wolfe, *The Limits of American Literary Ideology in Pound and Emerson* (Cambridge: Cambridge UP, 1993). Wolfe argues that the "Lockean individualist basis" of Pound's and Emerson's social criticism serves "to disarm and delimit their full economic and political implications by recasting what are properly issues of fundamental economic and political structure into problems of ethics and personal conduct" (7). The

*Notes to Chapter One*

problem with this formulation is that Emerson often complicates and challenges this individualism and the model of ethics as mere personal conduct associated with it.

11  Poirier, "The Question of Genius," in *Renewal of Literature* 86–87; "Writing Off the Self," in *Renewal of Literature* 196.

12  Joseph N. Riddel identifies these same energies with the aesthetic individualism that has defined the "Americanist" project since at least F. O. Matthiessen's *The American Renaissance*. Riddel's rigorous deconstructions of such enabling myths as "literature," "self," and "America" can be seen as clearing the way for recent attempts to reinvent the American literary canon as well as its enabling ideas of "America" and "Americanness." Riddel himself, however, resembles critics like Poirier and Harold Bloom, both of whom he criticized for not sufficiently deconstructing the "subject" of "American literature" (in all imaginable senses of the phrase), in that his criticism took the form of very close readings of classic American writers and the fascinating ambiguities, contradictions, ambivalences, and disjunctions of their language. See Riddel, "Decentering the Image: The 'Project' of 'American' Poetics?", in *Textual Strategies: Perspectives in Post-Structuralist Criticism*, ed. Josué V. Harari (Ithaca: Cornell UP, 1979) 322–58, and *The Purloined Letter*, ed. Mark Bauerlein (Baton Rouge: Louisiana State UP, 1995).

13  Donald Pease, *Visionary Compacts: American Renaissance Writings in Cultural Context* (Madison: U of Wisconsin P, 1987) 204, 232. In *The Rites of Assent*, Sacvan Bercovitch also emphasizes the "profoundly unsettling energies" of Emersonian individualism in the late 1830s and early 1840s. For Bercovitch, Emersonian dissent "testifies to the oppositional forms generated within the structures of society—in Emerson's terms, somewhere at the margins of culture, at some transitional moving point, perpetually inchoate because transitional on principle, between center and circumference" (349). Pease also locates "nature's law" in Emerson "in the transition from the thought to the thing or the thing to the thought, for that is the ever moving course of nature" (216). For all their differences of emphasis, Pease and Bercovitch agree with Poirier that the Emersonian self is not, in its most rigorous conception, the liberal subject that so many of Emerson's critics make it out to be. Indeed, the most peculiar and distinctive feature of Emersonian self-reliance is that Emerson would seem to posit no self on which to rely in the first place.

14  Emerson's conception of "the method of nature" prefigures the emphasis among twentieth-century systems theorists and ecologists on integrated wholes whose "specific structures arise from the interactions and interdependence of their parts." See Fritjof Capra, *The Turning Point: Science, Society, and the Rising Culture* (1982; New York: Bantam, 1988) 267. See also Capra, *The Web of Life: A New Scientific Understanding of Living Systems* (New York: Doubleday, 1996). For more general background to the rise of ecological metaphors of interdependence, see Donald Worster, *Nature's Economy: A History of Ecological Ideas* (1977; Cambridge: Cambridge UP, 1992). Though Worster criticizes what he characterizes as Emerson's aggressively self-centered view of nature, he writes at length about Thoreau's "romantic ecology" and its place in developing ideas of interdependence and mutuality (59–111). For a wide spectrum of views on the rise of systems theory in both scientific and nonscientific contexts, see "The Politics of Systems and Environments," a double-issue forum edited by William Rasch and Cary Wolfe in *Cultural Critique* 30 and 31 (1995).

15  William James would resort to a similar model, invoking phases of a single reality, in his description of how an object can be "taken" twice, both in the context of the objects alongside it and in the context of the thinker's thoughts. These might be called phases of a single reality, though they are simultaneous. See "The Knowing of Things Together" and "Does

*Notes to Chapter One*

'Consciousness' Exist?" (*W* 1:1057–76; *W* 2:1141–58). Emerson's rejection of a narrow, quasi-mechanistic analysis of mental processes and his turn instead to the interrelatedness of things and attitudes of feeling, awe, or love in which we can intuit something of this inter-relatedness anticipate phenomenologists' later emphasis on the role of a lived, prereflective phenomenal field in our constitution as purposeful human subjects. As chapter 2 will demonstrate, William James develops these insights into a more systematic reformulation of our understanding of the relationship between mind and world.

16  On the trope of abandonment, see Stanley Cavell, "Thinking of Emerson," in the expanded edition of *The Senses of Walden* (San Francisco: North Point Press, 1981) and Barbara Packer, *Emerson's Fall: A New Interpretation of the Major Essays* (New York: Continuum, 1982). Packer comments on how, in the conclusion to "Circles," the trope functions as a pun: "The way of life requires abandonment *of* the ossified circumference of past thought in favor of the new truth rupturing and pushing beyond it; it requires abandonment *to* that central principle of life, higher than reason or even faith, which in its first protests against all forms of limitation 'already tends outward with a vast force, and to immense and innumerable expansions' " (136–37). To this I would only add that part of what is being abandoned, at least in Emerson's most radical formulation of the problem, is what we typically call the "authentic self."

17  On Emerson and natural science, see Lee Rust Brown, *The Emerson Museum: Practical Romanticism and the Pursuit of the Whole* (Cambridge: Harvard UP, 1997). Linking Emerson's Coleridgian poetics with his interest in the scientific naturalism of his day, Brown suggests that " 'the whole' for Emerson is best described not as an object of faith or philosophical inquiry but as a project, a pursuit, a work discipline that employs many local positions of belief and skepticism, of renunciation and fresh commitment" (18–19).

18  On the problem of diminished rights, see especially Stanley Cavell's ongoing discussion of Emerson. Given that ideas are, as Cavell puts it in "Emerson's Constitutional Amending," "in the air," that they are "our life's breath," that they "become our words," and that many of them are obnoxious and sick ("slavery is supported by some of them and might have crushed the rest of them"), we have an obligation to choose our words with extraordinary care. As Cavell notes, "every word is a word spoken *again,* or against again" (25). In *Conditions Handsome and Unhandsome: The Constitution of Emersonian Perfectionism* (Chicago: U of Chicago P, 1990), Cavell calls this "aversive thinking": "We must become averse to this conformity, which means convert from it, which means transform our conformity, as if we are to be born (again)" (47). Genius should be an incentive to thinking, to uttering our every word in aversion to whatever conformities fill the air. As Cavell notes in "Emerson's Constitutional Amending," this can be an unpleasant and difficult task: "To think is to turn around, or to turn back (Wittgenstein says lead back), the words of ordinary life (hence the present forms of our lives) that now repel thought, disgust it" (14).

## 2   WILLIAM JAMES AND THE METAPHORICS OF TRANSITION

1  West, *American Evasion of Philosophy* 54.

2  See especially Walter Benn Michaels, *The Gold Standard and the Logic of Naturalism: American Literature at the Turn of the Century* (Berkeley: U of California P, 1987) and Priscilla Wald, *Constituting Americans: Cultural Anxiety and Narrative Form* (Durham: Duke UP, 1995). Wald summarizes this position nicely: "James was a conscientious reformer, liberal pluralist, and avowed anti-imperialist who sought to destabilize normative philosophical

*Notes to Chapter Two*

notions of selfhood by demonstrating 'that we are of one clay with lunatics and criminals.' Yet the metaphors of ownership through which he describes the self actually interfere with his inquiry. Gradually becoming traits of the self in the course of his discussion, more-over, those metaphors normalize patriarchal property relations that are consistent with the precepts of overseas expansion that he actively opposed" (261). For a different reading of James's pluralistic, anti-imperialist politics, see Frank Lentricchia, *Ariel and the Police: Michel Foucault, William James, Wallace Stevens* (Madison: U of Wisconsin P, 1988) and *Modernist Quartet* (Cambridge: Cambridge UP, 1994).

3   James uses the phrase (and chapter title) the "stream of thought" in the 1890 *Principles,* but revised both phrase and title to the "stream of consciousness" in the 1892 *Psychology: Briefer Course.* All citations from "The Stream of Thought" are from the more expansive *Principles of Psychology,* except where otherwise noted.

4   James's work in many ways anticipates phenomenology, especially the founding work of Edmund Husserl, Martin Heidegger, and Maurice Merleau-Ponty. On James and phenome-nology, see especially Bruce Wilshire, *William James and Phenomenology: A Study of "The Principles of Psychology"* (Bloomington: Indiana UP, 1968); James M. Edie, *William James and Phenomenology* (Bloomington: Indiana UP, 1987); and Richard Cobb-Stevens, "A Fresh Look at James's Radical Empiricism," in *Phenomenology: Dialogues and Bridges,* ed. Ronald Bruzina II and Bruce W. Wilshire (Albany: State U of New York P, 1982).

5   The significance of James's achievement in his conception of mind has long been recog-nized, though it is not very widely understood. Alfred North Whitehead presents James (specifically the James of the essay "Does 'Consciousness' Exist?', an essay also much ad-mired by Dewey) as his characteristic modern philosopher, exemplifying a new, emerging direction for nonmechanistic, nondualistic models of thought. See Whitehead, *Science and the Modern World* (1925; New York: Free Press, 1967) 139–56. In "The Structure of Aware-ness: Contemporary Applications of William James' Forgotten Concept of 'The Fringe,' " David Galin, a psychiatrist conducting research in forms of cognitive awareness, suggests that James's notion of the "nucleus/fringe" relation could provide "a bridging conceptual framework" that will show how cognitive and brain subsystems are "integrated into be-haviorally relevant systems in the whole brain and the whole person" (396). Galin offers a useful account of James's fringe, contextualizing it in a variety of later models of cognition. See Galin, "The Structure of Awareness," *Journal of Mind and Behavior* 15 (1994): 375–401. For another view of James's place in recent developments in human psychology, see Eugene Taylor, *William James on Consciousness beyond the Margin* (Princeton: Princeton UP, 1996).

6   For the background of James's interest in psychical research, see Perry, *Thought and Charac-ter of William James* (*TC* 2:155–72). Eugene Taylor approaches James's psychical researches with an eye to their relevance as authentic psychological research in "The Reality of Multiple States: Abnormal Psychology and Psychical Research," in *William James on Consciousness* 40–81.

7   Critics have long questioned pragmatism's conception of experience. Paul Jay has recently restated this criticism: "What this position ignores is the extent to which 'experience itself' is shot through with the processes we associate with signification and interpretation. There is no 'experience itself' that stands before or outside of these processes. Experience is con-stituted through them, not before or beyond them." This is essentially the same criticism posed by several of the participants in the May 1993 Paris colloquium recorded in the vol-ume *Deconstruction and Pragmatism.* If there is no "experience itself" outside processes of signification and interpretation, however, these same processes have no possible relevance

*Notes to Chapter Two*

except to signify and interpret the world we experience. To say we are not experiencing the world because language has intervened is no more useful than to say we are not experiencing it because all we ever experience are simple sense impressions. If the advantage of Jay's and the deconstructionists' perspective is to foreground the irreducible impact of culture on experience, the advantage of the pragmatist method is to cultivate agencies of transition as they are realized in experience. See Jay, *Contingency Blues: The Search for Foundations in American Criticism* (Madison: U of Wisconsin P, 1997) 25; *Deconstruction and Pragmatism,* ed. Chantal Mouffe (London: Routledge, 1996).

8   For James's revision, see "A World of Pure Experience" as printed in *The Meaning of Truth* (rpt. in *WWJ* 206).

9   Ralph Barton Perry documents the initial debate surrounding "The Will to Believe" in *The Thought and Character of William James* (*TC* 2:225–49). Perry summarizes the criticisms James immediately faced: "He was accused of encouraging *willfulness* or *wantonness* of belief, or of advocating belief for belief's sake, whereas his whole purpose had been to *justify* belief. He had affirmed that belief was voluntary, but had naturally assumed that, in this as in other cases, volition would be governed by motives and illuminated by reasons. His critics had accused him of advocating *license* in belief, whereas, on the contrary, his aim had been to formulate rules for belief" (*TC* 2:248). Commentary has not advanced considerably from the stage Perry describes: advocates of James's doctrine continue to emphasize the constraints that govern possible beliefs while critics emphasize the sheer absurdity of weighing voluntary belief so heavily. No doubt James's habit of championing the individual will obscures the restraining mechanisms on which he also insists.

10   This formulation appears in the later, revised text of *Psychology: Briefer Course.* In "The Consciousness of Self" chapter from *The Principles of Psychology,* James had written, "*If the passing thought be the directly verifiable existent which no school has hitherto doubted it to be, then that thought is itself the thinker,* and psychology need not look beyond" (*PP* 1:379). In his revision, James both pluralizes the formula, replacing the abstract-sounding "thought . . . itself" with "the thoughts themselves," and highlights his deconstruction of self by making these the concluding words of the chapter.

11   Because James did not merely shorten the chapter on "Will" for his *Briefer Course,* but often revised key concepts, I have quoted from "Will" as it appears in that volume.

12   James is anticipating one of the central aphorisms of his contemporary Nietzsche: "To transform the belief 'it *is* thus and thus' into the will 'it *shall become* thus and thus.'" Nietzsche has as hard a time locating this "will" as James: "Linguistic means of expression are useless for expressing 'becoming'; it accords with our inevitable need to preserve ourselves to posit a crude world of stability, of 'things,' etc. We may venture to speak of atoms and monads in a relative sense; and it is certain that the smallest world is the most durable — There is no will: there are treaty drafts of will that are constantly increasing or losing their power." See Friedrich Nietzsche, *The Will to Power,* ed. Walter Kaufmann, trans. Walter Kaufmann and R. J. Hollingdale (1901; New York: Vintage, 1968) 324, 380–81. On Nietzsche's conception of self and will, see Alexander Nehamas, *Nietzsche: Life as Literature* (Cambridge: Harvard UP, 1985) 170–99.

13   This essay exists in two forms, one as delivered to the American Philosophical Association at Columbia University on December 28, 1906, and subsequently published in the *Philosophical Review* in January 1907 and the other published in the more popular *American Magazine* in October 1907. The latter, cited here, appears in *The Writings of William James* (*WWJ* 671–83); the former appears in the Library of America's *Writings 1902–1910* (*W* 2:1223–41).

*Notes to Chapter Two*

1   William James, *Essays, Comments, and Reviews* (Cambridge: Harvard UP, 1987) 489.

2   Qtd. in Howard M. Feinstein, *Becoming William James* (Ithaca: Cornell UP, 1984) 146–47. Feinstein offers one of the best discussions of James's early pursuit of a career in the visual arts (103–45).

3   Santayana, "A General Confession," in *The Philosophy of George Santayana*, ed. Paul Arthur Schilpp (Evanston: Northwestern UP, 1940) 15, 16–17.

4   Ibid. 20; Santayana, *WGS* 1:393.

5   This passage is from "What Is Aesthetics," originally published in the *Philosophical Review* in 1904 and reprinted in *Obiter Scripta: Lectures, Essays and Reviews*, ed. Justus Buchler and Benjamin Schwartz (New York: Scribner's, 1936) 35. For a discussion of the transitional place of this essay in the development of Santayana's aesthetics, see Arthur C. Danto, "Introduction," *The Sense of Beauty*, vol. 2 of *The Works of George Santayana*.

6   Henry Samuel Levinson, *Santayana, Pragmatism, and the Spiritual Life* (Chapel Hill: U of North Carolina P, 1992) 3, 220.

7   This qualification regarding Plato appears in Santayana's work from first to last. It is important not to confuse the much-abused derogatory tag *Platonist* with Plato's actual body of writings: Plato's Platonism is everywhere complicated by his own anti-Platonic skepticism. Vincent Descombes, commenting in *Modern French Philosophy* (trans. L. Scott-Fox and J. M. Harding [1979; Cambridge: Cambridge UP, 1980]) on Jacques Derrida's reading of Plato, similarly concludes that "between the text by Plato and itself . . . there passes a 'scarcely perceptible veil', separating Platonism from itself. . . . A slight displacement, a slight play in the reading of the text, is sufficient to collapse the first into the second, the *wisdom* of the first into the *comedy* of the second" (151). The reductive *Platonist* subtracts Plato's comedy from his wisdom, or, in Santayana's terms, his poetry from his metaphysics. While the tag *Platonist* has a certain polemical force, it also obscures the complex "truth" of Plato's writings.

8   James similarly reversed the title of his 1889 essay "The Psychology of Belief" when he published it with only minor changes as "The Perception of Reality" in *The Principles of Psychology*. Both this change and the proposed change for "The Sentiment of Rationality" underscore the mutual relatedness, for James, of fact and belief.

9   Important cultural issues of sexuality, encoded into both Henry James's and Santayana's personal comportment, sensibility, and literary style, are very much at stake here. For a compelling analysis of William's anxieties in the presence of such open, receptive styles of being, see especially Ross Posnock, *The Trial of Curiosity*.

10  In *The Thought and Character of William James*, Ralph Barton Perry suggests that "closely allied to James's moral earnestness was his strong distaste for anything which he suspected of being decadent" (*TC* 2:251). Perry's emphasis on James's moral will, however just as a description of James's willed self-image, does tend to obscure the complex psychic tensions, and especially their cultural genealogy, that produced the willed self-image in the first place.

11  Thoreau cites the same passage from Tennyson's "Locksley Hall" in *A Week on the Concord and Merrimack Rivers*, anticipating James's variation with his own playful spin: " 'Through the shadow of the world we sweep into the younger day: / Better fifty years of Europe than a cycle of Cathay.' / Than fifty years of Europe better one New England ray!" See Henry David Thoreau, *A Week on the Concord and Merrimack Rivers, Walden, The Maine Woods, Cape Cod* (New York: Library of America, 1985) 126.

*Notes to Chapter Three*

12  James had reached this conclusion about Renan as early as 1876, when he reviewed *Dialogues et fragments philosophiques* in the *Nation*. He called Renan's book "an example of mental ruin — the last expression of a nature in which the seeds of insincerity and foppishness, which existed at the start alongside of splendid powers, have grown up like rank weeds and smothered the better possibilities." See James, "Renan's Dialogues," in *Essays, Comments, and Reviews* 327.

13  For Dewey's analysis of James's developing notion of consciousness and the self, see "The Vanishing Subject in the Psychology of James" (*LW* 14:155–67).

14  Dewey's deconstruction of subjectivity should be distinguished from most postmodern and poststructuralist deconstructions of the self. Michel Foucault describes his project in his 1971 essay "Nietzsche, Genealogy, History": "The purpose of history, guided by genealogy, is not to discover the roots of our identity but to commit itself to its dissipation. It does not seek to define our unique threshold of emergence, the homeland to which metaphysicians promise a return; it seeks to make visible all of these discontinuities that cross us" (162). Dewey's own emphasis on interdependent processes and the self's participation in and extension of those processes suggests that Dewey is less interested in such dissipation of the subject than in its effective transitional agency. In other words, Dewey does not set out to make visible the discontinuities that cross us so much as to orient us toward new and different realizations. See Foucault, *Language, Counter-Memory, Practice: Selected Essays and Interviews*, ed. Donald F. Bouchard, trans. Donald F. Bouchard and Sherry Simon (1977; Ithaca: Cornell UP, 1981) 139–64.

15  West, *American Evasion of Philosophy* 95.

16  Of the exceptions, I refer below to Thomas Alexander and Giles Gunn. It was John McDermott's *The Culture of Experience: Philosophical Essays in the American Grain* (New York: New York UP, 1976) that first pointed me toward *Art as Experience*. See also Richard Shusterman, *Pragmatist Aesthetics: Living Beauty, Rethinking Art* (Oxford: Blackwell, 1992), which usefully compares twentieth-century analytic aesthetics with pragmatism, though his treatment of pragmatism is limited to Dewey and the neopragmatists of the 1980s and 90s. Shusterman also provides provocative analyses of pragmatist aesthetics and popular culture.

17  For a comprehensive treatment of Dewey's aesthetic theory and its centrality to his philosophy of experience, nature, and culture, see Thomas Alexander, *John Dewey's Theory of Art, Experience, and Nature: The Horizons of Feeling* (Albany: State U of New York P, 1987).

18  Rorty, *Consequences of Pragmatism* 73; West, *American Evasion of Philosophy* 97.

19  Rorty, *Consequences of Pragmatism* xliv.

20  Rorty defines the "liberal ironist" in *Contingency, Irony, Solidarity* (Cambridge: Cambridge UP, 1989): "I borrow my definition of 'liberal' from Judith Shklar, who says that liberals are the people who think that cruelty is the worst thing we do. I use 'ironist' to name the sort of person who faces up to the contingency of his or her own most central beliefs and desires — someone sufficiently historicist and nominalist to have abandoned the idea that those central beliefs and desires refer back to something beyond the reach of time and chance. Liberal ironists are people who include among these ungroundable desires their own hope that suffering will be diminished, that the humiliation of human beings by other human beings may cease" (xv). West describes the "prophetic pragmatist" in *The American Evasion of Philosophy*: "The distinctive hallmarks of a prophetic pragmatist are a universal consciousness that promotes an all-embracing democratic and libertarian moral vision, a historical consciousness that acknowledges human finitude and conditionedness, and a critical consciousness

which encourages relentless critique and self-criticism for the aims of social change and personal humility" (232). See Rorty, *Contingency, Irony, Solidarity* 73–95, and West, *American Evasion of Philosophy* 226–39.

21 West, *American Evasion of Philosophy* 206. On West's sense of pragmatism's common ground with American religious traditions, see his discussion of Reinhold Niebuhr, as well as his comments on religion preceding his conclusion, in *American Evasion of Philosophy* 150–64, 232–35.

22 Ibid. 204.

23 Giles Gunn, *Thinking across the American Grain: Ideology, Intellect, and the New Pragmatism* (Chicago: U of Chicago P, 1992) 74; Richard Poirier, *Poetry and Pragmatism* (Cambridge: Harvard UP, 1992) 37.

24 Stephen C. Pepper, "Some Questions on Dewey's Esthetics," in *The Philosophy of John Dewey*, ed. Paul Arthur Schilpp (Evanston: Northwestern UP, 1939) 388.

25 See also *Experience and Nature*, where Dewey describes the function of aesthetics in ancient Greek culture, its later effect on classical Greek philosophy, and the impact of the seventeenth-century scientific revolution on ideas about the nature of nature as they were inherited from the Greeks (*LW* 1:72–90, 93–94).

26 In *Art as Experience*, Dewey carefully distinguishes "*an* experience" from experience per se. *An* experience is a discrete event that "runs its course to fulfillment" and involves a concomitant doing and undergoing (*LW* 10:42). Every aesthetic experience is "an experience." Indeed, as Dewey comments, "Even a crude experience, if authentically an experience, is more fit to give a clue to the intrinsic nature of esthetic experience than is an object already set apart from any other mode of experience" (*LW* 10:16–17).

## 4 SANTAYANA, DEWEY, AND THE POLITICS OF TRANSITION

1 Eliot's description of Santayana appears in a very critical 1898 letter to Hugo Münsterberg on Santayana's proposed advancement to assistant professor, cited in John McCormick, *George Santayana: A Biography* (New York: Knopf, 1987) 97. McCormick suggests that "since Eliot was not alleging psychiatric disorder, his use of 'abnormal' probably meant 'homosexual'" (97).

2 For a full and nuanced treatment of Dewey and democracy, see Robert B. Westbrook, *John Dewey and American Democracy* (Ithaca: Cornell UP, 1991). Bertrand Russell reflects the conventional marginalization of Santayana when he juxtaposes Santayana and James, suggesting that where James appreciated religion as a moral, democratic force, Santayana appreciated it "aesthetically and historically, not as a help towards a moral life." Russell misleadingly overstates the gap, both moral and intellectual, between James and Santayana, ignoring both student and teacher's steady if always qualified appreciation of one another's work. See Russell, *A History of Western Philosophy* (1945; New York: Simon and Schuster, 1972) 811. For Santayana's admiring reflections on James, see especially "The Genteel Tradition in American Philosophy" (*GT* 54–64); *Character and Opinion in the United States* (*CO* 39–60); and *Persons and Places: Fragments of Autobiography* (*WGS* 1:232–33, 238–39, 401–5). The best treatment of Santayana's political thought can be found in Henry Samuel Levinson, *Santayana, Pragmatism, and the Spiritual Life* 249–84. Levinson traces Santayana's "misgivings" about the Deweyan conception of democracy, comparing him to Nietzsche in his effort to "unmask ways in which democracy can rationalize cruelty or humiliation in the name of equality, by making personal anomalies that comprise individual distinction

*Notes to Chapter Four*

appear offensive or pathological" (250). He also examines the link for Santayana between public projects of social amelioration and naturalistic spiritual forms of life, a set of complementary impulses that defines what Levinson calls Santayana's "spiritual liberalism." For another view of Santayana's "critique of liberalism," see Noël O'Sullivan, *Santayana* (St. Albans, UK: Claridge, 1992) 78–102.

3 McCormick, *George Santayana* 367.

4 George Santayana, *Three Philosophical Poets: Lucretius, Dante, and Goethe* (1910; Cambridge: Harvard UP, 1922) 211–12.

5 See Levinson, *Santayana, Pragmatism, and the Spiritual Life* 3–4.

6 For an extended discussion of Dewey's *A Common Faith* in the context of Santayana and pragmatism, see Levinson, *Santayana, Pragmatism, and the Spiritual Life* 251–56.

7 On the "two psychologies of William James," see Herbert Schneider, *A History of American Philosophy* (1957; New York: Columbia UP, 1963) 495–503.

8 Dewey's theory of communication should be understood in connection with Peirce's semiotics, especially his treatment of the triadic structure of the sign. This affinity is apparent in one of Peirce's comments in a letter to Lady Welby: "Now a definition does not reveal the Object of a Sign, its Denotation, but only analyzes its Signification, and *that* is a question not of the sign's relation to its Object but of its relation to its Interpretant" (qtd. in John K. Sheriff, *The Fate of Meaning: Charles Peirce, Structuralism, and Literature* [Princeton: Princeton UP, 1989] 57). See Peirce, "Logic as Semiotic: The Theory of Signs," in *Philosophical Writings of Peirce*, ed. Justus Buchler (1940; New York: Dover, 1955) 98–119. For a discussion of "the nature of communication in Dewey's philosophy" grounded in Peirce's semiotics, see Victorino Tejera, *American Modern: The Path Not Taken. Aesthetics, Metaphysics, and Intellectual History in Classic American Philosophy* (Lanham, Md.: Rowman and Littlefield, 1996) 49–53.

9 Richard Rorty has written about the "contingency of language" in *Contingency, Irony, Solidarity*. Rorty's Deweyan pragmatism fuses with Wittgenstein's concept of the language game, Donald Davidson's discussions of metaphor, and Thomas Kuhn's treatment of the relation between normal science and scientific revolution to suggest that "*languages* are made rather than found, and that truth is a property of linguistic entities, of sentences" (7). Dewey would certainly agree with Rorty and his company of linguistic pragmatists that words are not designed to "fit" external realities. He would not, however, have considered truth a mere property of sentences because he would not have conceived of sentences so utterly abstracted from experience. Truth is not a property of sentences but rather of the shared social processes that sentences make possible, a view that in many ways takes its inspiration from Peirce's semiotics.

10 Because of limitations of space, I have not been able to examine in any detail Santayana's brilliant but neglected late writing on the subject of the realms of being, the first volume of which is devoted to the realm of essence. Suffice it to say that Santayana is everywhere aware of the long and densely problematic traditions preceding his own appropriation of such terms as *being, essence, matter, truth,* and *spirit*. In an important sense, his whole project is dedicated to recovering these terms for the modern imagination. Santayana, in other words, attempts to take philosophy behind the Socratic and post-Socratic traditions which have divided us from such primary philosophical terms. Though *Scepticism and Animal Faith* was written as the introductory volume to the series, Santayana also composed a preface for *The Realm of Essence* (1928), reprinted as the preface to the one-volume 1942 edition of *The Realms of Being*. This preface contains the best brief statement of Santayana's larger project. For a useful summary discussion of Santayana's late philosophy, see Timothy L. S. Sprigge,

*Notes to Chapter Four*

*Santayana: An Examination of His Philosophy* (London: Routledge and Kegan Paul, 1974); for a discussion of Santayana's use of such terms as *essence* and *spirit* with more of an eye to the contexts of pragmatism, see Levinson, *Santayana, Pragmatism, and the Spiritual Life,* especially his suggestive chapter "Comic Faith" (205-48).

11 Charles S. Peirce, "How To Make Our Ideas Clear," in *Writings of Charles S. Peirce: A Chronological Edition,* ed. Christian J. W. Kloesel, 5 vols. (Bloomington: Indiana UP, 1982-1993) 3:273.

12 On Santayana's view of "absolute truth," see the preface to *The Realm of Essence,* reprinted with the one-volume 1942 edition of *The Realms of Being:* "This relativity does not imply that there is no absolute truth. On the contrary, if there were no absolute truth, all-inclusive and eternal, the desultory views taken from time to time by individuals would themselves be absolute" (*RB* xv). This absolute truth "is no living view, no actual judgement, but merely that segment of the realm of essence which happens to be illustrated in existence" (*RB* xv). Though Peirce's language in "How To Make Our Ideas Clear" is decidedly more scientific, his description there of truth as "the result of investigation carried sufficiently far" is strikingly similar to Santayana's view. See Peirce, "How To Make Our Ideas Clear," in *Writings* 3:274. For another view of the relation between Santayana and Peirce, see Tejera, *American Modern* 79-116. Tejera notes Santayana's own passing acknowledgment of the influence of Peirce's semiotics, including Santayana's claim that if Peirce "had built his philosophy on signs," Santayana might himself "have been his disciple" (qtd. in *American Modern* 80).

13 On the novel's treatment of homosexuality, see Irving Singer's introduction to the 1994 MIT critical edition of the novel, vol. 4 of *The Works of George Santayana.* See also Ross Posnock's discussion of Santayana, Henry James, and Howard Sturgis in *The Trial of Curiosity* 193-220.

14 These lines were dropped from all early editions of the novel due to a printer's error—a manuscript page was apparently lost—but are restored in a textual note to the 1994 MIT critical edition of the novel.

15 Santayana's emphasis in *The Last Puritan* on the salutary effect of natural surroundings is also reflected in the talk's concluding invocation of the western forests and Sierras: "They suspend your forced sense of your own importance not merely as individuals, but even as men. They allow you, in one happy moment, at once to play and to worship, to take yourselves simply, humbly, for what you are, and to salute the wild, indifferent, noncensorious infinity of nature" (*GT* 63-64). Natural splendor, for Santayana, is at once a source of pleasure and a reminder of human limitation, precisely the sort of thing to wake Americans from their genteel, self-satisfied, and puritanical slumber.

16 Santayana had spent most of the war years in Oxford. In 1919, as he was completing the manuscript of *Character and Opinion,* he began a pattern of what John McCormick calls "geographical movements" that "he maintained until the outbreak of World War II in 1939": "Summers for the first few years he spent in Paris with [Charles] Strong, moving south by way of the Riviera or Florence to Rome, where he spent the winters in a hotel." In the winter of 1919-20, Santayana did indeed pass through Florence on his way to Rome. See McCormick, *George Santayana* 242.


## 5  HENRY JAMES AND THE DRAMA OF TRANSITION

1 As indicated in the introduction, James's comment appears in a letter to William James (*TC* 1:428).


*Notes to Chapter Five*

2 T. S. Eliot, "Henry James," in *Selected Prose of T. S. Eliot,* ed. Frank Kermode (New York: Harcourt, 1975) 151, 152.

3 For an excellent discussion of this scene with particular attention to its rhetoric of violence, see Ross Posnock, *The Trial of Curiosity* 221–49.

4 Qtd. in Roger Gard, ed., "Introduction," *The Critical Muse: Selected Literary Criticism,* by Henry James (New York: Penguin, 1987) 7.

5 Pound, "Henry James," in *The Literary Essays of Ezra Pound,* ed. T. S. Eliot (New York: New Directions, 1968) 331.

6 There are several fine studies of James's style that form a background to my own observations. See especially Dorothea Krook's essay "James's Late Style," appended to *The Ordeal of Consciousness in Henry James* (Cambridge: Cambridge UP, 1962) 390–413; Ruth Bernard Yeazell, *Language and Knowledge in the Late Novels of Henry James* (Chicago: U of Chicago P, 1976); Sharon Cameron, *Thinking in Henry James* (Chicago: U of Chicago P, 1989); and Millicent Bell, *Meaning in Henry James* (Cambridge: Harvard UP, 1991). See also Ian Watt's exemplary discussion of the first paragraph of *The Ambassadors* in "The First Paragraph of *The Ambassadors:* An Explication," *Essays in Criticism* 10 (1960): 250–74.

7 The 1985 Penguin edition of *The Golden Bowl* cited here and hereafter follows the revised text of the 1909 New York Edition.

8 Some of James's characters are subjected to such summarizing, conclusive judgment. Amerigo's assumptions about the shopkeeper are, from the narrator's point of view, dead on: he is a stereotypical Jew who shares his race's habit of scheming to make a buck. The anti-Semitic logic of this assumption is only reinforced when this particular shopkeeper proves, in regard to Maggie, to be the exception to the rule. James's description makes clear that the shopkeeper's second thoughts about selling the flawed bowl to Maggie are unaccountable, as if no Jew would normally display such qualms. James's representation of the Jewish shopkeeper in *The Golden Bowl* suggests that there are indeed limits to his ideal of unlimited perceptual responsiveness. As fine a focus as James puts on the novel's principal characters, the lens through which he views characters who fall outside the range of his favored class can be markedly dull.

9 The "case studies" of *The Turn of the Screw* are filled with such speculation. See most recently Peter G. Beidler, ed., *The Turn of the Screw,* Bedford's Case Studies in Contemporary Criticism (New York: Bedford, 1995).

10 For a discussion of surface and depth in the larger context of English prose traditions, see Richard Lanham, *The Motives of Eloquence: Literary Rhetoric in the Renaissance* (New Haven: Yale UP, 1976) and "*At* and *Through:* The Opaque Style and Its Uses," in *Literacy and the Survival of Humanism* (New Haven: Yale UP, 1983) 58–86.

11 As Leo Bersani has observed, "James's fiction is notoriously dense in what I suppose we have to call psychological detail, but it is remarkably resistant to an interest in psychological depth." See Bersani, "The Jamesian Lie," in *A Future for Astyanax: Character and Desire in Literature* (1976; New York: Columbia UP, 1984) 130. For another approach to James's anti-psychologist method, see G. L. Hagberg, *Meaning and Interpretation: Wittgenstein, Henry James, and Literary Knowledge* (Ithaca: Cornell UP, 1994).

12 The Norton Critical Edition of *The Ambassadors* cited here and hereafter follows the revised text of the 1909 New York Edition.

13 *Henry James Letters,* ed. Leon Edel, 4 vols. (Cambridge: Harvard UP, 1974–84) 4:767, 770.

14 Fanny may indeed be a parody of the Jamesian analyst, someone whose perceptive faculty is

*Notes to Chapter Five*

overindulged for lack of other interests. This would explain her perfectly ridiculous name, Fanny Assingham, with its triple evocation of what is generally acknowledged as the least enlightened part of the human anatomy.

15 Qtd. in Richard A. Hocks, *Henry James and Pragmatistic Thought* 52. Hocks offers a comprehensive and illuminating analysis of James's letter to Adams (71–112).

16 It is significant that James's dramas of sensibility are so often centered on female characters. For James, as for anyone of his age, sensibility is coded female, just as bold, heroic action would be coded male. Interestingly, a novel like *The Ambassadors* reverses the usual associations, contrasting the passive, ever-hesitating, and increasingly responsive Strether to Mrs. Newsome's fearsomely male control of the family fortune. What is most distinctive about James's fiction, however, is that the drama of sensibility is itself depicted as a great "adventure." If what William James wanted from Henry was a more conventional novel of heroic action, Henry recognized that his brother's psychology and pragmatism implied that a kind of heroic action was already taking place in any sensitive perception and developing awareness of the most ordinary, domestic social situations.

17 The 1985 Library of America edition of *The Portrait of a Lady* cited here and hereafter follows the text of the original 1881 Houghton, Mifflin edition.

18 For the revised New York Edition paragraph, see Henry James, *The Portrait of a Lady,* Scribner Rpt. Ed. (1908; Fairfield, N.J.: Augustus M. Kelly, 1977) 4:436.

19 For a detailed reading of Isabel's return to Rome as a type of triumph, see Robert Weisbuch, *Atlantic Double-Cross* 289–95.

## 6 GERTRUDE STEIN AND THE MOVEMENT OF WORDS

1 Michael Levenson suggests in *A Genealogy of Modernism: A Study of English Literary Doctrine 1908–1922* (1984; Cambridge: Cambridge UP, 1988) that modernism became an official institution in 1922, not so much with the publication of *The Waste Land* or *Ulysses* as with the founding of the *Criterion,* "because it exemplifies the institutionalization of the movement, the accession to cultural legitimacy" (213). By 1922, Stein had written dozens of what are now regarded as her major works: *Three Lives* (finished in 1906, published in 1909), *The Making of Americans* (begun in 1903, jump-started in 1908, and completed in 1911, though unpublished until 1925), *Ada* (written in 1910, published in 1922), *A Long Gay Book* (written in 1911–12, published in 1933), *Tender Buttons* (published in 1914), and many portraits, including those of Picasso, Cézanne, Matisse, and Mabel Dodge (all of them written in the early 1910s). Apart from her notoriety as the author of long stretches of sheer nonsense, Stein's prominence would only follow from the 1933 publication of *The Autobiography of Alice B. Toklas,* a tour de force of literary gossip, but far less challenging in form than anything she had previously written. The various dates of composition, about which there is sometimes controversy, are taken from the excellent headnotes in *A Stein Reader,* ed. Ulla E. Dydo (Evanston: Northwestern UP, 1993).

2 Edmund Wilson, *Axel's Castle* (New York: Scribner's, 1931) 252–53. It should be noted that Wilson did at least take Stein's writing seriously enough to include his discussion of her writing in his book.

3 Reprintings in the past dozen years include: *Mrs. Reynolds* (Los Angeles: Sun and Moon, 1987); *Operas and Plays* (Barrytown, N.Y.: Station Hill, 1987); *Useful Knowledge* (Barrytown, N.Y.: Station Hill, 1988); *Tender Buttons* (Los Angeles: Sun and Moon, 1990); *Everybody's Autobiography* (Cambridge, Mass.: Exact Change, 1993); *Geography and Plays* (Madison:

*Notes to Chapter Six*

U of Wisconsin P, 1993); *Stanzas in Meditation* (Los Angeles: Sun and Moon, 1994); *How To Write* (Los Angeles: Sun and Moon, 1995); *Last Operas and Plays* (Baltimore: Johns Hopkins UP, 1995); and *The Making of Americans* (Normal, Ill.: Dalkey Archive, 1995). Other important publications in this period include the 1993 *A Stein Reader*, ed. Ulla E. Dydo, and the two 1998 Library of America volumes cited here, *Writings 1903–1932* and *Writings 1932–1946*, ed. Catharine R. Stimpson and Harriet Chessman.

4   One of the earliest and most important feminist readings of Stein is Catharine Stimpson's "The Mind, the Body, and Gertrude Stein," in *Critical Inquiry* 3.3 (1977): 489–506. For a reading of Stein drawing on French feminist theory, see Marianne DeKoven, *A Different Language: Gertrude Stein's Experimental Writing* (Madison: U of Wisconsin P, 1983), as well as her essays in *Gertrude Stein and the Making of Literature*, ed. Shirley Neuman and Ira B. Nadel (Boston: Northeastern UP, 1988) and *Rereading Modernism: New Directions in Feminist Criticism*, ed. Lisa Rado (New York: Garland, 1994). Marjorie Perloff's essays on Stein, including a chapter in *The Poetics of Indeterminacy: Rimbaud to Cage* (Princeton: Princeton UP, 1981) 67-108 and an article in *Gertrude Stein and the Making of Literature*, have drawn attention to Stein's relationship to international avant-garde movements. For other approaches to Stein in a revisionary modernist context, see Ellen E. Berry, *Curved Thought and Textual Wandering: Gertrude Stein's Postmodernism* (Ann Arbor: U of Michigan P, 1992), and Bob Perelman, *The Trouble with Genius: Reading Pound, Joyce, Stein, and Zukofsky* (Berkeley: U of California P, 1994) 129-69. On Stein and contemporary avant-garde poetics, see bpNICHOL, "When the Time Came," in *Gertrude Stein and the Making of Literature* 194-209, and Charles Bernstein, "Professing Stein / Stein Professing," in *A Poetics* (Cambridge: Harvard UP, 1992) 142-49.

5   Marianne DeKoven, "Gertrude Stein and the Modernist Canon," in *Gertrude Stein and the Making of Literature*, ed. Neuman and Nadel 10-11.

6   Russell, *A History of Western Philosophy* xv, 230.

7   In his 1918 essay "Provincialism the Enemy," Pound links James to Galdos, Turgenev, and Flaubert, suggesting that "the whole fight of modern enlightenment is against" provincialism. James, Pound further comments, "was, despite any literary detachments, the crusader, both in this internationalism, and in his constant propaganda against personal tyranny, against the hundred subtle forms of personal oppressions and coercions" (189). In another 1918 essay on James, he describes these "personal oppressions and coercions" in a footnote: "What he fights is 'influence', the impinging of family pressure, the impinging of one personality on another; all of them in the highest degree damn'd, loathsome and detestable" (296). Hence, the "emotional greatness in Henry James' hatred of tyranny" (297). "Idiots," he comments bluntly in "Provincialism the Enemy," "said he was untouched by emotion" (189). See Ezra Pound, "Provincialism the Enemy," in *Selected Prose: 1909-1965*, ed. William Cookson (New York: New Directions, 1975), and "Henry James," in *Literary Essays of Ezra Pound*, ed. Eliot 295-338.

8   On Stein and modern art, see especially Wendy Steiner, *Exact Resemblance to Exact Resemblance: The Literary Portraiture of Gertrude Stein* (New Haven: Yale UP, 1978).

9   William Carlos Williams, "The Work of Gertrude Stein," in *Selected Essays* (1954; New York: New Directions, 1969) 116, 117-18.

10   Qtd. in Joseph Frank, "Spatial Form in Modern Literature," in *The Widening Gyre* (New Brunswick: Rutgers UP, 1963) 53-54. The article originally appeared, in somewhat different form, in consecutive issues of the *Sewanee Review* in 1945.

11   Ibid. 55.

*Notes to Chapter Six*

12 The description is from a catalog in the Harvard archives and is quoted in Linda Wagner-Martin, *"Favored Strangers": Gertrude Stein and Her Family* (New Brunswick: Rutgers UP, 1995) 34.

13 A number of critics have recently argued for the important influence of this research on Stein's developing experimental prose style. See especially Priscilla Wald, *Constituting Americans* 267–73.

14 See, for example, Jayne L. Walker, *The Making of a Modernist: Gertrude Stein: From "Three Lives" to "Tender Buttons"* (Amherst: U of Massachusetts P, 1984) 2–18. Richard Poirier also links Stein and William James in *The Renewal of Literature* and *Poetry and Pragmatism.*

15 For *Psychology: Briefer Course,* James would revise the sentence: "As the English associations arise, the sound itself appears to change" (*W* 1:296). Thus James removes even the lingering sense of agency implicit in the initial formulation, "As we seize the English meaning. . . ." As the revision suggests, the self is only another set of established associations which in no way precedes or determines what associations will "arise."

16 See Lisa Ruddick, " 'Melanctha' and the Psychology of William James," *Modern Fiction Studies* 28.4 (1983): 545–56, and "Fluid Symbols in American Modernism: William James, Gertrude Stein, George Santayana, and Wallace Stevens," in *Allegory, Myth, and Symbol,* ed. Morton W. Bloomfield (Cambridge: Harvard UP, 1981) 335–53. In *Reading Gertrude Stein: Body, Text, Gnosis* (Ithaca: Cornell UP, 1990), Ruddick underscores James's influence on Stein's early writing, but argues that Stein eventually came to reject what Ruddick describes as James's disapproval of untrained, random selectivity. I would suggest instead that Stein aggressively pursues aspects of self that James admired with profound and altogether terrified ambivalence. Nor is Stein unappreciative of this terror, as "Melanctha" demonstrates with striking clarity.

17 Richard Bridgman, *Gertrude Stein in Pieces* (Oxford: Oxford UP, 1970) 57.

18 On the problem of Stein's representation of race in "Melanctha," see Milton A. Cohen, "Black Brutes and Mulatto Saints: The Racial Hierarchy of Stein's 'Melanctha,' " *Black American Literature Forum* 18.3 (1984): 119–21. Cohen offers a useful chart correlating skin color and personality traits, demonstrating the racism implicit in Stein's "bottom natures," not only in Stein's representation of the rough, violent nature of darker skinned Blacks but also in her association of whiteness with the capacity to sustain complexity and contradiction. See also Michael North's illuminating discussion of the racial codes in "Melanctha" in "Modernism's African Mask: The Stein-Picasso Collaboration," in *Prehistories of the Future: The Primitivist Project and the Culture of Modernism,* ed. Elazar Barkan and Ronald Bush (Stanford: Stanford UP, 1995) 270–89.

19 Richard Poirier has aptly described "Melanctha" as "the first great story of homosexual cruising, of endlessly perambulating and unsettled desire, of literally wandering the streets searching for an object that might excite desire, but with no intention of locating that object in familiar, approved, or communally endorsed figures, and with no aspiration to settle down with the Jeffs of this world, especially when they do become available." See Poirier, "Pragmatism and the Sentence of Death," in *Wild Orchids and Trotsky,* ed. Edmundson 315.

20 Stein, *Everybody's Autobiography* 274.

21 Ibid. 274.

22 Stein, *A Long Gay Book,* in *A Stein Reader,* ed. Dydo 239. As Ulla E. Dydo points out in her headnote, it is in the last section of *A Long Gay Book* (from which this passage is taken) that Stein develops the technique she will later utilize in *Tender Buttons* (151).

*Notes to Chapter Six*

## 7 WALLACE STEVENS AND THE PRAGMATIST IMAGINATION

1 While there is wide agreement about Stevens's Romantic inheritance, there is little agreement about just what that inheritance is or how it affects his poetic modernism. Joseph Carroll offers a useful and comprehensive reading of Stevens's effort to "update" British Romantic traditions in *Wallace Stevens' Supreme Fiction: A New Romanticism* (Baton Rouge: Louisiana State UP, 1987). Harold Bloom, in *Wallace Stevens: The Poems of Our Climate* (1976; Ithaca: Cornell UP, 1980) and in his many essays on Stevens, has provided the most forceful (and eccentric) account of Stevens's Romantic inheritance, offering especially illuminating comparisons to Emerson and Whitman. Marjorie Perloff also associates Stevens's poetics with Romantic and symbolist traditions, though she highlights the ways in which this background compromises Stevens's modernity and differentiates him from the antilyrical avant-garde. See Perloff's essays, "Pound/Stevens: Whose Era?", originally published in *New Literary History* in 1982 and reprinted in *The Dance of the Intellect: Studies in the Poetry of the Pound Tradition* (Cambridge: Cambridge UP, 1985) 1–32, and "Revolving in Crystal: The Supreme Fiction and the Impasse of Modernist Lyric," in *Wallace Stevens: The Poetics of Modernism,* ed. Albert Gelpi (Cambridge: Cambridge UP, 1985) 41–64.

2 Many critics have written about Stevens's elusiveness under various headings. See, for example, Helen Vendler, "The Qualified Assertions of Wallace Stevens," in *The Act of Mind: Essays on the Poetry of Wallace Stevens,* ed. Roy Harvey Pearce and J. Hillis Miller (Baltimore: Johns Hopkins UP, 1965) 163–78. See also Charles Altieri, "Why Stevens Must Be Abstract, or What a Poet Can Learn from Painting," in *Wallace Stevens: The Poetics of Modernism,* ed. Gelpi 86–118.

3 The major critical trend among scholars of Stevens's poetry in the 1990s has, not surprisingly, been to examine Stevens's relation to historical reality. See especially Alan Filreis, *Wallace Stevens and the Actual World* (Princeton: Princeton UP, 1991) and *Modernism from Right to Left: Wallace Stevens, the Thirties, and Literary Radicalism* (Cambridge: Cambridge UP, 1994), as well as James Longenbach, *Wallace Stevens: The Plain Sense of Things* (Oxford: Oxford UP, 1991).

4 Stevens, *Sur Plusieurs Beaux Sujets: Wallace Stevens' Commonplace Book,* ed. Milton J. Bates (Stanford and San Marino: Stanford UP and Huntington Library, 1989) 77, 81; Stevens, *CPP* 747. James's comment in the letter to Wells is discussed in chapter 5 above.

5 Lentricchia, *Ariel and the Police* 14–15, 20.

6 Stevens's peculiar anxiety is reflected in a letter he had written to William Carlos Williams describing what struck him as the "casual character" of the poems in Williams's 1917 volume *Al Que Quiere!* and stating his own "distaste for miscellany," which he cites as "one of the reasons I do not bother about a book myself." When he finally does "bother," it only exacerbates his own self-doubt, as is evident in a letter to Harriet Monroe, dated October 28, 1922, in which he describes his poems as "horrid cocoons from which later abortive insects have sprung" (*LWS* 231). What stands out most here is Stevens's apparent revulsion, evident again in a 1928 letter in which he reveals the "horror" that attended his reading of proofs for *Harmonium* (*LWS* 251). The language here suggests something harsher and more damning than mere authorial modesty. Stevens's letter to Williams appears in Williams, "Prologue to *Kora in Hell,*" in *Imaginations,* ed. Webster Schott (New York: New Directions, 1970) 15.

7 On Nietzsche and truth, see especially Alexander Nehamas, *Nietzsche: Life as Literature* 42–73. Nehamas cites the following passage from *Beyond Good and Evil:* "The falseness of

*Notes to Chapter Seven*

a judgment is not for us necessarily an objection to a judgment. . . . The question is to what extent it is life-promoting, life-preserving, species-preserving, perhaps even species-cultivating. . . . To recognize untruth as a condition of life—that certainly means resisting accustomed value feelings in a dangerous way: and a philosophy that risks this would by that token alone place itself beyond good and evil" (55).

8  In his late essay "The Relations between Poetry and Painting," Stevens adapts the phrase "decreation" from Simone Weil to describe this process: "She says that decreation is making pass from the created to the uncreated, but that destruction is making pass from the created to nothingness. Modern reality is a reality of decreation, in which our revelations are not the revelations of belief, but the precious portents of our own powers" (*CPP* 750). On "decreation," see Roy Harvey Pearce, "Toward Decreation: Stevens and the 'Theory of Poetry,'" in *Wallace Stevens: A Celebration,* ed. Frank Doggett and Robert Buttel (Princeton: Princeton UP, 1980) 286–307.

9  For the relation between Nietzsche and the "anti-master-man," see David Bromwich, "Stevens and the Idea of the Hero," *Raritan* 7.1 (1987): 1-27.

10  "Anatomy of Monotony" is one of the poems Stevens wrote in the early 1930s when, after six years of what appears to have been total poetic silence, he began writing poetry again. Harold Bloom aptly describes this and the handful of related poems from this period as "uniformly elegiac, as though hymning a dead poetic self." In "Anatomy of Monotony," the brilliant sky merely serves to accuse the freshly awakened poet of a lingering poetic impotence. The anti-master-man of the later "Landscape with Boat" also reacts against the still-brilliant sky, though Stevens is by this time more in control of this anxious response. He stages the anti-master-man's reductive passion only to insist on the association between an expansive poetic self and the general magnification both symbolized and actualized by the sky. See Bloom, *Wallace Stevens* 88.

11  For an extended discussion of "The Snow Man," see Jonathan Levin, "Life in the Transitions: Emerson, William James, Wallace Stevens," *Arizona Quarterly* 48.4 (1992): 76-97.

12  William Bronk, *Life Supports: New and Collected Poems* (San Francisco: North Point, 1981) 134–35.

# Index

*Index*

*Index*

*Index*

*Index*

*Index*

2-4/6

19 –
31
42